Competition Policy and the Transformation of Central Europe

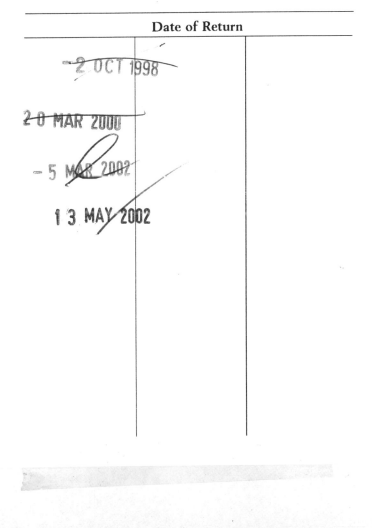

The cover shows an engraving of the annual fair in the Great Hall of Prague Castle, made in 1607 by Aegidius Sadler (*c.* 1570–1629), who from 1597 lived and worked in Prague at the court of Rudolph II. We are most grateful to Christopher Mendez for his kind permission to reproduce the engraving.

Competition Policy and the Transformation of Central Europe

John Fingleton
Eleanor Fox
Damien Neven
Paul Seabright

Centre for Economic Policy Research

The Centre for Economic Policy Research is a network of over 300 Research Fellows, based primarily in European universities. The Centre coordinates its Fellows' research activities and communicates their results to the public and private sectors. CEPR is an entrepreneur, developing research initiatives with the producers, consumers and sponsors of research. Established in 1983, CEPR is a European economics research organization with uniquely wide-ranging scope and activities.

CEPR is a registered educational charity. Institutional (core) finance for the Centre is provided by major grants from the Economic and Social Research Council, under which an ESRC Resource Centre operates within CEPR; the Esmée Fairbairn Charitable Trust; the Bank of England; 19 other central banks and 40 companies. None of these organizations gives prior review to the Centre's publications, nor do they necessarily endorse the views expressed therein.

The Centre is pluralist and non-partisan, bringing economic research to bear on the analysis of medium- and long-run policy questions. CEPR research may include views on policy, but the Executive Committee of the Centre does not give prior review to its publications, and the Centre takes no institutional policy positions. The opinions expressed in this report are those of the authors and not those of the Centre for Economic Policy Research.

19 June 1996

25–28 Old Burlington Street, London W1X 1LB
Tel: (44 171) 878 2900
Fax: (44 171) 878 2999
Email: cepr@cepr.org

Contents

List of Tables

Acknowledgements

The writing of this book was enabled, supported and encouraged by a large number of people and by several institutions over the past two years. The authors would like particularly to thank the Directorate General II (Economic and Financial Affairs) of the European Commission for financial support, and Joan Pearce (of DGII) for her encouragement of this research. The European Centre for Advanced Research in Economic (ECARE) at the Université Libre de Bruxelles provided valuable logistic and other support and is owed a particular debt of gratitude by John Fingleton, who spent six months sabbatical there while working on this book. Eleanor Fox gratefully acknowledges research support from the Filomen D'Agostino & Max E. Greenberg Faculty Research Fund at New York University School of Law. The Centre for Economic Policy Research assisted our research in many ways, quite apart from the publication of this book. We should like to thank everybody from CEPR who helped with this project and especially Tessa Ogden, Kate Millward, Sarah Northcott, Constanze Picking, and Richard Portes.

This work could not have been undertaken without the assistance of the competition offices of the four Visegrad countries. We are particularly grateful for their patient and painstaking work in providing us with data and in helping us to understand the detailed nuances of competition policy. In particular, we should like to thank Zdenik Foit and Sonja Matachová of the Czech Ministry of Economic Competition, Gizella Györki, Peter Pogácsás, Josef Sáarai of the Hungarian Office of Economic Competition, Andrzej Cylwik, Eva Kaliszuk and Andrej Sopocko of the Polish Anti-monopoly Office and Danica Paroulková and Pavel Frano of the Slovak Anti-Monopoly Office. Communications with Eva Miklaszewska and Tadeuz Skoczny greatly helped our understanding of competition policy in

Poland. Meetings and communications with Anna Fornalczyk and Ferenc Vissi were of enormous value, not just in understanding competition policy in their respective countries. In the European Commission, Stefaan Depyper, Thinam Jakob and Claude Rakovsky of Directorate General IV (Competition Policy) of the European Commission and provided much encouragement and helpful advice.

We would also like to thank our research assistants Roxanna Ionici (in Lausanne), Cloda Lane (in Dublin), Maurizio Pappalardo (in New York) and Tomas Karakolev, Gabor Bognar, and Milosz Rojek (in Cambridge). Finally, we would like gratefully to acknowledge the helpful suggestions and comments of several people, many of whom read and commented on an earlier version of this book, They include Pierre Buigues, Carolyn Brzezinski, Shyam Khemani, Alexis Jacquemin, Massimo Motta, Paulo Moura, Jerzy Osiatynski, Russell Pittman, Frances Ruane, Gérard Roland and Sally van Siclen. None of the above individuals or organizations bears any responsibility for any errors of fact or expressions of opinion in this book, which are those of the authors alone.

Although all four authors take joint responsibility for the book as a whole, a disproportionate share of the organization of the research and the preparation of the manuscript has been borne by John Fingleton. The other three authors would like to express their appreciation of his leading contribution to the work.

Foreword

Since 1989 the countries of Central and Eastern Europe and the Former Soviet Union have witnessed unprecedented economic, political and social transformation. This has included remarkable progress in the move from a system of central planning to the use of markets as a means of allocating resources and in the introduction of new institutions and laws governing these markets. The maintenance of competition, however, requires the design and implementation of effective policy to limit the distortionary effects of individuals or organizations who might seek to obstruct it. The Czech Republic, Hungary, Poland and Slovakia have been particulary successful in this regard.

This volume examines the implementation of competition policy in Central Europe during the 1990s. It analyses the statutes of the countries and the structure of the institutions established to implement competition policy. These countries have been operating competition policies since the transition process began, and a large body of case law has been established, which the authors also discuss. This is therefore a very timely contribution to the policy debate on the challenges of the next stage of transition.

The authors combine rigorous economic analysis with careful and informative assessment of competition policy so far. The result is an insightful and innovative study, which CEPR is very pleased to publish. It will be required reading for researchers and policy-makers in both competition policy and the political economy of transition. It will also help to illuminate these countries' paths towards accession to the European Union, where competition policy is essential underpinning for the Single Market.

The work for this volume was initially undertaken as part of a CEPR study on Competition Policy in Central and Eastern Europe, financed by a grant from the Directorate-General for Economic and Financial Affairs of the European Commission, to which we are very grateful. The opinions expressed are those of the authors writing in their personal capacities. Neither the European Commission nor CEPR takes any responsibility for these views, and CEPR takes no institutional policy positions.

Richard Portes
8 July 1996

Executive Summary

This study finds that remarkable progress has been made in the implementation of competition policy in the four Visegrád countries (the Czech Republic, Hungry, Slovakia and Poland), despite enormous obstacles, but also that important challenges lie ahead. Our research suggests that competition policy has a particularly significant role to play in transition economies, relative not just to those in established market economies but also, more surprisingly, to what was expected at the outset of transition. The reallocation of resources across industries has not been as radical as expected and new and existing corporate control mechanisms are not yet fully effective. As a result, much of the transition process in the next few years is likely to depend on and be driven by product-market competition. Factors like free trade, free entry to markets and foreign direct investment which typically encourage product-market competition in established market economies are still relatively ineffective in transition economies In addition, market structures and behavioural habits are still a matter of concern. In effect, there is a striking gap between the still-weak state of product-market competition and the task that it is expected to perform. In these circumstances, rules on the conduct of firms have a central role to play in the transition process.

The development of competition policy in the Visegrád countries has been impressive. Competition laws and institutions were introduced in all four countries during 1990 and 1991 and a large body of case law (over 1200 decisions) has since been established. The statutes are broadly similar to the Treaty of Rome, reflecting the approximation required by the Association Agreements. The competition offices are relatively politically involved (one is a ministry and the others have inputs to wider policy-making) and, in all countries, have been staunch advocates of competition policy in the public domain, suggesting greater *de facto* independence. The coverage of competition policy is similar to that in established market economies. The offices face similar problems too, for example enforcing policy where there are regulatory or professional barriers to entry. The adoption of competition policy was relatively uncontroversial at the beginning of transition. We find that this consensus is dissipating, especially as interest groups realize that competition policy may block transactions that benefit them and are tempted to bring pressure to bear on the decision-makers.

The caseload reveals a preponderance of abuse of dominance cases, a lenient approach towards mergers and a surprising lack of action against hardcore cartels (i.e. bid-rigging, price-fixing or market division). Detailed examination of the case law suggests that clear standards have still to emerge. Small market actors are clamouring for the attention of the enforcement authorities to remedy unfair outcomes of differential bargaining power, and governments are inclined to use competition offices to control prices or to implement industrial policy objectives. In particular, the competition laws of the Visegrád nations reflect three problems that could be remedied within the existing framework of their laws.

The first problem is that within the large number of abuse of dominance cases, many involve allegations of unfair bargains or unfair strategies in a contract relationship, with a small proportion of resources devoted to monopolistic abuses that impair market entry or expansion. We believe that Visegrád competition policy could play a much stronger role in market reform if the agencies self-consciously devoted the predominant share of their resources to market-improving efforts, including enforcement against cartels and monopolistic exclusions, as well as advocacy before other agencies of pro-market policies. To do so, it will be necessary for the competition offices to distinguish between problems involving fairness and redistribution between two parties and those that entail marketwide effects. Record-keeping of the agencies could usefully include statistical categories that show the proportion of resources devoted to cases likely to have significant market-wide effects.

Second, the competition officials and judges are still moving along a learning curve. In some cases the analysis of what is a market, whether a firm is dominant, and whether a practice helps or hurts competition needs improvement. Sometimes we note technical shortfalls. At other times we sense a conflict of goals – helping small firms versus improving productive efficiency. We observe that the offices and their staffs are constantly increasing their technical proficiency, and that many are working hard to do so. We support and encourage this learning process.

Third, it is not clear to us that the business community sufficiently knows and understands the competition rules, nor that the remedies imposed for egregious violations are sufficiently punitive to make the law a 'credible threat'. We recommend much more clarity in the law, much heavier fines for egregious violations and more publicity and advocacy regarding the law. Publication and availability of all decisions, and guidelines, e.g., for mergers, would aid this effort. We also consider reform of the existing institutional structures to be desirable to improve transparency of competition policy and to guarantee the political independence of the competition offices. In terms of the former, we recommend that trade, industrial and competition policy decisions be taken by separate institutions, with clear written reasoning for decisions so that the economic trade-offs may be clearly observed, debated and evaluated. To enhance political independence, we recommend that the individuals deciding cases and the heads of the competition offices be appointed in a manner that tends to immunize them from external influence or pressure. This is necessary to ensure that neither the selection of cases for investigation nor the decision-making process is distorted by political or other pressures. Financial independence of the competition offices would be extremely helpful. This would tend to insulate the offices from budgetary pressures used as a lever.

Agreements with the European Union require the Visegrád countries to approximate EU competition policy in principle. This is a positive policy, because it provides a helpful urgency to development of competition policy, which is central to the transition process. However, there seems little ground for further detailed approximation of the laws and policies of the Visegrád countries to those of the European Union in preparation for integration into the internal market. Our examination of the case law and other material suggests that the remaining differences between the law and its application in the Visegrád countries and in the EU are not ones that matter for the integration of factor- and product-markets or for the readiness of the countries for EU membership. Given the nature of the problems faced by transition economies, further forced approximation of the detail of the law might not be beneficial, in terms of either moving the law and its application closer to that of the EU or the aims of approximation. It may even reduce the overall readiness for membership of the countries concerned. It may also deflect attention from the more serious problem of ensuring that the application of competition law and policy should remain reasonably objective in the face of the substantial political pressures to distort it for the private advantage of particular interest groups.

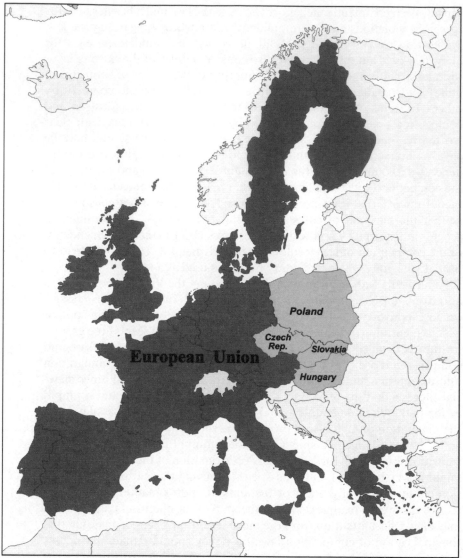

Poland

Czech
Rep.

Slovakia

European Union

Hungary

The European Union and the Visegrád countries

1

The Rationale for Competition Policy

1.1   Introduction

The period since 1989 has witnessed an unprecedented process of economic, political and social transformation in the countries of Central and Eastern Europe and of the former Soviet Union. Although the process has differed considerably in the different countries and regions, a central and common theme has been the switch from some variant of the system of central planning to the use of markets as the means to allocate resources. This increasing reliance on the market has been accompanied by major political changes and by the rapid establishment of new institutions and laws. This transformation has been most far-reaching in the countries of Central Europe.

Given the importance and centrality of markets in the overall transition process, the specific rules and institutions under which markets operate have a fundamental and formative role to play. This book is concerned with those rules and institutions that referee economic competition, namely those that govern the interaction between producers and the effects of producers' actions on consumers. Competition is necessary precisely because it is not enough simply to provide a basic framework of law to enable private agreements to be enforced. In the absence of explicit competition policy, there is a very real risk that the competitive process might be obstructed or distorted by the actions of private parties or the organs of the state itself.

The abrogation of price and other market controls and the consequent development of competition can be expected to lead to substantially more efficient allocations of resources than those attained under central planning, enabling consumers to a greater extent to purchase those goods and services that they choose, rather than those that the state formerly chose to supply. Thus the benefits from competition policy are likely to be considerable. There are some who would go further, seeing competition policy in a wider context of personal liberty, but that is beyond the scope of this book.

We examine the experiences of four countries, namely, the Czech Republic, Hungary, Poland and Slovakia, collectively known as the Visegrád[1] countries, that were among the earliest to abandon central planning and have undertaken the most fundamental reforms. Their competition policies date from the early stages of transition, and have now been in operation for several years, with an impressive volume of case law already produced. We document their policy approaches and seek to assess their operation and effectiveness. The experiences of the Visegrad countries are important not just in themselves but also in providing insights for other countries that have begun or are contemplating a somewhat similar transition. Our investigations also shed light more generally on the paradoxical nature of economic competition, a process of rivalry among free economic agents that must be scrupulously refereed if it is to work effectively.

1.2   What is Competition Policy?

What is meant, then, by competition policy? In a general sense the term refers to those tools of public policy that lay the foundation for markets or facilitate the creation and growth of efficient and competitive firms that can both deliver goods and services to the nation's own citizens (and inputs to intermediate businesses) and engage in trade and competition in international markets. In contrast to this broad notion of competition policy, a narrow definition confines it to a set of rules governing the conduct and transactions of enterprises, commonly known as 'anti-trust' rules. Although for much of this book our focus will be on the narrower sense of the term, it is important to set this in the context of its broader definition.

In its narrow sense competition policy, in the form of competition law, would prohibit anti-competitive action and transactions by enterprises (anti-trust rules). It would also expose state-owned enterprises to these same anti-trust rules, and would not grant exemptions from anti-trust except where justified by market failures. In its broader sense, competition laws would additionally entail all aspects of the proposition that neither governments nor commercial enterprises shall stand in the way of market competition. It would prohibit or limit government powers in the following areas: in imposing tariff and non-tariff barriers to trade; in restricting foreign investment and the freedom of establishment of business; in controlling prices and adopting overly broad trade-restraining laws; and in granting state aids. Where markets are supplied by state-owned monopolies whose ownership and structure were designed to reflect different conditions in the past that no longer prevail, competition policy (again in its broader sense) would support any changes in ownership and structure that would result in greater efficiency. In the case of formerly planned economies, questions of privatization and restructuring would thus come under any broad definition of competition policy.

Whether broadly or narrowly defined, competition policy can also be illuminated by pointing out what it does not include. In any economic system, it might be feared that greater competition might expose vulnerable people or businesses to the random vicissitudes of the market. They might therefore wish to adopt a set of 'fairness' rules, on the basis that competition is not fair and that there should be a check against it. These type of fairness rules are not part of competition policy. They may be desirable in the same way as are redistributive policies designed to redress inequalities in access to economic opportunity, but since they are in conflict with competition policy in that they put a check on the working of markets, a wisely designed legal system would be clear about the distinction and the trade-offs.[2]

Similarly, industrial policy (e.g. policy to save or create jobs or build national champions regardless of possible anti-competitive impacts domestically) is not competition policy and may often conflict with competition policy. In a well-designed system, industrial policy decisions would be taken in a transparent manner, enabling any trade-off with competition policy to be clearly observed, and to be debated and evaluated on its relative merits.

In cases of natural monopoly (where a single firm can supply the market at significantly lower cost than any group of competing firms), it follows by definition that competition does not work to produce best results for consumers. Regulation is normally the chosen instrument to deal with this problem. Given that some degree of competition may be introduced into even a substantially regulated industry, regulation is not necessarily in conflict with competition policy: indeed, there may be synergies.[3] Regulation is also appropriate in other circumstances where markets fail. Typical situations are inadequate information about product quality, externalities such as those caused by pollution or the need for an adequate provision of public goods.

All these other forms of public intervention in the economy differ from competition policy in that they aim to rectify possible inefficiencies or inequities arising from over-vigorous or undesirable rivalry between economic competitors. Competition policy, by contrast, is directed at ensuring that such rivalry exists in the first place, in the face of many efforts by the parties involved to block it or to diminish its intensity.

As we discuss below, the constraints that prevail in transition economies may create greater pressures (than in established market economies) for competition policy to be designed or implemented so as to protect people from the excesses of the market. In terms of fairness, competition policy might be expected to provide protection from exploitation by the suddenly emerging captains of business or by greedy entrepreneurs seeking opportunities to exploit others before markets have the chance to develop. In industrial policy, greater pressures might exist to protect employment in a rapidly changing industrial environment. Given the absence (and history) of price controls, there might be pressure to adopt a different basis for setting price-caps in the regulation of natural monopoly from that which exists in an established market economy. Thus there is a considerably greater risk that in transition economies the key purpose of competition policy could be confused with other, possibly very worthy, policy objectives.

1.3   Why Does Competition Policy Matter?

Although the conditions of perfect competition in the sense known to (or from) economics textbooks are too demanding ever to be observed in practice, there are ample theoretical and empirical reasons to think that a vigorous degree of competition between private economic agents will yield substantial efficiency benefits.

Broadly speaking, weak or absent competition poses two distinct problems for the efficiency of resource allocation. The first, known as *allocative inefficiency*, arises because monopolists produce less than competitive firms: they raise prices in pursuit of profit, knowing that the consumers they lose at the margin are worth less to them than the consumers they keep but overcharge. This distorts the allocation of resources in the economy because relative prices faced by consumers no longer reflect relative costs. There is an overall welfare loss for society because some consumers are forced out of the market or consume less (known as the Harberger triangle because of its shape when represented under a demand curve). There is also a transfer of resources from consumers to producers (or their shareholders) in the form of higher profits. This will not generally imply a loss in the aggregate welfare of society except in the case where the owners of firms are foreign.

The second problem posed by inadequate competition, and one of potentially greater magnitude, is that monopolistic firms often use inefficient and costly methods of production. If competition is vigorous a firm that fails to minimize costs would, in principle, be driven out of business (or onto the margin of the market) by more efficient firms. This is not true of monopoly. In practice, there are two independent dimensions to productive inefficiency. One is that a firm may not fully exploit economies of scale, because it produces at inappropriate levels of output.[4] The other is that firms may produce any level of output at higher cost than is necessary because they face no challenge to do so cheaply: as Hicks put it many years ago, 'the best of all monopoly profits is the quiet life'. This latter phenomenon is often described as *X-inefficiency* and we discuss it in some detail below.

The consequences of monopoly in one market are felt in other markets (although these should not be added to the above costs, being merely alternative manifestations of the social costs). Demand for factors of production is reduced because output is lower, resulting, for example, in unemployment and lower demand for capital and other inputs. Downstream producers face higher costs, so that prices in these markets will be higher than they would otherwise be. One consequence is that an economy with a monopoly in its non-traded upstream markets (such as legal and financial services or transport) will be less competitive internationally.[5] A third effect is that consumer demands in other markets will be distorted by relative prices and by income effects (richer shareholders or managers, poorer consumers). These negative macroeconomic effects of monopoly have recently received wide attention in the economics literature.[6]

What can we say about the empirical importance of these effects? Estimates of the welfare losses from monopoly for actual economies have typically focused on the measurement of allocative inefficiency and have come up with very small magnitudes (no more than one or two percentage points of gross domestic product for the US economy).[7] Furthermore, we know that market power is not necessarily damaging in terms of aggregate consumer and producer welfare if it offsets other distortions in the economy. For instance, given what we know about the failures of credit and other financial markets to finance risky investments, monopoly profits may represent a valuable offsetting source of internally generated investment finance. Hence it is often argued that, although monopoly may have harmful effects, these are not serious in practice.

Any benefits of monopoly power can accrue only if the resulting rents are realized in the form of profits and if those profits are reinvested in promising ventures. Because of failures of corporate control, monopoly may instead lead to inefficiency and 'the quiet life'. In such cases there may be no retained earnings for investment; even if there are, the temptation for managers to invest them in pet projects or to finance empire-building may be hard to resist. In these circumstances the losses associated with monopoly power may be much larger than the Harberger triangles of conventional theory.[8] Empirical evidence suggests that, even if markets are imperfectly competitive, it may not matter very much whether the number of participants in the market is one, two, or (say) half a dozen (see Bresnahan and Reiss, 1991). There is also evidence that high barriers to entry (and the consequent low risk of challenge by outsiders) may encourage productive inefficiency.

Competition policy is an appropriate response to the reality that monopoly is prevalent, because of the considerable incentives that exist for firms in a market to avoid or prevent competition, and that monopoly entails welfare losses. Nevertheless, the task facing competition policy is far from straightforward, for a number of reasons. Typically, competition policy involves legislation and implementing institutions. The nature of both the legislation and the institutions may be much influenced by the political pressures generated by the distribution of the gains and losses from competition policy. In any one market, for instance, if policy succeeds in achieving efficiency, many consumers benefit by a very small amount, and a relatively small number of producers (shareholders, workers, managers) lose considerably. Although economic theory suggests that the total gain exceeds the total loss, losers are likely to form a more focused and power-ful political lobby so that, in political economy terms, the forces against any particular competition policy measure may outweigh those in favour even when total welfare would improve. Such political pressures can distort competition policy, especially in terms of exempting sectors or activities from competition (policy). For example, a country may open its markets to foreign trade, importing stronger competition into domestic markets for traded products, but neglect to implement (or enforce) competition policy in the domestic non-traded sector.

If there are market failures in some markets, competition may reduce welfare rather than enhance it.[9] As we mentioned above, natural monopoly is a case in point. On the other side, the perception that competition may reduce welfare can inhibit progress. An example that is relevant both in the European Union (EU) and in the Central and East European countries (CEECs) is that of state-owned monopolies in sectors like communications, transport and energy. For various reasons, these were not previously run along profit-maximizing lines but instead were used to create or increase employment, resulting in overstaffing. Competition in such industries might actually increase unemployment rather than reduce it, making it pos-sible to argue (erroneously in many cases) that competition would reduce welfare.

At any given moment there certainly are pockets of monopoly power in different sectors of the economy, and the profits resulting should attract new entrepreneurs. This process of continual replenishment of monopoly power by new entry from outside might lead, as the Austrian economist Josef Schumpeter hypothesized many years ago, to a much more dynamic and progressive form of capitalism than either textbook static monopoly or perfect competition would lead us to believe. Another way to express this is to say that monopoly power itself may not be a bad thing provided there is sufficient continuing competition for the chance to be a monopo-list. Against this, it can be argued that the circumstances that create monopoly power are often precisely those that make it difficult for existing monopolists to be replaced by new ones, especially in R&D-intensive industries where this argument is often thought to have greatest applicability.

Another argument sometimes advanced for adopting a relatively relaxed attitude to monopoly power is that, if trade is sufficiently liberalized, foreign competition should provide the necessary discipline for domestic firms, even those that face little domestic competition. The question of whether foreign trade can substitute for domestic competition policy, or whether trade liberalization might, in contrast, make domestic competition policy more necessary (as was argued by the *Cecchini Report on the European Single Market*, for example) is a difficult one that does not admit of a straightforward resolution (see Neven and Seabright, 1995). It is certainly true that there are a number of important circumstances where foreign competition may provide the necessary discipline for a firm that is apparently a domestic monopolist. In particular:

1. Where the goods produced may be easily imported, incur low transport costs and are not dependent on distribution networks or after-sales service, monopoly pricing by the domestic firm will be difficult.
2. Foreign firms may be less likely to join a domestic cartel, and more likely to leave any cartel they have joined.
3. Even in cases in which some degree of monopoly pricing on the domestic market is possible, if the monopolist competes on export markets it will be less inclined to enjoy its monopoly rents in the form of high costs.

However, it is also clear that there are circumstances in which foreign competition will be inadequate:

1. In many services that are location-specific (such as retailing or distribution).[10]
2. Where transport and distribution costs are high (whether because of monopoly in these sectors or because of natural factors), and where foreign goods therefore face a significant mark-up or other disadvantage on the domestic market.
3. Where product standards or other regulatory barriers artificially segment the domestic from the world market.[11]

Sometimes foreign competition may actually provoke more aggressive anti-competitive behaviour from domestic firms than would be likely to occur in its absence, although this may be more of a risk when there are few potential competitors and conditions less applicable to the former command economies than to transition economies liberalizing within a free trade area.[12] Overall, while foreign competition can play an essential role in disciplining domestic firms, it is unrealistic to expect it to do the whole job.[13]

In summary, the need for competition policy arises because the free functioning of the market does not always guarantee effective competition and the absence of effective competition may entail substantial welfare losses for a society.

1.4 What is Transition?

The requirements and role of (and benefits from) competition policy in the aftermath of central planning are not obviously identical to those in an established market economy. In order to understand better the exact nature of such differences, it is useful to outline the main features of the transition to a market economy, namely, the legacy of central planning.

At the outset of transition, it was widely expected that movement towards a market economy would result in major restructuring. Such restructuring could, in principle, take three main forms. First, to the extent that the broad economic structure of the planned economies was different from that of market economies of comparable prosperity (notably in being more heavily industrialized and having a less developed service sector), it was likely that transition would involve substantial transfers of resources between sectors of the economy. Second, because the allocation of resources to different kinds of economic activity had been determined by central planning, once prices were liberalized there would be a sharp divergence between profitability levels in different activities. Indeed, Hare and Hughes (1991) estimated that at world prices whole sectors would not only be unprofitable but would also produce negative value added.[14] It was therefore expected that there would be a sharp contraction in unprofitable and an expansion in profitable activities. Third, the incentives for efficient management of individual firms had previously been weak: substantial efficiency gains might therefore be hoped for from the improved organization and management at the individual firm level. In particular, the boundaries of economic organizations were not determined by profit or efficiency incentives. Substantial recomposition of assets, especially the reduction in size of large conglomerate firms, was thus also expected.

Product-market competition arising from the liberalization of prices was intended to drive and motivate this deep and widespread process of restructuring and reallocation of resources within and across industries. Section 2.1 below examines and evaluates the extent to which this has happened. Here we briefly evaluate the state of industrial structure at the outset of transition in terms of the key dimensions of the pattern of economic activities, the organizational characteristics of firms and ownership and corporate control.

1.4.1 The Pattern of Activities

Output decisions under central planning were not determined by price signals or, if they were, these signals did not reflect real opportunity costs and financial performance standards. There is some systematic evidence that this resulted in a distorted allocation of resources across sectors. Hare and Hughes (1991) attempted to evaluate the distortions associated with central planning by seeing to what extent the profitability of sectors of the economy at world prices was correlated with their profitability at previous controlled prices. They found only a moderately positive rank correlation (across sectors), equal to about 0.6 for Hungary, Czechoslovakia[15] and Poland. This was what led them to predict substantial sectoral reallocations.

Central planning also affected the balance between industry, services and agriculture, given that a striking feature of command economies was its emphasis on material production at the expense of less physically tangible output such as services. In particular, these economies featured a relatively high concentration of the labour force in agriculture relative to Western market economies. Given the possibility of rapid (labour-saving) technological progress in agriculture and the inferred existence of a large unsatisfied demand for services, most observers (for instance, CEPR, 1990) predicted that the transition would entail a significant shift in production from manufacturing and agriculture towards services.

As Table 1.1 shows, the distribution of employment across sectors was indeed biased against services in all countries before the transition relative to the twelve countries of the European Union. The services share of employment in Hungary and in Czechoslovakia in 1988 was similar to that

Table 1.1 Allocation of employment across sectors

	Agriculture 1988	Industry[a] 1988	Services 1988
Poland	27	38	35
Hungary	19	36	45
Czechoslovakia	15	45	43
EU-12 (1986)	8	32	59
Ireland (1979)	19	32	48

Source: ILO Statistical Yearbook, 1993; Czech Quarterly Statistical Bulletin, 1995; Irish Labour Force Survey. All figures are percentages.
Note:
[a]Industry includes construction.

Table 1.2   Standard deviation of employment shares across industries, 1989

	Czechoslovakia	Hungary	Poland	Germany	UK
Standard deviation	4.28	3.47	3.24	4.56	3.36

Source: *UN Statistical Yearbook.*

found in Ireland (the EU state with the lowest services share) in 1979, with an even lower figure for Poland, perhaps suggesting that income levels rather than central planning can explain the low services shares. The distribution between industry and agriculture varied, with industry being particularly dominant in Czechoslovakia in contrast to almost one third of the labour force in agriculture in Poland.

The integration and coordination of production across countries was another supposed characteristic of central planning that affected industrial structure (see, for instance, CEPR, 1991). Under such a system, each country could be expected to have specialized in relatively few industrial sectors (CEPR, 1990). However, this does not mean that they were significantly more specialized overall. Table 1.2 reports the standard deviation of employment shares across sectors in 1989 (summarizing Table A1.1 in Appendix 1). These data suggest that the overall degree of specialization across industrial sectors in the economies now in transition was not atypical compared with Germany and the United Kingdom. Germany and the Czech Republic have similar diversity in their industrial structures, as do Hungary, Poland and the United Kingdom.

A third and related feature of central planning was its concentration on standardized and tangible outputs, eschewing complex technological processes and product differentiation (see, for instance, Nuti, 1988). The allocation of labour across industries presented in Table A1.1 in Appendix 1 offers a partial confirmation of this view, to the extent that the transition economies had specialized in both labour-intensive sectors (e.g. clothing and footwear) and heavy industries (e.g. iron, steel and machinery). By contrast, sectors intensive in human capital, such as pharmaceuticals and transport equipment, were underrepresented. Given that these are industries dominated by multinationals in established economies, it is not surprising that they have not grown indigenously.

1.4.2   The Organization of Firms

Production in the CEECs was conducted using economic organizations, known as 'combinates', which differed substantially from Western-style firms. The size and boundaries of these combinates were not determined by profitability or common features of production, but rather by wider considerations which included political and social elements (Hirschausen,

Table 1.3   Average number of employees per firm, 1989

	Czechoslovakia	Hungary	Poland	Germany	UK
Manufacturing	2772	327	521	162	33.00
All industries	2782	362	603	165	NA
Coefficient of variation	0.63	1.41	1.04	1.09	1.97

Source: *UN Industrial Statistics*, 1991.

1995a; Joskow, Schmalensee and Tsukanova, 1994). Thus they integrated industrial production with social services (housing, health care, etc.) and activities of social control (party administration, unions, prisons). The introduction of markets and financial performance standards would therefore be likely to change incentives for the organization of economic activities towards those with potential to increase productive efficiency, resulting in a recomposition of assets into more specialized firms.

Another closely related feature was the relatively large size of economic entities, as dictated by the need to simplify the implementation of economic planning and control (as well as to produce inputs that were hard to find in conditions of shortage). There is evidence for this in Table 1.3, which reports the average number of employees per firm in 1989. Firms in Czechoslovakia were particularly large, with an average of more than 2500 employees in the manufacturing sector. This compared with just 33 in the United Kingdom and 162 in Germany. Polish firms, although smaller, were still three to four times as large as German ones, whereas Hungarian firms were 'only' twice as large. As a consequence of these large production units, production, and often sales, were highly concentrated at the national level.

The dispersion of firm size across industries is also revealing (for the detail see Table A1.2 in Appendix 1). In market economies, average firm size tends to vary across industries, depending on scale economies and the stage of maturity of the industry. To examine this we consider the coefficient of variation of firm size across sectors (Table 1.3). The variation found in Poland is not markedly different from that in Germany and that in Hungary is greater. Czechoslovakia was a clear outlier, with a particularly homogeneous distribution of firm size across sectors. This confirms the widespread belief that central planning had a greater effect on industry structure in Czechoslovakia than in other economies now in transition.

1.4.3   Ownership and Corporate Control

In command economies, most economic entities were directly controlled by the state. As Table 1.4 reveals, private firms did not account for more than 15% of value added (the Polish figure is infested by the inclusion of agriculture). This is very small by comparison with EU levels of private

Table 1.4 Private sector share of GDP, 1989

Czechoslovakia	Hungary	Poland
11	15	29

Source: EBRD (1995). Figures in per cent.

ownership and expenditure (public expenditures in the EU represent about 40% of GDP and about 25% if transfers are excluded). Governments in transition economies were typically more heavily involved than EU governments in the provision of market services. New forms of corporate control therefore had to emerge following the progressive transfer from public to private ownership.

The process of industrial restructuring in transition economies could therefore have been expected to be particularly deep,[16] involving both a reallocation of resources across activities and a recomposition of firms in terms of size and scope. As the systems of corporate control that would normally direct the process of restructuring were not well established, product-market competition assumed a particular important role as the fundamental driving force behind restructuring (Mayhew and Seabright, 1992). To put it another way, if the carrot of profitability was limited in its effectiveness, the stick of competition would have to do correspondingly more work. However, a virtuous circle seemed possible: to the extent that the process of restructuring encouraged entry, growth of smaller firms and rivalry among existing firms, monopolization and collusion become less likely.

1.4.4   The Role of Competition

The legacy of central planning means that the role of competition, as opposed to competition policy, in transition is likely to be different from what it would be in an established market economy. With the inherited industrial structure and the lack of competitive habits, outcomes may have been very far from those that would have prevailed in a market-based system. Given this, the effect of increased product-market competition can be expected to be widespread and profound. Moreover, competition in the product market is likely to have effects on corporate control, factor markets and the political and social life of the countries (just as there are effects in the opposite direction). Thus competition in the product market is one of the very fundamental forces driving the transition process, as well as being caused by it.

At the most general level, competition can be expected to facilitate consumer choice. The command economies entered the reform era with an economic structure characterized by small numbers of large firms, accustomed to only a limited degree of rivalry in the product market. The main rivalry they would have known would have been that for government favours, for example using political contacts to gain preferential access to supplies rather than directing economic resources towards producing goods in the quantities and qualities consumers might desire. At the same time, these societies had been used to highly concentrated power structures and the expectation that most producers of goods and services (like most citizens) would simply do as instructed.

As a result, the opening up of markets to rivalry has assumed an importance in the command economies that is only partly economic. It is also about autonomy and the dispersion of power. People whose economic independence (e.g. ability to change employment or to set up in business) was previously thwarted by the state should not now fear that it will be thwarted by monopolies. Only their ability to supply to customers on terms the latter find attractive should determine whether they succeed in their aspirations. Likewise, consumers should be able to exercise choice, not merely because this will enable them to obtain the goods and services they prefer but also because they no longer wish to be told how to live.

Inadequate competition, then, threatens the ability of citizens in the formerly planned economies to exercise autonomy and choice. But it also threatens their standard of living directly, in ways that are familiar from the experience of market economies.

1.5 Competition Policy in Transition

So why do transition economies need competition policy (i.e. explicit prohibitory rules)? They need competition, certainly, but the abolition of central planning (and consequently the liberalization of prices and removal of quantitative output targets) already represents a major stride in that direction. Why do more?

The liberalization of prices and markets may not be sufficient to ensure competition. The very nature of transition may inhibit the development of competitive industry structures, because of high barriers to entry. There are several reasons to believe that new or small firms may face barriers to entry or growth:

1. Credit to new firms is heavily restricted, not only by generally tight financial conditions, but more specifically because existing large (and typically state-owned) firms receive priority access to available funds, be it through deliberate policy or due to banks' desires to shore up their existing portfolios.
2. In the fragmented markets of transition economies, many of the scarce assets needed by new firms if they are to mount a credible challenge to

existing monopolists (such as land, premises or distribution networks) are either unavailable or continue to be allocated in distorted ways that favour existing firms.

3. Imperfect enforcement of hard budget constraints on enterprises means that competition from new entrants to an industry may be less likely to drive out existing monopolists than in a more mature market economy; and knowing this, new entrants are less likely to mount a challenge to existing monopoly power in the first place.[17]

Such factors will be compounded if the restructuring that accompanies privatization does not prioritize the creation of competitive market structures. When a combinate is privatized, many of its divisions may not compete directly with each other. However, when a large production unit supplying the entire country or region is being privatized, it may be possible to restructure it horizontally into independent entities that will subsequently compete against each other in the product market. Privatization agencies face a difficult conflict in such cases: the privatization of the unrestructured monopoly would likely yield considerably more revenue than the privatization of competing entities. This danger is reduced in two senses by effective competition policy. First, privatized monopolies are less likely to be able to erect barriers to entry or to abuse their market powers. Second, the market will recognize that a monopoly is less valuable in the presence of effective competition policy so that the privatization agency will not face such a stark trade-off between revenue and competition.

More generally, the depth of restructuring itself matters for the design of competition policy in several ways. One obvious implication is that the task of competition agencies is unusually demanding, as many firms and industries are likely to warrant attention. Another, less obvious, implication concerns the institutional role of competition agencies: a deep and widespread process of restructuring will typically involve serious conflicts of interests between the government, managers, workers and consumers. In this context, the role required of competition agencies is likely to be more activist than usual; the design of the institutions in charge of competition policy is likely to be particularly important, especially where it affects the balance of power between the various interest groups. Competition agencies might expect to find the ratio of abuse of dominance cases to mergers and cartels to decline over time as the industry structure becomes less concentrated.

The fact that restructuring occurs rapidly may alter the priorities of competition policy. The evaluation of existing competition may be short-lived if firms are shifting resources out of an industry or if existing firms are undertaking deep restructuring. Similarly, the evaluation of potential competition may be equally short-lived if an industry attracts new resources. Finally and more importantly, the stance taken by competition agencies may affect the pace of restructuring and its final outcome. For instance, if potential competition is underestimated, excessive restraints may be imposed on large incumbent firms, which in turn reduces the speed with which they restructure. Such issues are, of course, common in established market economies, in particular for industries with rapid technological developments. Industry representatives have long advocated a specific anti-trust treatment for high-technology industries in market economies and anti-trust agencies have to some extent responded to these arguments (for instance, the EC block exemptions on research joint ventures or the US treatment of licensing in high-tech industries). In the context of transition economies, the question of how to implement a competition policy with rapidly changing industry structures is particularly pressing given the scale of potential resource reallocation across industries and the scale of firm restructuring within industries.

1.6 Adapting Competition Policy to the Needs of Transition

We have indicated why societies seeking to create a market economy from the debris of central planning will wish to use competition policy to influence the evolution of their economic structures. We have sought to reconcile this with the central philosophy of a market economy, according to which many of the most important decisions in this process are made by the undirected actions of independent economic agents. Nevertheless, many questions remain unanswered. In particular, the precise role and importance attached to competition policy will depend on the desired goal of the evolution, upon the kind of market economy the society's decision-makers wish to see emerge. Market economies differ considerably from each other, with respect to their economic structures, the role of the state in the economy, the level of inequality and the concepts of law that underpin economic relations. Such differences may seem minor compared to the fundamental differences between planned economies as a group and the market economies as a group, and one might think that the overwhelming priority for economies in transition is simply to adopt one of the frameworks of law and philosophies of state intervention appropriate to market economies without too much concern about fine points of detail.

However, it would be unwise to presume that the law and policy appropriate to an already-established and fully functioning market economy are also suited to an economy still in transition to such a state. There are two distinct reasons for thinking otherwise. First, the many important differences between transition and market economies with respect to their initial economic conditions mean that the effects (and therefore the social costs) of anti-competitive structures and conduct may be very different from those in a market economy. This may happen in a number of ways. Collusion (explicit or implicit) between the leading firms in a market may be much more damaging in the absence of a competitive fringe of smaller firms to challenge the cartel. Market foreclosure (preventing new firms from entering the market) is both more possible and more damaging when there are fewer firms in the market in the first place. Weak corporate control (whether due to state ownership, public subsidies or protection, or to underdeveloped capital markets) means that firms are more likely to enjoy the fruits of market power in the form of high costs and low levels of quality and innovation. Since all competition policy judgements (like all forms of state intervention in the economy) involve striking a balance between the costs of action and the costs of inaction, the fact that inaction, and the consequent unfettered exploitation of market power, is typically more costly in transition than in market economies means that the authorities will and should resolve this balance in different ways. Cases will be brought that might be considered unimportant in market economies, and offences will be defined that might otherwise seem marginal. On the other hand, the vastly greater uncertainty about general economic conditions in the turbulence of transition means that the authorities will need simpler and less subtle rules of action, and may well wish to trust less in the discretion of public agencies.

There is a second reason for thinking that competition policy may have a greater urgency in transition economies. In the absence of certain kinds of intervention to police the competitive process, the credibility of the transition to a market economy itself may be in doubt. An economy may remain for a long time sluggishly trapped in a cycle of weak competition, low productivity and slow growth if large firms with monopoly power are able to prevent new entry into established markets, if government ministries intervene to distort foreign or domestic trade, if access to credit, land, infrastructure or distribution outlets prevents new firms from competing vigorously or if cartels merely replace state bureaucratic planning with corporate bureaucratic planning. This is a particular risk in some of those (often non-traded) sectors producing inputs into other production processes, whether these are items of infrastructure or certain business services. The output of such sectors may be essential to the ability of downstream firms to compete effectively on international markets, and weak competition or low productivity in these sectors may have social costs significantly higher than calculations of private cost might lead one to conclude.

Our analysis of competition policy in transition, then, will take into account the need to have a different competition policy from that in an established market economy both because there is more work to do and because it must remove some of the obstacles that may prevent the goal of a market economy from being reached at all. But in addition to the fact that competition policy has a subtly different task to perform in transition than in market economies, it is important to be aware that it also faces different constraints. As we have already mentioned, uncertainty is much higher in the process of transition, and the authorities have much less scope for comparing conditions in one market or area of the economy with those in other, presumably more competitive, ones. Economic performance (whether revealed in profits and other financial indicators or in real economic variables) is much harder to evaluate in the turbulence of transition than when conditions have settled down and current conditions are a more reliable guide to future prospects. And, as we discuss in Section 2.2 below, the political constraints faced by policy-makers, and therefore their scope for implementing actions that have differential effects on various interest groups in society, will typically be different.

For all these reasons it is important to assess the achievement of competition policy in transition economies by broader criteria than simply by the extent of conformity of their laws and practices to international best practice, even if there were an unchallenged consensus as to what that best practice is. Our procedure here will be to describe both the task and the constraints facing competition policy, then to give an account of what has actually been achieved, and finally to evaluate that achievement in the light of that task and those constraints.

1.7   The Structure of this Book

The remainder of this book consists of eight chapters. Having set out in this first introductory chapter the rationale for and the task facing competition policy in transition economies, in Chapter 2 we look more closely at the constraints under which competition policy must operate. First, we consider in some detail the economic structures inherited from central planning. Next, we look at the political constraints on competition policy. What are the interest group pressures to which it has been and will continue to be subject? We go on to look at factors determining how effectively the rule of law operates in transition economies, since these will determine the credibility of the entire framework of competition policy. All these constraints can be thought of as internal to the societies concerned. The final section of Chapter 2 outlines and discusses the constraints implied by their external relations, notably their wish to become members of the European Union. In Chapter 3, we draw together the threads of the discussion by suggesting how these constraints together might influence the desirability of various alternative approaches to competition policy. We set out some criteria that such a policy should meet, criteria that will help in the evaluation of the developments we subsequently document.

Chapters 4 and 5 describe the systems of competition policy that have been put in place in the countries of our study. By 'systems' we understand the body of statute law (outlined in Chapter 4) and the institutions that have been charged with implementing such law and the associated procedures. Although the distinction between statute and case law is to some extent artificial, we prefer to think of the case law as reflecting the performance or functioning of the systems concerned rather than their structure. Chapters 6 to 8 therefore analyse the functioning of the systems, looking at the case law (in Chapter 6), the overall scope and reach of competition policy (in Chapter 7), and the consistency and credibility of its institutions (in Chapter 8). Each chapter contains a summary or evaluation and Chapter 9, the Conclusion, makes an overall assessment of the findings, and draws conclusions for the countries themselves, for other countries in transition, and for the policies of the European Union.[18]

Notes

1. This collective noun, which we use through the book, arises from an agreement signed at Visegrád in Hungary in December 1991. Other terms used are EU (European Union) and CEECs (Central and East European Countries), a category that includes more than just the Visegrád countries.
2. This point is discussed in detail in note 14 in Chapter 6.
3. Our concern is to distinguish competition policy in its narrow sense from the regulation of natural monopoly which we consider to be part of competition policy in its broader sense. This distinction matters more for transition economies because of the possibility that regulation of natural monopoly could cause competition agencies to be confused with the previous price-control offices, an issue we address in detail below.
4. Even in a competitive market, it is not clear that firms will make the best use of scale economies, as illustrated by the results on excess entry. For example, with competition (in quantities) and free entry, the equilibrium number of firms will be greater than that which would maximize welfare.
5. Fingleton (1993) uses a simple model to show that the effectiveness of competition policy is greater, the more sectors of the economy are covered.
6. See Dixon and Rankin (1994) for a survey of this literature. See Layard, Nickell and Jackman (1991) regarding imperfect competition models and unemployment.
7. See Bresnahan (1989) and Schmalensee (1989) for surveys of empirical studies of market power and performance.
8. For a discussion of the issue in relation to airlines, see Good, Roller and Sickles (1993).
9. This is an example of the theorem of second best.
10. See Fingleton (1995) for a detailed discussion.
11. Aghion (1993) argues that the pro-competitive effect of trade will be rather weak when products are vertically differentiated so that high-quality Western goods are not in competition with low-quality East European goods.
12. See Neven and Seabright (1995). Aghion (1993) argues that whereas state-owned enterprises may withstand competition from importers, the emerging private sectors may not be in a position to do so. In his view, because it is important to nurture the emerging private sector, full trade liberalization should be avoided. This is an infant industry-type

argument which takes on particular force, however, because of the unusual constraints (in factor markets) faced by the emerging private sector in transition economies.

13. Fung (1992) examines the effect economic integration has on promoting competition and shows that under some circumstances integration will retard competition. He concludes that competition policy must still be actively enforced even when economies are becoming increasingly open.

14. A sector is unprofitable if the value of its output, net of input costs, is insufficient to reward the associated factors of production (capital, labour and land). It produces negative value added if the value of its output is less even than the value of its inputs.

15. We use the name Czechoslovakia in all references to statistics obtained before the formation of two independent states.

16. For instance, relative to the industrial restructuring observed in market economies undertaking structural reforms, such as those in Latin America in the 1980s.

17. Feinberg and Meurs (1994) argue that liberalization and competition policy may not break down the very high barriers to entry in transition economies and suggest that specific policy measures are required to facilitate sufficient entry.

18. Updates of information contained in this book may be obtained on the World Wide Web at www.economics.tcd.ie/jfinglet/CEC/update.

2

The Constraints on Competition Policy

2.1 Evidence on the Economic Process of Transition

This chapter examines the constraints under which competition policy must operate in transition economies. Before considering those constraints imposed by politics and interest group pressures, and by the external relations of the countries concerned, we turn first to the nature of economic transition itself. What has the evidence of the first few years since the end of central planning shown us about the nature of this process, about how long it takes and about its amenability to influence by deliberate policy?

We argued above that the legacy of central planning led many observers to expect profound changes in industry structure during the transition, involving both substantial shifts of resources between economic sectors and restructuring within industries. This section describes what has happened during the first years of transition. As far as shifts of resources between sectors are concerned, we find there has been a major increase in the size of the services sector (as expected), but surprisingly little systematic movement of resources between industrial sectors when considered at a more disaggregate level. The evidence on restructuring within firms presents a mixed picture, with cost-cutting and labour-force reductions by many firms but relatively little fundamental reorientation of product lines and overall competitive strategy. An examination of ownership and the mechanisms of corporate control suggests that major changes have occurred, but that much remains to be done (for example, many of the most difficult privatizations have yet to be undertaken). Overall, this suggests that the active process of market entry by new firms and exit by old ones has not taken place on the scale that was envisaged. As a consequence, an active competition policy may be even more important than was originally thought.

Table 2.1 Basic economic features of the Visegrád countries

	Czech Republic	Hungary	Poland	Slovakia
Population (1994, millions)	10.3	10.3	38.6	5.5
GDP/capita (ecu, 1995)[a]	7551	5223	4376	5392
GDP/capita relative to EU (%)	52.2	34.6	29.0	35.7
GDP growth (year to end-1995)	5.0	1.5	7.0	7.4
Inflation (year to April 1996)	8.5	24.4	20.5	6.0
Ecu exchange rate (June 1996)	34.44	184.66	3.34	38.38
Area (km²)	78 864	93 030	312 685	49 035
Population density	131	111	123	112

Source: Slovak Economic Sheet, *Financial Times*.
Note:
[a]Per capita GDP in 1995 measured in purchasing power parity.

Table 2.2 Shares of allocation of employment across sectors, 1994, 1988

	Agriculture		Industry[a]		Services	
	1994	1988	1994	1988	1994	1988
Poland	23	27	32	38	45	35
Hungary	15	19	35	36	50	45
Czech Republic[b]	9	15	42	45	49	43
EU-12 (1986)	8		32		59	
Ireland (1979)	19		32		48	

Sources: *ILO Statistical Yearbook*, 1993 and 1994; *Quarterly Statistical Bulletin of the Czech Republic*.
Notes:
[a]Industry includes construction.
[b]The 1988 figure is for the former Czechoslovakia.

We therefore go on to examine direct evidence concerning the nature of rivalry between firms. We focus on factor markets, the process of entry, foreign direct investment, import pressure, horizontal concentration, behavioural and collusion habits and vertical integration. On all fronts, we find encouraging signs but also reasons for significant caution. It seems that industry structures and the nature of competitive rivalry remain significantly different from those in established market economies. The task of competition agencies in transition economies will have its own particular character for some time to come.[1] Table 2.1 presents some general background statistics on the four countries.

2.1.1 The Pattern of Activities

Reallocation of Resources across Industries

Since 1988 there has been a significant fall in the share of agriculture and a rise in the share of services (see Table 2.2) in total economic output.[2] The

Table 2.3   Reallocation across industries, 1989–93

	Poland	Hungary	Czech Republic	UK (1989–93)
Standard deviation	26.89	22.99	22.47	10.36
Weighted average	−23.59	−29.84	−34.13	−5.73
Coefficient of variation[a]	−1.14	−0.77	−0.66	−1.81
Laurence index[b]	0.09	0.09	0.07	0.03

Source: UN industrial statistics, authors' calculations.
Calculations are based on 30 sectors. The data comprise the percentage change in the share of each sector between 1989 and 1993.
Notes:
[a]The coefficient of variation is the standard deviation divided by the mean. If the variability of the shares is thought to be related to the depth of the recession, this measure is more appropriate.
[b]To calculate the Laurence index, one takes half the absolute value of the change in the share of each sector and sums across sectors. This measure is used if the variability of the shares is not related to the depth of the recession.

share of employment in industry fell in the Czech Republic where it was unusually high. Overall, we observe that, from different initial sectoral shares, all transition economies have moved towards the shares observed in market economies. A significant amount of adjustment is still needed before there is complete convergence of sectoral shares to those typical of market economies.

As we discussed in Chapter 1, even within the manufacturing sector, substantial reallocation of resources was expected across activities as prices were liberalized, the tax system simplified and financial performance monitored. Manufacturing output fell on average by about 30% between 1989 and 1993 (see Table A1.3 in Appendix 1 for details of variation at the subsectoral level). Table 2.3 shows that there has also been a shift in the relative importance of the various sectors, as the standard deviation of the change in output exceeds 20% in all three countries. But it is unclear whether these differences in output change across sectors are associated with genuine long-term shifts in resources in response to changing economic incentives, or whether they reflect temporary changes in demand during a recession. As a benchmark, Table 2.3 also reports the standard deviation and coefficient of variation of the changes in output observed in the United Kingdom during the last recession. It appears that the dispersion of output responses in the United Kingdom relative to the mean output response (as measured by the coefficient of variation) was higher than that observed in transition economies during the period 1989–93. This comparison suggests that the differences in output change across sectors observed in transition economies may have been rather small given the severity of the recession they have all experienced. If, however, a severe recession explains a greater average output drop but not a greater dispersion of output changes across sectors, the Laurence index suggests that the

Table 2.4 *Ex ante* profitability and changes in production, 1989–93

Country	Rank correlation	*t*-statistics
Czechoslovakia	−0.13	−0.59
Hungary	0.20	0.99
Poland	0.005	0.02

Sources: UN industry statistics (1995); Hare and Hughes (1991); authors' calculations.

dispersion of output responses in the Visegrad countries is indeed greater than that in the United Kingdom.

Even if there has been a reallocation of output across sectors, has this been in response to long-term economic incentives or merely to random shocks? One way to explore this question is to compare the changes in output by sector with the calculations of *ex ante* profitability of industrial sectors (at world prices) that were made by Hare and Hughes (1991). If these *ex ante* profitability calculations are a reliable indicator of the expected returns to investment in that sector once prices are liberalized, a positive correlation would tend to confirm that resources are being efficiently reallocated, with more profitable sectors growing at the expense of less profitable ones. Table 2.4 presents the rank correlation (across sectors) between profitability indices and observed changes in output. For Czechoslovakia and Poland, the correlation is close to zero and far from significant. It is positive but not quite significant for Hungary. Overall, this suggests either that the profitability indicators computed by Hare and Hughes (1991) are not very reliable or that the observed changes of output have more to do with the recession than with long-term structural change. However, one reason the Hare and Hughes indicators may be unreliable is that they purport to measure the average profitability of resources employed in a particular sector (using the existing technologies that characterize production in that sector). This may be a poor guide to the marginal profitability of new investment in that sector, which may well use quite different production methods.

This test may be too demanding; a weaker test is to sort sectors into six categories from lowest to highest, first, in terms of a profitability indicator and second, in terms of the change in production that they experienced between 1989 and 1993. These rankings provide slightly stronger support for the hypothesis that resources have been reallocated across sectors in response to the adjustment towards world prices and thus that the observed changes in output are associated with structural shifts. Nevertheless, the evidence overall suggests that the process of resource reallocation across sectors has been, at best, limited, at least until early 1994. One explanation is that the substantial restructuring that was expected had yet to occur.

Another is that the potential for achieving efficiency gains by substantial resource reallocations between sectors was originally somewhat over-played.

The view that substantial reallocation may still be expected is supported by the observation that relative prices have kept changing long after the initial liberalization, at least in Poland (*OECD Country Study, Poland,* 1994). Both in 1991 and 1992, the standard deviation of price changes across industries was around 25 whereas relative prices tended to stabilize in 1993. The data provided by Flek (1995) for the Czech Republic also confirm a significant turmoil in relative prices in both 1991 and 1992. If a significant lag can be assumed between changes in relative prices and the reallocation of resources, additional restructuring should still be expected, especially in the Czech and Slovak Republics which initiated the transition later than Poland.

Additional evidence on restructuring across industries for the Czech Republic is provided by Flek (1995). He sorts industrial sectors into three groups according to the evolution of their sales between 1989 and 1992. One group records a 10% increase in its share of overall sales (from about 35% to 45%), a second records a similar decline (from about 45% to 35% of overall sales), with the third group's share remaining unchanged. Relative prices deteriorated in the second (declining) group but improved in the first, which includes mostly energy-intensive industries (fuel, electricity, iron and steel, chemicals). This suggests that data on volumes would indicate greater cross-industry stability than that reported by that author. Interestingly, it also appears that the increase in energy prices has been passed on to final consumers.[3] According to Flek (1995), the increase in output prices observed in the first group of industries (which are notoriously concen-trated) results from the exercise of market power. He also concludes that the reallocation of output across industries is deceptively limited.

Whether or not substantial reallocation of resources across sectors can still be expected, the observation that relatively little reallocation has taken place so far has a clear implication: namely, that reliance on an active process of entry and exit across industries as a means to foster rivalry may be unduly optimistic. The development of competition within industries is therefore a particularly urgent task. The evaluation of dominance by estab-lished firms and the control of collusive behaviour by newly separated enti-ties may be of considerably greater importance in these transition economies than in their developed neighbours.

Restructuring at the Firm Level

Restructuring at the firm level can be detected either by changes in the boundaries of the firms through bankruptcies, spin-offs and mergers or by

Table 2.5   Average number of employees per (manufacturing) firm, 1992

	Czechoslovakia	Hungary	Poland	Germany	UK
Average firm size (1989)	2722	327	521	162	33
Average firm size (1992)	570	68	467	160	31
Change 1989–92 (%)	−80	−79	−10		

Source: UN industry statistics, 1995.

Table 2.6   Size distribution of manufacturing firms, 1989, 1993

Czechoslovakia[a]	0–25	25–200	201–500	501–1000	1001–2000	>2000
1989	0.0	0.1	1.3	6.1	18.9	73.6
1993	10.6	11.3	13.6	14.3	14.9	35.3

Hungary[b]	20–50[c]	51–100	101–300	301–500	501–	1001–	2001–	>5000
1989	2.0	2.5	9.3	7.0	14.2	22.0	24.8	18.0
1994	7.1	9.2	22.2	11.25	19.8	15.9	9.36	5.1

UK[b]	1–50	51–100	101–200	201–500	501–2000	>2000
1988	28.11	8.43	10.06	14.90	11.27	35.66

Sources: HMS Business Monitor, Czech Statistical Yearbook, Statistical Yearbook – Hungary 1990 and 1994.
Notes:
[a]The Czechoslovakia data are share of output by size class, expressed in percentages.
[b]The Hungarian and UK data are employment shares, expressed in percentages.
[c]The exclusion of the smallest firms and the low weight given those small firms included in the output or employment shares account for the low average number of employees in Table 2.5.

changes in their business strategies (including marketing and production strategies). Restructuring may affect competition if a firm is restructured horizontally into competing units, but may have little effect on competition if the different units are operating in separate markets.

Table 2.5 shows that average firm size (as measured by employees per firm) shrank by 80% in the former Czechoslovakia and Hungary between 1989 and 1992 (see also Table A1.4 in Appendix 1 for details at the sectoral level). At the end of this period, Hungarian firms were smaller on average than German firms. The average Polish firm, by contrast, had shrunk by only 10%: both Polish and Czechoslovak firms remained large by Western standards.

Statistics on average firm size are highly sensitive to absolute numbers of firms registered (even if these firms are unimportant in terms of either output or employment). A more useful indicator may therefore be the distribution of manufacturing output or employment by firm size: this is presented in Table 2.6. Relative to the United Kingdom, the small firms (with less than 50 or 100 employees) are still relatively unimportant in both Hungary and the Czech Republic. In the case of Hungary, this is compensated with firms in the middle of the distribution, up to 500 employees. For the Czech Republic, in contrast, this is compensated by firms at the upper

range of the distribution. In both cases, the importance of the largest firms
has approximately halved since 1989.

Of course, such drastic changes in the importance of large firms and in
the average firm size might be due to the entry of many small ones, the exit
of some large firms, substantial reductions in the size of existing firms
through split-ups or redundancies – or any combination of the three.

It seems that redundancies account for some of the observed change:
according to Bouin and Grosfeld (1995), employment has been reduced by
as much as 32% among large firms in the Czech Republic and 37% in
Poland between 1989 and 1993, where output fell on average by about 40%.
According to Grosfeld and Roland (1995), a similar pattern can be
observed in Hungary. Once again, it may be that the nature of transition
(here measured by average firm size) may have more to do with the fact that
all firms reduced employment during the recession than with any more
qualitative transformation.

In terms of bankruptcies, the evidence is mixed: as many as 22 000
liquidations and bankruptcies occurred in Hungary during 1991–3. This
seems large by comparison with France, a country five times larger, which
records some 5000 bankruptcies per annum. Data by size of enterprise
were not available, however, and it is not clear whether the threat of bankruptcy is credible for large firms. Case study evidence reported in Carlin,
Van Reenen and Wolfe (1994) suggests that large firms may still be protected from bankruptcy by government subsidies and soft loans. A similarly cautious assessment seems to be warranted for Poland, where
according to Grosfeld and Roland (1995), 288 state-owned enterprises have
either filed for liquidation or have been liquidated between 1990 and 1993,
relative to an average population of more than 7500 state-owned enterprises (OECD, 1994c). Although such a rate of bankruptcy is far from negligible, survey evidence suggests that large firms, at least in 1993, were
confident that they would be bailed out in case of potentially fatal difficulties (reported by Pinto, Belka and Krajewski, 1993, and Carlin, Van
Reenen and Wolfe, 1994). According to OECD (1994c), a lax official policy
toward aspects of tax and social security is still an important source of
financing for large firms in difficulties. In the case of the Czech Republic
even more caution seems to be required as the bankruptcy law was passed
only in April 1993.

Direct evidence on the number and significance of spin-offs and break-
ups is scarce. For the Czech Republic, the first wave of large-scale privatization led to important break-ups (Zemplinerova, 1994) But in general such
drastic restructuring has met with important resistance in all countries.

Overall, this evidence suggests that workforce reductions by existing
firms constituted the main factor behind the fall average firm size (in addition to entry, as we discuss below). This conclusion is supported in the case

Table 2.7 Cumulative distribution
of output by firm size: Czech
Republic

	1989	1993
10 largest firms	13.1	10.7
20 largest firms	17.9	15.1
50 largest firms	26.3	23.7
100 largest firms	38.9	34.1
200 largest firms	58.0	47.5

Source: Zemplinerova (1995).

of the Czech Republic by the remarkable stability of the share of output accounted for by the very large firms (see Table 2.7). Equivalent data for other countries are not available.

Industrial restructuring does not result solely from layoffs, break-ups and bankruptcy. Indeed, the ultimate success of restructuring activities requires the development of new business strategies. We use the term strategic restructuring to describe the development and implementation of a strategy for the firm that embodies its production process, its internal organization and management, the distribution and sale of its product and the identification of its competitors. Direct evidence on this aspect of restructuring, is of course, difficult to gather. Enterprise surveys provide useful insights into this matter and suggest that few firms have, as yet, developed business strategies worthy of the name.[4] According to enterprise surveys, most firms have instead adopted 'defensive' measures, aimed at ensuring the immediate survival of the enterprise (see, for instance, EBRD, 1995). Workforce reductions are clearly the most important form of such defensive restructuring (and the data presented above are consistent with this view). The absence of business strategies is confirmed by Carlin, Van Reenen and Wolfe (1994), who distinguish between deep, passive and ambiguous restructuring. They find that most firms have undertaken either minimum change or ambiguous change, the latter referring to change that may not be compatible with the development of a market economy in the longer term.

Most studies find very few cases of deep (strategic) restructuring. Moreover, they observe that such cases are almost always associated with the presence of a foreign partner (either foreign take-overs or joint ventures). A phenomenon of importance for competition policy is that foreign partners have in many cases targeted firms and industries with substantial market power. They have often obtained substantial guarantees from the government in terms of protection from potential competitors. According to Carlin, Van Reenen and Wolfe (1994, p. 234), well-publicized cases like the purchase of Skoda by Volkswagen are not isolated. The clear pattern emerging from their surveys is that foreign ownership is associated with the existence and consolidation of market power (see also Voszka, 1993, for additional evidence).

One of the most common form of 'ambiguous' restructuring seems also to be associated with the exercise of market power. Carlin, Van Reenen and Wolfe (1994) report a number of cases studies (in Poland and Hungary) where an existing firm either used its dominant position to increase a price or took active steps to eliminate remaining competitors. At the same time, firms in such positions have also tended to reduce their labour force more than others. This suggests that monopoly rents may have been used to finance redundancies.

Overall, the evidence on restructuring gathered above suggests that while a lot has been achieved to reduce overstaffing in the enterprises created under central planning, much remains to be done in terms of the development of new business strategies. According to most observers (Carlin, Van Reenen and Wolfe, 1994; Zemplinerova, 1995; OECD, 1994b, EBRD 1995), the disappointing progress made in terms of restructuring is due to inadequate incentives in terms of both product-market competition and corporate governance. We turn to these questions next.

Corporate Control and Public Ownership

A variety of forms of corporate control can be observed during the first few years of transition. The following forms can be distinguished (see, for instance, Earle, Estrin and Leshchenko, 1995; EBRD,1995): state ownership (either directly or via a national property fund), control by insiders (workers or managers in the organization), control by investment privatization funds (private sector funds established by voucher privatization), control by other domestic outsiders (banks, private shareholders), and foreign control. For those firms that remained in the state sector, corporate control has evolved since the beginning of transition, as budget constraints have been hardened within governments. Nevertheless, it is striking that the share of the public sector in transition economies remains large. Table 2.8 shows that the public sector still accounted for at least 40% of GDP in each

Table 2.8   Private and public sector shares of GDP, 1994

Country	Private sector	Public sector
Czech Republic	56	44
Hungary	52	48
Poland	56	44
Slovak Republic	44	56

Sources: EBRD (1994) and OECD (1994b,c, 1995).
Figures in per cent.

economy in 1994. In addition, one cannot expect that remaining state enterprises will be privatized in the near future; in Poland, the number of large combinates was reduced by only 45% between 1989 and 1995 and the privatization of the remaining combinates will require more complex restructuring than early privatizations.[5] A similar pattern is found in Hungary where the (recently merged) privatization agencies still had, in mid-1995, 631 potentially difficult cases to handle, out of a total of 2015 enterprises from 1990 (data from OECD, 1995). The situation in the Czech Republic is more advanced with about 80% of government assets expected to have been transferred to the private sector by the end of 1995. Slovakia stood in stark contrast: the privatization process has stalled and less than 50% of state enterprises had been privatized by the end of 1994.

It is beyond the scope of this discussion to make a detailed analysis of the existing evidence on the effectiveness of the various systems of corporate control that have emerged (see Earle, Estrin and Leshchenko, 1995; Katsoulacos and Takla, 1995; and others reported in EBRD, 1995). Nonetheless, we can report a number of striking observations.

First, from the evidence across countries it is remarkable that the path of reform, and hence the relative importance of various forms of corporate control, does not seem to matter very much. Hungary, Poland and the Czech Republic have implemented radically different processes of privatization (for instance, restructuring before privatization in Poland compared to privatization before restructuring in the Czech Republic). But the symptoms of ineffective corporate control are prevalent in all countries. All systems seem to have significant shortcomings: for instance, budget constraints for state-owned firms in Poland and Hungary may not be as hard as desirable (with extensive inter-firm credits, soft loans, tax arrears and subsidies apparently persisting) (see, for instance, Anderson, 1996). Investment privatization funds in the Czech Republic may not be as effective as had been hoped.[6] There is also evidence (as we discuss in Section 2.2 below) that existing managers have in many circumstances managed to consolidate their control over existing corporate assets rather than being replaced, as had been widely expected.

Second, one can look at comparative evidence about different systems of corporate control within countries. This evidence (consisting mostly of enterprise surveys) is complex but generally sobering. Strategic restructuring is mostly associated with foreign ownership, and differences between control by state, insider, domestic outsider and investment privatization funds do not seem to matter very much (see EBRD, 1995). This possible irrelevance of alternative forms of corporate control is reinforced by some econometric studies. For instance, Lizal, Singer and Svejnar (1995), controlling for firm and industry characteristics, find that the behaviour and performance of split-up firms is no different from those that have not been restructured.

Significant progress may, of course, take place in the future, with mass privatization now under way in Poland, the second wave of privatization in the Czech Republic, the further consolidation of the Czech Republic's investment funds and, more generally, the accumulation of managerial talent. At the same time, it may be unwise to rely completely on such (somewhat speculative) improvements without emphasizing product-market competition. If anything, given the fact that product-market competition and corporate governance create incentives that are to some extent substitutes for one another, the experience of the restructuring that has taken place so far seems to reinforce the case for a more activist approach to product-market competition. The profound changes in industry structures that are still likely to take place in the next few years also require a competition policy enforcement which is capable of adapting to such a rapidly changing environment.

2.1.2   Product-market Competition

The effectiveness of product-market competition can be assessed in a number of ways. In what follows, we look at entry, import competition and the potential for collusion and the exercise of dominance by established firms.

Entry and Factor Markets

A large number of new enterprises have been formed in all transition countries, especially in the trade and service sectors. Table 2.9 shows that the number of enterprises in Hungary has increased by a factor of ten since the beginning of transition, this consisting of a sixfold increase in manufacturing and an increase of more than fifty times in services. Most of these new firms tend to be very small, with less than 10 employees, and tend to remain

Table 2.9   Growth of number of enterprises with legal status, Hungary

Sector	Percentage change, 1988–94
Industry	578
Building	505
Home trade[a]	6568
Total	836

Sources: *European Economy* (1991); *Statistical Bulletin – Hungary* 1995.
Note:
[a]Home trade includes, in 1994, wholesale and retail trade, financial intermediation, real estate, hotels and restaurants.

Table 2.10   Size distribution of enterprise, Hungary. Share of the number of firms by employment classes (%)

	1–10	11–20	21–50	>50	>301	Unspecified
1988	18.7		14.5	28.2	23.3	15.3
1993	58.3	26.0	8.1	6.2	1.4	
Manufacturing	47.5	23.9	13.6	11.5	3.4	

Sources: European Economy (1994); Statistical Bulletin – Hungary 1995.

Table 2.11   Legal entities and private entrepreneurs, 1994[a]

	Slovakia	Hungary	Czech Republic	Poland
Legal Entities				
Agriculture	2467	5547	7883	18 119
Manufacturing	5687	19 038	15 662	28 269
Construction	2832	9604	8531	14 865
Services[a]	21 038	39 223	73 004	59 122
Total	51 606	101 247	180 313	120 375
Entrepreneurs				
Agriculture	24 240	22 493	91 936	na
Manufacturing	48 999	257 245	168 051	na
Construction	47 711	na	124 912	na
Services[b]	143 680	na	485 556	na
Total	290 961	778 036	938 221	1 800 000

Sources: Statistical Bulletins of the Czech Republic, Slovakia and Poland.
Notes:
[a]Data are for the end of 1994 for the Czech Republic and Slovakia but September 1994 for Poland.
[b]Services include wholesale and retail trade, financial intermediation, real estate, hotels and restaurants (the Czech Republic and Slovakia) and business activities (Poland).

small, even in the manufacturing sector (see Table 2.10). Comparison with the United Kingdom, a country about five times the size of Hungary, with 1.6 million legal units and 812000 legal units in services, suggests that the number of enterprises in Hungary could increase further by a factor of three before it reaches the UK level.

According to Table 2.11, the development of small private enterprises is particularly rapid in the Czech Republic, which has 80% more legal entities than Hungary, despite being roughly the same size. A 50% increase in the number of legal entities in the Czech Republic would be sufficient to attain the kind of structure observed in the United Kingdom. But Slovakia has, relative to its size, fewer independent entrepreneurs than either Hungary or the Czech Republic (which have a similar density of entrepreneurs). Poland (about five times larger than Hungary) has remarkably few legal entities and private entrepreneurs (about 1.8 million according to the Polish *Statistical Yearbook* for 1994). It may be that part of this phenomenon for the Czech Republic is explained by its long border with the rich German state of Bavaria, with small enterprises selling cross-border.

The implications for competition of such an evolution of the number of legal entities is hard to interpret. First, despite the large increase in the last few years, there remain fewer small firms than in market economies of equivalent size. Second, there is some evidence that new firms enter at very small scales of production, in comparison with established market economies where new firms enter at a scale which is about 25–30% of the average incumbent (see Geroski, 1992). By contrast, in the Czech Republic's manufacturing sector, average entry occurs at less than 5% of the scale of the average incumbent. It may be the case that entry at such small scale has a lower disciplinary effect on incumbents than the typical entry observed in established market economies.

At present, there is no direct evidence (to the best of our knowledge) about the growth of new entrants. In established market economies, effective competition can be provided by a few successful entrants which experience very fast growth in the first few years of their existence. But there are reasons to think that conditions in transition economies may restrain such growth.

If access to labour does not seem be a major issue, as suggested by Konings, Lehman and Schaffer (1995) and Rutkowski and Sinha (1995), access to finance and managerial talent may be more of a hurdle. According to Table 2.12, retained earnings are the most important form of investment finance in transition economies – to a high degree relative to United Kingdom standards. On this basis, Grosfeld and Roland (1995) conclude that access to credit may be a significant problem. However, such a high proportion of internal finance is not unusual in financial systems like that of Germany, although the German financial system may not be very effective at the provision of venture capital.[7] Whatever the appropriate point of comparison, the share of bank credit (the main source of finance for small firms) remains very low, at least in Poland and the Czech Republic In addition, this level of bank credit is small relative to the high demand for finance that one would expect during the transition process, especially with so

Table 2.12   Sources of investment finance, 1993

	Poland	Czech Republic	Hungary	Germany[a]
Retained earnings	63.3	72.7	54.2	61.7
Subsidies	4.7	4.8	26.1	6.9
Bank credit	8.7	16.8	3.4	15.7
Other	23.5	5.7	16.3	15.0

Sources: Grosfeld and Roland (1995); Edwards and Fischer (1994).
Note:
[a]The German data cover the period 1980–90.

many small entrants. These stylized facts provide indirect evidence that financing may be a hurdle for small entrants in transition economies. At the same time, much of the academic and policy debate on financial reform in transition economies has focused on the consolidation of bad debt and the provision of finance to existing firms. Venture capital has been relatively neglected (see, for instance, EBRD, 1994, or Anderson, 1996).

Access to managerial talent may also be a significant hurdle. Carlin, Van Reenen and Wolfe (1994) suggest that there is little evidence of a developing market for managers. The existing stock of managerial talent may be highly specific to the particular firms and industries in which it originated. In command economies, managers had strong incentives to develop their contacts with potential suppliers of inputs, and to lobby government agencies in order to ensure the survival of their enterprises. Such networks of contacts have lost some value with the transition, and, in any event, are difficult to transfer across firms or industries. This may partially explain why new entrants cannot easily attract good managers.

Foreign Direct Investment

To the extent that foreign firms can import managerial talent and upgrade technology faster than domestic firms, they can undertake restructuring more quickly and provide effective competition in the short term. As indicated above, there is indeed evidence that deep strategic restructuring (as defined on page 27 above), is often associated with the presence of a foreign investor.

Overall, foreign direct investment flows in transition economies have been modest, at least until 1995. Between 1989 and early 1994, these four countries received 18.5 billion ECU by comparison with an annual outward flow of investment by EC countries of about 49.2 billion ECU, but have received as much as 11 billion ECU for 1995 alone. However, investments are highly concentrated in a small number of large projects: the largest ten projects account for more than a third of total investments in all countries and as much as 80% in the Czech Republic (see Table 2.13). In each country, the manufacturing sector accounts for about half of the investments and the motor car industry consistently figures as a major recipient.[8]

Table 2.13   Foreign direct investment, 1989–95

	Czech Republic	Hungary	Poland	Slovakia
Cumulative investment (billion ECU)	7.1	13.2	8.4	0.9
Largest ten investors	5.7	4.1	2.8	0.4
of which motor cars	1.3	1.2	0.3	0.1

Sources: National banks, UN/ECE, *Business Central Europe*.

As foreign direct investment is highly concentrated in a few projects and sectors, it is unlikely to have a general impact on competition and restructuring across all sectors. However, the figures reported here may underestimate the importance of foreign firms in a more important respect: a foreign presence may be felt without direct investment, as, for instance, with a licence, marketing or distribution agreement. In the case of Hungary, the Anti-monopoly Office suggests that about one firm in five has some involvement with a foreign partner.

In those sectors where there has been foreign investment, it should not be assumed that there is a beneficial impact on competition. Often foreign investors have acquired large firms with substantial domestic market shares and have negotiated significant import protection. The motor car industry is a case in point. Volkswagen has a 65% market share in the Czech Republic while Fiat accounts for 52% of the Polish market (and 88% of the market for small cars). Both companies have obtained substantial import protection (15% and 35% tariffs, respectively). Peugeot is currently negotiating for the establishment of a joint venture with Dacia, the Romanian car producer, and is rumoured to be demanding an increase in import duties from 12% to 30%, as part of the deal.[9]

In those industries where foreign direct investment is taking place, the impact of foreign firms on restructuring should still not be underestimated. Business reports (see *Business Central Europe*, 1995, 1996) suggest that there are significant spill-overs from the presence of foreign firms on the rest of the industry, in terms of technological upgrading and the incentive to restructure. This is particularly important in vertical relations, where a foreign supplier or buyer has an impact on the downstream or upstream local firm.

Import Competition

It is often argued that opening markets to international trade and import competition is the most important stimulus for the promotion of competition. Such an argument has been advanced for transition economies, especially in view of their size and integration under central planning.

According to the EBRD (1994), the CEECs have drastically liberalized their trade regimes. Controls on imports have in general been abolished but restrictions have been maintained in all countries for 'sensitive products'. These include agricultural products, textiles, clothing, steel and coal in the Czech and Slovak Republics. In 1989–90, trade between the members of the former Eastern trading alliance (COMECON) collapsed and import flows shifted towards member countries of the Organization for Economic Cooperation and Development (OECD). Imports from the EU in particular rose quickly during 1991 and 1992. Thereafter, a number of import restrictions were reintroduced. For instance, Hungary progressively

Table 2.14 Import penetration,
ratio of imports to GDP

	1992[a]	1994[a]
Czech Republic	12.5	40.3[b]
Poland	7.3	18.3[c]
Hungary	16.9	35.3
Slovak Republic	12.2	36.0[d]
Belgium	72.0	
UK	25.0	

Sources: EBRD (1994), OECD country
studies and Eurostat. Figures are per
cent.
Notes:
[a]1992 figures are at purchasing power
parity and 1994 figures at current prices
and exchange rates.
[b]Includes trade with Slovakia.
[c]1993 figure.
[d]Includes trade with the Czech Republic.

increased its basic tariff from 11% in 1991 to 16% in 1994. The Slovak
Republic introduced a 10% surcharge in 1994. Poland increased its tariff
from 9% on average in 1991 to 11% for industrial products and 18% for
agricultural goods in 1993. Particular restrictions were also introduced for
bilateral trade among transition economies (with the Czech and Slovak
Republics currently in the middle of a tariff war) (see Faini and Portes,
1995, for full details).

The situation in 1992 was still such that transition economies were relatively closed to foreign trade (see Table 2.14). This conclusion is confirmed
by Hamilton and Winters (1992), who estimated, using a technique known
as a 'gravity' model, that at current income levels imports in transition
economies could increase by a wide margin (up to five-fold increases from
the EC for instance).[10] However, the estimates are very sensitive to the estimates of GDP that are used. The figures in Table 2.14 use EBRD data
where GDP is estimated at international prices, which seems to be
appropriate given that imports are estimated at international prices.
However, if one uses estimates of GDP at domestic prices and translates
them at current exchange rates, import penetration appears to be significantly higher. The latter calculation makes import penetration as high as
35–40%. This is still much below the figure observed in a Western economy
of similar size and central location, such as Belgium.

Aggregate figures do conceal large differences at the industry level.
Zemplinerova and Stibal (1995) provide estimates of import penetration
(i.e. imports as a percentage of apparent consumption) at the industry level
for 1989 and 1992 in the Czech Republic. These calculations suggest that,

for most industries, import penetration has increased moderately (i.e. by less than 10 percentage points) between 1989 and 1992. There are some important exceptions. Imports have surged in industries like business machines, where import penetration has increased from 8% in 1989 to 98% in 1992, and in the 'Other Transport' category from 4% to 47%. In other industries, like furniture, coal and oil processing equipment, optical equipment and communication equipment, import penetration has fallen substantially (i.e. by 10–25 percentage points).

Further insights on the competitive impact of imports can be found in a detailed study of trade flows in transition economies (between 1988 and 1994) by Hoekman and Djankov (1996). These authors find surprisingly little change in the commodity composition of exports, which supports the observation earlier that the pattern of activities has not changed markedly. However, they find substantial changes in trade flows within traditional export categories. There is a large increase in imports but a detailed analysis of these flows reveals that firms in transition economies have been importing intermediate goods, mostly machines and components, to upgrade their production, so that the intra-industry trade which prevails in those industries reveals some vertical specialization. Accordingly, the observed increased in intra-industry trade cannot be directly associated with increased competition for the final output.

One important form of trade known as outward processing, whereby foreign firms send semi-finished products to transition economies for (mostly labour-intensive) processing and subsequent re-import, is an extreme form of vertical specialization within industries.[11] In such circumstances, imports have little impact on domestic competition (except insofar as domestic firms compete for outward processing contracts). According to Corrado, Benacek and Caban (1995), outward processing trade accounts for as much 60–80% of exports in the textile industry and 20–30% in leather and footwear. Even in industries like electrical machinery, precision instruments and furniture, outward processing trade may account for 15–20% of exports (see Hoekman and Djankov, 1996).

Overall, this evidence suggests that the effect of imports on domestic competition is likely to be limited.[12]

Dominant Firms

The discussion of restructuring, entry and import competition thus far suggests that significant improvements have been made in terms of labour productivity, that numerous entrants challenge incumbents though at a very small (and thus probably inefficient) scale, and that import competition is relatively weak. In this section we examine whether dominant firms have survived in spite of the market changes.

Data are available only for the Czech Republic, but these may provide a useful benchmark, given that the Czech economy is clearly more dominated by large firms (as outlined in Table 2.5 above). Zemplinerova and Stibal (1995) compute the four-firm concentration ratio adjusted for imports and exports. The ratios measure the cumulative market share of the four largest domestic firms in apparent consumption. (They differ from the usual four-firm concentration ratios as the identity of foreign firms is not known and foreign firms may sometimes be among the largest four firms.) The latest data are for 1992 (but the 1993 numbers may be very similar, as the unadjusted data for 1993 are similar to those reported for 1992 and the ratio of imports to exports did not change during 1993).

The figures in Table 2.15 indicate that concentration ratios have fallen, with the unweighted average across sectors falling from 39 to 30, as a result of the various changes described above (labour shedding, entry, imports). Most of the concentration ratios reported here would not, with a few exceptions, immediately attract attention from competition agencies in market economies. Indeed, the concentration ratios observed in the United States in 1987 at a similar level of aggregation (two digits) are of the same order of magnitude (see Joskow, Schmalensee and Tsukanova, 1994) and often higher. Table 2.15 also provides a European benchmark, namely the

Table 2.15 Concentration ratios: Czech Republic and EU

Czech categories Four-firm domestic ratio	1989	1992	EU 3-digit category Five-firm ratio	1987
Foodstuffs	17	13		
Tobacco	69	69	Tobacco	56
Textile	18	16	Miscellaneous textiles	19
Clothing	39	23	Clothing	4
Leather and shoes	65	45	Footwear	6
Wood products	54	29		
Paper	59	39	Paper	16
Printing and publishing	44	27	Printing and publishing	9
Oil and coal processing	60	69		
Chemicals	30	20	Basic chemicals	25
Rubber and plastics	41	34	Rubber	46
Non-metals	21	19		
Metal	53	55	Iron and steel	40
Metal construction	23	27		
Machinery	12	8		
Business machines	59	2		
Electrical machines	18	16	Electrical machines	17
Communication equipment	15	10		
Optical, medical	4	13	Medical instruments	27
Cars and trailers	62	47	Motor vehicles	63
Other transports	38	37		
Furniture	19	15		
Recycling	90	53		

Sources: Zemplinerova and Stibal (1995); Davies and Lyons (1996).

five-firm concentration ratios for the EU-12 in 1987.[13] These concentrations ratios are provided for a selected number of three-digit industries. As the Czech data refer to what corresponds to EU two-digit industries, the comparison should be made carefully as one would expect four-firm concentration data at the three-digit level in the Czech Republic to be higher than those reported here. The industries selected for the comparison are broad three-digit industries for which this discrepancy should be smallest. On the other hand, concentration at the level of a country like the Czech Republic can be expected to be much larger than that at the level of the EU. The comparison confirms that the concentration observed in the Czech Republic is not out of line with that observed in the EU. There are, however, a number of industries like footwear, printing and publishing and clothing which are very fragmented in the EU and still strikingly concentrated in the Czech Republic.

Nevertheless, there is an important reason for caution before concluding on the basis of four- or five-firm concentration ratios that there is no problem of dominance. This is that, for the Czech Republic, the four-firm concentration ratio is sometimes very close to the one-firm concentration ratio. For instance, in the tobacco, paper, car, oil and coal processing, rubber and plastics industries, the four-firm concentration ratio is close to the market share of the largest firm. Single-firm concentration levels of this order of magnitude would certainly attract attention of competition agencies in Western economies.[14]

Collusion Habits

Estrin and Cave (1993) argue that managers in centrally planned economies had a habit of cooperating with colleagues in similar enterprises in order to fulfil their obligations (or to pretend to do so) to their superior. For instance, there was a common practice of trading inputs across enterprises. The industry surveys analysed by Carlin, Van Reenen and Wolfe (1994) tend to suggest that managers have often attempted to continue such practices. For instance, the creation of holding companies ('amalgamations') with firms in closely related product markets can be seen as an attempt to enhance cooperation. The powerful trade associations that have emerged (see Joskow, Schmalensee and Tsukanova, 1994) may serve the same purpose. These may be rational responses by managers to insecurity, but such responses may warrant particular attention by competition agencies.

Command economies also exhibited a high degree of vertical integration, and this increased over the 1980s in response to systemic failures (see Jaskow, Schmalensee and Tsukanova, 1994). As the supply of inputs was increasingly poorly coordinated, managers reacted by setting up their own production facilities for key inputs. According to enterprise surveys (see

Pinto, Belka and Krajewski, 1993; Carlin, Van Reenen and Wolfe, 1994), many enterprises (in Poland, Hungary and the Czech Republic) have also reacted to the insecurity associated with transition by creating links that either replicate former mechanisms of supply or establishing relations with firms in vertically related sectors. Such links may either be informal or take the form of cross-ownership. Their importance should not be under-estimated in a environment where the rule of law is not firmly established.

Summary

The main conclusion that arises from this overview of industry structures is that the state of competition in industry in transition economies is still far removed from that in established market economies. Surprisingly little reallocation of resources across industries has taken place. Reliance on an active process of entry and exit across industries to foster rivalry may be unwarranted. In addition, it seems that significant structural changes (mainly labour shedding) may have taken place but true strategic restructuring is rare. The mechanisms of corporate control have yet to improve significantly. Product-market competition should give much of the incentive to restructure, but only if it is reasonably vigorous. Relative to established market economies, there are more dominant firms and entry is discrete. Although entry is widespread, its effectiveness must be questioned because of the very small size of entrants. The impact of foreign direct investment has until recently been relatively modest, especially because investment has been concentrated on a small number of specific sectors. Import competition is weak, especially as these economies remain relatively closed. Finally, firm managers may be attempting to achieve within the market the non-competitive outcomes previously achieve by central planning. If anything the existing evidence on enterprise restructuring reinforces the need for prohibitive competition rules.[15] This is especially true as the process of restructuring will depend more on change within existing industries and sectors than on substantial transfers of resources across sectors. In particular, given the weakness of entry, competition agencies should accord high priority to preventing the entrenchment of dominance (either singly or in collusion) by existing large firms.

2.2   Political Constraints

2.2.1   *The Political Background to Competition Policy*

When legislatures pass laws to regulate competition and governments establish institutions to implement these laws, they do so not only because they have become convinced by abstract reasoning of the need to police the competitive process but also because they face political pressures of various kinds. By this we mean that politically powerful individuals and groups have expectations and make demands of the political system whose fulfilment implies government intervention in the competitive process in some way. These pressures may be internal, like the pressures to curb the power of the large trusts that led to the passage of the Sherman Act in the United States in the late nineteenth century. They may be external, as in the competition regimes imposed in occupied Germany and Japan after the Second World War, fuelled by the Allies' belief that pre-war militarism and rearmament in these two countries had owed something to the monopoly power of large engineering corporations. The pressures may be direct, as when there is lobbying for the passage of laws regulating monopolistic practices, or indirect, when legislators come to believe that interventions are required for the achievement of other objectives they are under pressure to deliver, such as stable prices or increased industrial output.

In this section, we analyse these pressures. Explicit analysis can be valuable for two reasons. First, it can help to explain why countries differ in the laws and institutions they adopt. Of course, countries differ for other reasons too: they may have inherited different economic structures, or they may be open to foreign competition to different degrees, and these factors may make it appropriate to adopt different policies. Nevertheless, sometimes policies differ not because of their expected consequences but because of their constituencies: those political interests that believe they have something to gain or lose from the way competition is regulated. Interest groups may, for historical, economic or ideological reasons, be better organized in some countries than in others, and there may be a different tilt in the balance of power between them in different countries.

Second, understanding the political pressures to which competition policy is a response can alert us to the constraints under which it must operate in the future. If a competition agency has been established in the first place in response to the demands of certain interest groups, then it may need to ensure that these groups are satisfied if it is to be able to continue to function effectively. None of this implies that political pressures completely determine economic policy, nor that sincere beliefs about the public good are irrelevant to the actions of legislators and officials. But political pressures certainly affect the constraints within which conceptions of the public good can be expected to work. In the rest of this book we are much concerned with discussing the importance of competition policy for the public good. In this section we attempt a tentative assessment of the surrounding political constraints.

We shall mainly consider the general ways in which the political pressures that have led to the adoption of competition laws and institutions differ in transition economies, considered as a group, from those in existing market economies. But we shall also use specific evidence from the four countries in our study to look at differences in political pressures across the transition economies, asking to what extent these may explain differences in the laws and policies adopted. We shall explicitly address the question of how these pressures may constrain future policy, and in what ways they may be harnessed to make future policy more effective.

A word about the structure of our argument. In examining differences between countries in the nature of interest group pressures, we are not implying that cultural or ideological differences may be ignored. Nevertheless, there is already evidence that apparent cultural differences between countries in attitudes to markets and economic reforms may owe more than has previously been supposed to differences in institutional constraints and opportunities and less to differences in fundamental habits of thought. For example, Shiller, Boycko and Korobov (1991) cite questionnaire evidence comparing attitudes of citizens of New York and Moscow to various aspects of economic reform, including the acceptability of price increases in response to shortages and inequality in the distribution of benefits of reform. They find clearly that 'notions of fairness are very situation-specific: flower-sellers are unfair if they raise their prices, while landlords who do so [when improved transport facilities raise the desirability of housing] are usually not. Notions of fairness are not country-specific' (p.389). These findings are reinforced by the discovery that Russians show no greater tendency to blame speculators for shortages than do Americans, and no greater opposition to the idea that incentives, including income inequality, are necessary for the organization of society.[16] The authors did find some slight evidence of greater resistance among Soviet citizens to the replacement of barter by financial transactions, and 'less warm attitudes towards business', as well as 'more of a concern that the government may later nationalize private enterprises'. But overall it seems reasonable to conclude that while lesser familiarity with the characteristics of market society may make Soviet citizens more cautious, there is no evidence of fundamental differences in values that might lead to a radically different conception of what any market society can be expected to deliver. The possibility of such fundamental differences in values should not be ruled out, but explanations in terms of different information, opportunities or constraints should be explored first. This will be our approach in what follows.

2.2.2 General Pressures in Transition Economies

All the industrialized societies that forswore central planning at the end of the 1980s have as a result faced, to varying degrees, political pressures that

are different from those in market economies. Perhaps the most fundamental of these pressures has arisen from the fact that common sense
implied even at the start of the transition, and experience has subsequently
confirmed, that economic reform would involve major redistribution of
assets and incomes. More pertinently (since even in more normal times the
lottery of a market economy is constantly creating new winners and losers),
it was likely that this redistribution would not be just random but would be
predominantly directed away from individuals and groups who had been
especially favoured under the former regimes. This redistribution might but
need not have been accompanied by an increase in overall inequality.
Newbery (1995) shows that relative price changes (which were only one
component of economic reform) did not have an appreciable effect on
inequality in Hungary from 1988 to 1993 (nor did they in the United
Kingdom over the same period). He concludes from this that taxes and subsidies had been poorly targeted, from a distribution point of view, prior to
the reform. This may have been intentional: central planners may have had
other objectives in mind in distributing subsidies. It is also consistent with
his evidence to argue that (1) economic reform may still increase inequality, but because of differential access to assets and profit opportunities
rather than because of relative price changes; (2) even if it does not do so
overall, the likely losers from reform may be better organized and more
politically powerful than gainers.

All the societies concerned were therefore characterized by the presence
of groups of people, some of them previously powerful – who had every
reason to expect that their economic value to a market economy would be
small compared with the privileges they currently enjoyed, and who consequently and understandably wished to prevent, slow down, or alleviate the
process of reform. The extent to which these groups continued to enjoy
influence under the new regimes varied a great deal between groups and
between countries: factory managers as a group were undoubtedly a better
organized lobby than pensioners, and the large trade unions continued to
wield much more political influence in, say, Romania than in the Czech
Republic, due to the more comprehensive political transition in the latter
country. Although economic reform in any country always creates certain
groups of losers who may wish to impede the reform, the losers in the formerly planned economies were more identifiable, better connected and typically more desperate than their equivalents in any existing market
economies. However, the political system that had supported them had also
been much more dramatically discredited.[17]

The mere fact that reform would threaten existing privileges does not,
however, explain by itself why the interests of potential losers should constitute an important political constraint on the reform process. There are
two main reasons for this. First, the very inefficiency of the planned

economies might have been thought to offer ample opportunities to compensate losers while still leaving clear gains for the rest of society. Indeed, there is a paradox: the more inefficient the initial state of the economy, the greater the potential gains available in the aggregate from reform, and consequently, one might suppose, the easier it should be to ensure that nobody loses from reform and some groups strictly gain. Yet the almost universal experience, whether in the former planned economies or elsewhere, is that it is harder to implement reforms, the more severely distorted is the economy to begin with. Why? The answer almost certainly lies in the fact that, for any economy to be functioning in a distorted state, significant groups must be receiving large rents. A reform that raises these groups' marginal productivity may nevertheless leave them worse off if it reduces the element of rent they receive. And reform typically does reduce at least some rents, since these are usually linked to the control of resources (assets or jobs) which it is the purpose of the reform to redistribute. So unless a means is found to compensate such groups for the loss of these rents they will do their best to frustrate the reform.[18] But compensation is typically difficult. Many of the economies of Eastern Europe and the former Soviet Union were so severely distorted that they contained many enterprises, even whole sectors, producing negative value added (Hare and Hughes, 1991). In theory, such a situation provides the simplest possible prescription for reform: closing down an enterprise instantly raises GDP even if nothing else is done with the resources employed. In practice, of course, managers and workers in such enterprises must have been receiving benefits far above their marginal product, and even with generous unemployment benefits they may be much worse off unemployed. Even those who *ex post* would realize that they had become better off (for instance, by rapidly finding new employment) might not feel sufficiently confident of such a prospect *ex ante* to welcome the reform.

A second reason why the threat to existing privileges need not constitute an insuperable obstacle to reform has become apparent in the time since the reform process began. This is that significant numbers of those who enjoyed privileges under the previous regimes have proved highly adept at benefiting from the transition, usually because of their access on favourable terms to valuable corporate assets. Although many commentators (such as Bolton and Roland, 1992) thought that one of the major advantages of reform (including via privatization) would be a widespread replacement of existing factory managers, in practice and in all countries there has been a considerable entrenchment of existing managers, both in positions of control and often as owners (a phenomenon that may partly explain the weak impact of mechanisms of corporate control that we discussed in Section 2.1 above). Whether this has been because existing managers were in fact better suited to managing firms than had previously been thought, or because of advantages of incumbency unrelated to competence, is harder to say. In Hungary, for example, an early vote on the confirmation of company managers was widely expected to result in sweeping changes but in fact confirmed around four-fifths of existing appointments.[19] There has also been strong criticism of the degree of discretion granted to the Hungarian State Property Agency in arranging privatizations.[20] In the Czech Republic there has been criticism by the Ministry for Economic Competition of the tendency of enterprises facing privatization that 'refused to give the necessary data to authors of competing privatization projects' (*Hospodarske Noviny*, 18 February 1992). In addition, the post-reform governments have proved enthusiastic proponents of appointing their own political supporters to leading corporate positions in both state-owned and private enterprises.[21]

The fact that some of those who might have been expected to lose out from economic reform have been able to reap some of the early fruits of reform has had some unexpected results. First, among the CEECs, the election of governments composed of or with strong links to former Communists has not, contrary to some early fears, seen a substantial reversal of the general direction of economic reform (a conclusion that it is too early to draw in the former Soviet Union). Those who were previously powerful may be persuaded of the virtues of reform without becoming supporters of the first-generation reforming governments. As Peter Bod, President of National Bank of Hungary and former Minister of Industry, expressed it: 'The new opportunities offered by a market economy benefited first and foremost the former ruling strata, owing to their advantageous initial position. It does not follow from this, however, that the former party secretary who is now a major merchant would support the new government' (Blejer and Coricelli, 1995, p.120). The fact that former Communists nevertheless became reformers may be an example of what Bolton and Roland (1992) argue to be one of the most compelling arguments for gradualism in reform, namely that it may persuade potential losers that they may after all have something to gain from the process and thereby assist in the creation of constituencies for the most difficult parts of a reform package. Leszek Balcerowicz, former Polish finance minister, advanced a similar hypothesis about the dynamic process of creating constituencies for reform when he claimed that 'entrepreneurs, whose numbers had been growing rapidly, were on the whole in favour of the market economy. People employed in the private sector, too, were on average more supportive than those in the state sector. Therefore, the rapidly growing share of the private economy outside agriculture has some positive political implications for the market-oriented reform' (Blejer and Coricelli, 1995, pp. 116–17).

However, it is also quite possible that this same process, while ensuring that reforms are not wholly reversed, has made it easier for them to be distorted in subtle ways. The formerly powerful may have had privileged access to industrial assets, but those assets were far from being equally productive. For every factory manager who is able to prosper in the new economic environment there will be another whose products are unsalable and who is therefore on the lookout for subsidies and protection from competitors. The fact that factory managers may have been appointed partly on the basis of political connections under the old regimes can be expected to have helped rather than hindered them in the new environment. Control by insiders may have helped to fragment the potential opposition to reform, but it has posed dangers to the coherence and effectiveness of that reform.

The simple fact of a conflict between winners and losers from reform, though central to the predicament of all the formerly planned economies, is not the whole story. There were many other features of these economies giving rise to expectations from and demands upon their political systems as reform progressed. It is convenient to group these pressures into those resulting from:

1. The absence of market habits and institutions under central planning;
2. The speed with which old habits and institutions had to be abandoned;
3. The persistence, nevertheless, of some habits and institutions more appropriate to central planning than to the market economy.

We consider these in turn.

The Previous Absence of Market Habits and Institutions

The high degree of horizontal integration of firms meant that behaviour which would be considered collusion in a market economy was a natural (indeed, the only natural) way for firms to operate within the central planning system (see Joskow, Schmalensee and Tsukanova, 1994). Learning to compete required firms to conceive of each other in a wholly new way, and has often produced a certain bewilderment among managers at the idea that price-fixing or market-sharing, for instance, might be socially harmful and therefore illegal. A recent incident in the Czech Republic illustrates this clearly.

The government had wished to see unleaded petrol sold more cheaply than the leaded variety, but was afraid that differential tax rates would lead to tax evasion. A government minister, Mr Dlouhy, met with representatives of the main oil companies in December 1995 and arranged common prices, which would have involved a degree of cross-subsidization of unleaded by leaded fuel. It does not seem to have been anticipated that this decision would be investigated as an instance of price-fixing by the Ministry of Economic Competition (see *Lidove Noviny*, 3 January 1996), even though the illegality of such an agreement would be routine in Western Europe or the United States.[22] The case has yet to be adjudicated, but the MEC has already complained of political interference in its activities. The Czech Republic's prime minister made a speech condemning the action of the MEC as 'absurd' (*Lidove Noviny*, 14 February 1996), and the MEC itself has protested publicly against 'the irresponsible politicization of its work' (*Svobodne Slovo*, 20 April 1996), although the arguments were somewhat muted by the injury of the minister in a car accident.

The associated high levels of industrial concentration have given rise to concern that economic liberalization or privatization would not work without prior dissipation of monopoly power. It is hard to know how widespread was this concern. Joskow, Schmalensee and Tsukanova (1994) report that many Russian policy makers were genuinely convinced of the dangers of liberalization in the presence of monopoly. However, Johnson and Kowalska (1994) report the results of a Polish opinion poll in 1991, in which respondents were asked to name likely beneficiaries of the reform process. Less than one per cent named 'monopolists', who came twenty-first in the list behind such examples as 'foreign capital' and 'the Church and priests'. It may be that this discrepancy reflects a difference between Russia and Poland; it is also possible that policy makers in both countries perceived the danger as more serious than did the public at large; yet another possibility is that the antipathy towards foreign capital encompasses an implicit identification of foreign capital with monopoly. Certainly, the 'monopoly power' explanation for the initial drop in Polish output after the 1990 reforms has featured much in subsequent debates among economists (Schaffer, 1992; Calvo and Coricelli, 1992).

The lack of experience of many managers with contractual bargaining has led them to look to competition authorities for help in their negotiations with one another. As we see below, the legislation in Poland and Hungary explicitly forbids 'onerous contract terms', and no country clearly establishes the principle of *caveat emptor* in negotiations between firms. In other words, the distinction between the regulation of the competitive process and the protection of specific competitors has been particularly blurred in the formerly planned economies. This may also have led to considerable pressure for protection of the first generation of entrepreneurs. In market economies new firms are those most likely to be threatened by bankruptcy, but in transition economies there were often unrealistic expectations of the future for entrepreneurs, and a consequent tendency to turn to the authorities for help in the course of economic difficulty. This effect has been exacerbated by the wide scope of bankruptcy legislation in some cases, especially in Hungary.[23]

Consumer activism was almost non-existent under central planning, both because it was politically suspect and because in situations of excess demand for consumer products there was nothing to be gained from complaining about product quality; consumers were typically glad to be able to obtain any goods at all. As a result, consumer lobbying is, as a general rule, even weaker than in market economies, but competition authorities sometimes come under strong pressure to be general champions of the consumer interest, since private or voluntary consumer organizations have previously been so weak.[24]

Profiteering was usually a crime under central planning, and there remains a reluctance in transition economies to see profits as being in any way necessary for the encouragement of risk-taking (in spite of the fact that the risks to be taken are in many respects greater).

The weakness of many governments' fiscal mechanisms (the absence at the beginning of the reform period of anything resembling VAT and a high degree of reliance on profits taxes; see Hussain and Stern, 1993) has led them, and especially their finance ministries, to be particularly appreciative of the fiscal benefits of monopoly, both when firms are in state hands and for the privatization revenue they generate.

Labour markets were poorly developed under central planning. In addition the comprehensive association of social benefits (health, education, holidays) with membership of an enterprise has made unemployment a prospect even more to be feared in transition economies than it is in market economies (Atkinson and Micklewright, 1993). The fact that in many families more than one adult works full-time may also limit the ease with which labour can move in search of jobs. Overall there is evidence of a very low rate of job-finding of unemployed people (Jackman, 1995).

The Speed of Reform

The speed of price liberalization has led to substantial bursts of inflation even in countries where there has been comparative macroeconomic stability (such as the Czech Republic). There is an understandable temptation for governments to blame these price increases on the greed of monopoly, and consequent pressure for price control of monopoly enterprises has been strong.[25] The fiscal weakness alluded to above has been exacerbated by the depth of the recession in many countries.

Likewise, the fact that many firms have been in difficulties beyond their control and only weakly related to their long-term prospects (because of the collapse of foreign trade, or arrears in customer payments, for example) has added plausibility to arguments to the effect that the state must intervene to support struggling enterprises rather than let competition inexorably take its course. Even where these arguments have been well-grounded they have added to the atmosphere of uncertainty as to the rules under which firms are supposed to be competing.

The comprehensive retreat of the state from many areas of economic and social life has sometimes made it difficult to legitimate state action in areas that would be considered uncontroversial in market societies (enforcement of contract law and even of civil order, though the latter has been a much more severe problem in the former Soviet Union than in central Europe). During the passage of competition legislation a number of parties voiced concerns about the powers that would be thereby granted to the organs of the state. The Association of Young Democrats (a Hungarian parliamentary party) sought guarantees that complaints of abuse of dominance would not provide opportunities for the state to interfere unjustifiably with market mechanisms, especially since the greatest burden on the economy, they claimed, was the overweight state. In Poland in 1990 one MP, Ms Anna Dynowska, objected to the proposed powers of the new AMO on the grounds that they would be like 'handing a razor to a monkey'. She subsequently repeated her anxiety in an interview for the newspaper *Rzeczpospolita*, saying that the powers envisaged were not like loading a gun with blank cartridges purely for deterrence but were tantamount to live ammunition. Even the AMO president, Dr Anna Fornalczyk, pointed out that, taken literally, the law would allow the AMO to control over 70% of industrial output, a state of affairs that was evidently nonsensical.

The Persistence of Old Habits and Institutions

Notwithstanding the comprehensive retreat of the state from many areas of economic life, in all the transition economies there have been, though to widely varying degrees, certain institutions that have persisted into the reform phase, or (more commonly) institutions that have been abolished but whose personnel have been transferred elsewhere and given powers not unlike their old powers. The most common manifestation of this phenomenon has been the transfer of staff responsible for price control from ministries of finance or of central planning to work in the competition offices (though Poland has been an exception to this general trend). But there are others; such as the transformation of parts of the central planning bureaucracy into trading associations, for example, or the creation of financial industrial groups. Sometimes such institutions can appear to be imaginative responses to the coordination failures of economies in transition, and there is some empirical evidence that they may help in creating incentives for enterprises to make necessary structural adjustments. But they also have significant anti-competitive potential (Joskow, Schmalensee and Tsukanova, 1994).

Allied to this has been an understandable wish on the part of politicians to retain residual powers to control economic variables such as prices which have an important impact on the living standards of the population. In the face of the enormous uncertainty generated by the reform process there has been a reluctance to abandon such powers, in case the experiment goes horribly wrong. This is in addition to the tendency which politicians may have not to limit their discretion in general.

Economics was subordinate to politics under central planning. In a rather obvious sense therefore, the abolition of central planning has been viewed as a political and not a purely economic process. Competition policy has not been treated as the kind of narrowly technocratic activity with which it is frequently associated in market economies. This has advantages in that the newly created competition offices are often headed by individuals with substantial political influence. It has corresponding disadvantages in that decisions may be openly politicized, and competition agencies may be easily and frequently overruled because of the political visibility of their activities.

Sometimes legal and constitutional provisions may give wide scope to the offices to intervene in market activities in the name of fairness. For example, Article 70.B.1 of the Hungarian Constitution says that 'Everyone who works has a right to emolument that corresponds to the amount and quality of the work performed' (see Elster, 1994, p. 63). Likewise, prohibitions of 'onerous contract terms' in competition statutes can potentially license significant state involvement in what might more normally be considered free contractual relations between parties (as we discuss in Chapter 4 below).

Overall, these political pressures and factors have posed a very difficult set of challenges for the competition offices in formerly planned economies. In particular, expectations of what competition policy can achieve are often unrealistically high. Competition offices are often presented with extremely ambitious goals (ranging from supporting weak firms in their contractual bargaining to scrutinizing the privatization process and sometimes even to tasks such as preventing intimidation that are more properly matters for the police), while simultaneously being granted limited *de facto* powers with which to pursue these goals. Although the resources, particularly in terms of personnel, available to competition offices in transition economies have typically been generous compared to those of their counterparts in many market economies (as we indicate in Chapter 5 below) these have not necessarily been matched by a political willingness to grant the offices real power. On paper the powers of the offices are often sweeping, but in practice their ability to enforce decisions against well-connected economic agents is much more limited. As we shall see, in the right combination of circumstances competition offices have been able to provide an effective voice in favour of competition and against special interests, often to a degree that would be envied by their counterparts in market economies. But under unfavourable circumstances they have been placed in the unenviable position of being empowered to do little while being blamed for a great deal.

2.2.3 Political Mandate

Finally, we consider the political mandate of the competition offices, as revealed by the political consensus at their foundation and the existence of a tradition of competition policy in the region.

It is striking that in all four countries the establishment of competition offices was a far less controversial matter than many other components of the overall reform process. There was no serious parliamentary opposition in any country to the initial competition legislation. In Czechoslovakia (as it then was) there were no votes against the adoption of the Law for Protection of Competition in January 1991. The new law of the Slovak Republic was likewise passed unopposed in November 1993 (although it nearly failed because of the initial absence of a quorum). In Hungary, parliamentary discussion was confined to points of detail, with no fundamental disagreement about the bill's main purpose, and the bill was eventually passed by 290 votes to 2 with a single abstention. The lack of public controversy in Hungary may also have owed something to the fact that the parliamentary debates coincided with the far more newsworthy nationwide cab-drivers' blockade from 25 to 29 October 1990, in protest against rises in petrol prices. In Poland there was some argument about the agency's powers (as cited above), but no major challenge to the law's main form.

Evidence of this kind may be interpreted in one of two ways. We may conclude that there was little opposition because there existed a substantial social consensus in favour of competition policy. Alternatively, there may have been little understanding of what competition policy entailed and widespread apathy about the whole issue. Superficial evidence (such as the problem of mustering a quorum in the Slovak parliament) certainly points to the latter rather than the former interpretation.

However, there are some considerations pointing in the other direction. In all the four countries there existed a substantial legislative tradition of competition regulation. The reformers in Poland adopted the civil code from 1934, and a strong competition policy had been part of the activities of a government that in the 1930s faced a highly cartelized economy. A law on unfair competition (drafted originally under the terms of a Franco-Polish commercial treaty of 1923) was passed in 1930, and an anti-cartel law in 1933. Although these laws were not formally repealed, they were not enforced under the Communist regime, but concern with monopolies resurfaced during the 1980s, and in 1987 Poland passed new anti-monopoly legislation in the socialist bloc. The First Czechoslovak Republic had passed a Law Concerning Cartels and Private Monopolies in 1933, which was repealed in the 1950s. Hungary's competition legislation dated from 1923, and was replaced by new laws in 1984 and then in 1990. All this suggests that (unlike in the former Soviet Union) competition legislation was a reasonably familiar object in the CEECs, and the notion that free competition might need to be policed was not as paradoxical as it may have seemed further east. The legitimacy of the agents of the state in enforcing competition policy has never therefore been under fundamental political threat during the 1990s.

2.2.4 Summary

What has this evidence about the political constraints upon competition policy taught us? The passage of competition laws and the establishment of competition agencies in all the countries we have studied was initially much less controversial than many of the other components of the reform programmes these countries were undertaking. Competition policy seems therefore to be an excellent example of the kind of gradualist reform whose main purpose is described by Dewatripont and Roland (1995) as being to build constituencies for further reform. However, it is important to note that this argument does not imply that the implementation of competition policy should itself be gradualist. In effect, Dewatripont and Roland's argument claims that if there are two policies, A and B, between which there are important complementarities, implementing A before B may help to create support for B if A is initially less unpopular than B and the success of A increases the perceived gains from implementing B. This is certainly an argument for implementing B more slowly than would otherwise be desirable, but it is simultaneously an argument for implementing A as fast as possible (so as to be able to create the most favourable conditions for B). Policy A is best described as a non-gradual component of a gradualist overall programme. We may conclude, therefore, that the relatively non-controversial character of competition policy has made it an ideal early component of economic reform, part of whose purpose is to make other less palatable components acceptable. For that very reason, it is desirable for it to be implemented rapidly, fully and effectively.

2.3   Constraints on the Rule of Law

The effectiveness of competition law must be considered in the wider context of the legal system of a society. An effective framework of law, both criminal and civil, can be thought of as an institution that participants in the economy use to structure their economic activities and to resolve disputes. It has in many societies the character of a public good, and is provided by the state. It is nevertheless a public good with a rather special character, in that it usually depends upon a culture of trust: people on the whole obey the law and carry out their contractual obligations to respect one another's property and to refrain from prohibited acts because they expect the law to be enforced, and conversely, it is feasible to enforce the law because spontaneous compliance can be expected to be reasonably high. It also has some characteristics of a local public good, in that patterns of compliance and the rigour of enforcement can vary between regions within a country. Where such variations are significant they may have an important impact on the ability of a region to attract economic resources, and even on long-run patterns of economic growth (see Putnam, 1993, for an illuminating application of this argument to the history of Italy).

A culture of trust cannot be taken for granted. Trust, like reputation, is built over time and supported by the repeated observation that the law is indeed enforced. When trust is established, the rule of law operates as a self-fulfilling mechanism. However, when a society is passing through a major social transformation, the necessary culture of trust may be lacking and the ability of the state to supply this public good may be in doubt. This will arise in particular if the state has been widely discredited as part of the social transformation, so that it faces a problem of legitimacy.[26] In such circumstances other rival suppliers may attempt to fill the gap, providing the services of contract enforcement and even the maintenance of civil order, even if they do so far less effectively than a properly functioning state would be able to do.

Varese (1994), following work on Italy by Gambetta (1988, 1993), suggests that the growth of organized crime in the former Soviet Union cannot be seen simply as a symptom of the breakdown of the system of criminal justice. He argues that the inability of the state to provide an adequate infrastructure for and enforcement of *contract* law has provided the opportunity for organized crime to substitute itself for the state system. Mafia protection is not just taxation by terror; it typically involves the provision of a service, namely the enforcement of contractual undertakings by one's business partners, that for a variety of reasons is inadequately supplied by the state. In transition economies, a major reason for inadequate state supply could be the sudden and dramatic increase in the demand for such contract-enforcement services, arising from the massive transfer of property into private hands. Although organized crime gangs often diversify into other activities such as narcotics and weapons supply, the widespread tolerance of their activities by ordinary citizens is explicable only in terms of their role as providers of services that are necessary to entrepreneurship. In periods of stability the state may be a much more efficient supplier of such services than the private sector, since (among other reasons) the state controls a larger territory and is therefore able to enforce contracts over a wider geographical area (disputes between businesses under the protection of different criminal gangs are settled much more arbitrarily and with greater uncertainty than disputes between businesses within the same territory). But for the former Soviet Union, these are not ordinary times.

The CEECs have seen a much less serious growth in organized crime than in the former Soviet Union, though their mafia is by no means negligible: for instance, the Institute of Criminology of the Czech Republic reports that as much as 16% of businesses in Prague were threatened with extortion in 1994 (see *Business Central Europe*, December 1995/January 1996)). This is partly because the CEECs maintained stronger state legitimacy than in the former Soviet Union and accordingly have been able to establish more quickly a credible system of civil law (often based on civil codes from the pre-Communist era). It is also because large-scale demobilization of armed forces personnel in the former Soviet Union has created a larger pool of private sector entrepreneurs in the contract-enforcement business, as Varese reports. Nevertheless, some of the threats to the rule of law that are highly visible in the former Soviet Union are not ones that countries further west can afford to ignore. In particular, they underline the crucial lesson that organized crime reflects an inadequacy not just in the criminal law but also in the civil law. Indeed, the absence of a credible civil and commercial system of law may provide the initial spur to the organized criminality of which violence and disorder are but a symptom. The experience of the former Soviet Union is particularly dispiriting in view of what we know about the persistence of cultures of distrust. A failure by the state to establish the credibility of the rule of law may take a very long time to redeem.

To the extent that trust is built by repeated interactions, people need to be convinced to experiment with the legal system and should not be disappointed. From this perspective, it seems that a legal system should have the following features. First, people should broadly accept the objectives of the law and the values it defends: the imposition of legal systems and regulations from outside may be detrimental to the establishment of a culture of trust. This suggests that the people concerned should participate in the formulation of the law and that 'transplanting' should be avoided. The process through which people build up ownership of the law is also delicate. In order to ensure a wide acceptability of the legal system, it may matter that all people concerned have the opportunity to be heard. This implies that the process by which law is formulated and enacted matters considerably for the overall effectiveness of the legal system. Thus the credibility of a legal system may be associated with the quality of its democratic institutions.

Second, it may be desirable early in the existence of a legal system to place particular emphasis on simple rules that are easy to implement and monitor, even at the expense of the greater discretion that would allow for more differentiation of the law according to particular circumstances. Simple rules that are well understood are likely to encourage people to experiment with the emerging legal system, whereas general rules that allow the courts wide discretion may be ineffectual and, in extreme cases, that could facilitate abuses of power that might discourage people from operating within the legal system. As people's trust in the legal system is enhanced and courts become more competent, the balance could be tilted more in favour of general rules that may be interpreted by the agencies and the courts.

The effectiveness of law does not just depend on the background culture: issues such as the credibility of penalties will also matter. These issues are too large to treat here, but by way of example, consider the issue of who should bear the penalties of competition law. Company fines fall on the owners, as do fines on managers that are transferable. On the other hand, criminal sanctions for managers are not transferable. Other penalties, such as public apology[27] are similarly non-transferable, but may have less disincentive effects on entrepreneurship than criminal sanctions and fines. In a situation where the law is very clear-cut and admits little discretion, penalties on decision makers may be more efficient than penalties on owners. On the other hand, with new laws or with areas where the legality is more ambiguous (such as vertical restraints), it may be more efficient to levy penalties on owners, in order that managers may be partially insured against the adverse consequences of their decisions. An additional constraint in transition economies may arise if the market for managers does not work well or if good or versatile managers are in short supply.

2.4   The External Constraint: Membership of the EU

2.4.1   The Association Agreements with the EU

The EU has signed Association Agreements with a number of CEECs governing relations between each of them and the EU. These Agreements have been signed for ten countries so far, and the four Visegrad countries were early signatories. The Agreements contain separate rules both for conduct affecting trade between the CEEC signatory and the EU Member States (i.e. law in the free trade area) and for the national law of each of the CEEC nations (see Hoekman and Mavroidis, 1994, and Smith, 1995, for detailed analyses).

With respect to the law in the free trade area, the Association Agreements are modelled upon the Treaty of Rome. However, there is no equivalent to Article 85(3) – that is, there is no provision allowing for the possibility of exemptions for agreements that restrict competition – and there is no provision for mergers. Importantly, the Agreements do not contain any explicit allocation of jurisdiction to EC institutions, Member State institutions or joint institutions (unlike, for instance, the EEA Agreements). To the extent that EC law covers agreements which have their effects in the EU (see the *Wood Pulp* decision), nothing would prevent both the EU and the relevant transition country from claiming jurisdiction at the same time. Following the Agreement, such cases are supposed to be dealt with according to the principles of traditional comity – the (potentially symbolic) rule that countries should take each other's interests into account – and positive comity – the rule that one contracting party can request another one to undertake proceedings. Finally, and most importantly, the Agreements expressly require that any practices that may distort competition be 'assessed on the basis of criteria arising from the application of the rules of [the EC Treaty]' (Articles 62(2), 63(2).[28] As a consequence, associated CEECs have committed themselves to apply the entire case law on competition arising from the Treaty of Rome, at least in regard to matters affecting trade between them and the EU. Any assessment as to whether this implementation is adequate will be undertaken by the Association Councils established under the Agreements.

Regarding national law, the Association Agreements state, at Article 68:

> The Contracting parties recognize that the major precondition for [the country]'s economic integration into the Community is *the approximation of that country's existing and future legislation to that of the Community*. [The country] shall use its best endeavours to ensure that future legislation is compatible with Community legislation. (Emphasis added.)

By reason of this clause, the CEECs are required to harmonize their national law with that of the EC. The Agreements require that transition countries implement these rules within three years in cooperation with the EU and under the aegis of the Association Councils. There is room for debate about the meaning of the word 'approximation' in Article 68 of the Association Agreements. Some policy makers and officials argue for a broad and general significance of the word, such as 'to bring into general harmony'. By this interpretation, it would be sufficient for the nations to incorporate and carry out the general principles of EC competition law with an eye towards establishing a sympathetic legal and economic system.

Support for this point of view may be drawn from the fact that the EU Member States themselves have the right – consistent with EC law – to choose their own style of domestic legal regime. National competition systems as diverse as those of the United Kingdom, France and Germany co-exist with one another and with EC law. While some Member States of the EU are now choosing to harmonize their domestic competition law with that of the EU, they retain their right to design their domestic regime.

2.4.2 The White Paper

A different point of view is expressed in the European Commission's White Paper on Enlargement (1995) which considers a more specific compatibility of national law with EC law. It takes the view that the CEECs should adopt as national law, not only EC rules but also EC case law. In this respect, the White Paper demands more of the CEECs than of the EU Member States.

The White Paper acknowledges this distinction. It observes that Member States need not align their domestic law with EC law because EC law is 'directly effective' within their states; that is, EC competition law is automatically a part of each Member State's national law whenever trade between Member States is affected. Supremacy and direct effectiveness of EC law brings the law home to the people and into the national system, and ensures a uniformity of law when trade is affected.

The White Paper continues:

> For the CEECs, the situation is obviously different [from that of the Member States]. An obligation of approximation was considered indispensable because there could be no extension of Community law to them as is the case for Member States [through the direct effectiveness doctrine]. Such an approximation is therefore necessary *inter alia* to ensure that economic operators can be sure to act on a level playing field, and in order to prepare the CEECs' economies for future membership (Competition appendix, p. 56).

Thus, the argument goes, EC law (to the extent it is applicable) is self-executing in Member States, but not in the CEECs. Therefore some mechanism is necessary to bring EC law into the legal systems of the CEECs. A mandate to put the EC rules into place in the national systems of the CEECs could play this role. It is also argued that the economies of the CEECs are so small and that in such a high number of cases transactions within these nations will affect trade with the EC or its Member States, that it would be unduly burdensome, if not impossible, for a CEEC to maintain two sets of rules and regulations in tandem.

For these reasons the White Paper envisions that the CEECs must accept a high level of detail of EC competition law. The White Paper states that 'the key elements' of EC competition law must be put into place in the CEECs; and that EC group exemptions and notices 'must be considered as constituting key elements of the Community competition system'.[29]

2.4.3 Assessment

The basic problem here is that in cases where trade between transition countries and the EU is affected, EC law does not apply directly. Judicial institutions in transition countries will have to rule on such cases, and the

EU cannot affect their decisions. In particular, the evaluation of whether trade between the transition countries and the EU is affected is undertaken by the competition agencies of the relevant transition country, subject to coordination within the Association Council (following the principles of comity). Accordingly, there may be some situations in which competition agencies in transition countries will find that their domestic law applies even though the EU finds that the provision of the Association Agreements should apply. By asking the transition countries to apply EU rules to domestic matters, the White Paper resolves this potential conflict. In all cases, EU rules (or their approximation) would apply.

It appears therefore that because the EU cannot ensure that transition countries will interpret the scope of the Association Agreements in the way it finds appropriate, it wishes to impose on the transition countries the obligation to apply its own rules on all cases. An alternative (perhaps simpler) solution could be to define precise rules for determining the scope of the Association Agreements, similar to those found in the EEA Treaty.

All this would not matter if approximation were not potentially costly for the transition countries. There are, however, some good reasons to think otherwise. EU law and practice are not natural candidates for implementation on the domestic level. Indeed, such law and practice have only been applied at a transnational level so far. If anything, the correct target for approximation should be the intersection of national laws, procedures and practices rather than those of the EU. But it is not clear what such an intersection would consist of, given that competition policy (i.e. law and implementation) varies a great deal both among EU Members States themselves and between the Member States and the European Commission. The mere observation that such an intersection may be difficult to find throws into question the very idea of approximation. It also implies the paradoxical conclusion that the White Paper is urging candidates for membership to adopt the *acquis communautaire* without the principle of subsidiarity!

It has been argued above that the industry structures of the transition countries are likely to differ, even into the medium term, from those found in countries with established market economies and that transition countries operate in a different institutional environment requiring the progressive establishment of a rule of law. These institutional factors indicate that some flexibility to adapt competition policy to the circumstances of transition may be highly desirable.

Notes

1. We endeavour to make comparisons with EU economies of similar size where possible, but the benchmark will also vary according to data availability.
2. This is true in other transitions economies in the region also, but not in Romania.

3. Whereas producer prices increased by 80% between 1989 and 1992, energy prices rose by more than 160%.
4. These are summarized in Carlin, Van Reenen and Wolfe (1994) but see also Grosfeld and Roland (1995) and EBRD (1995). Primary studies of importance include Belka *et al.* (1995), Earle, Estrin and Leshchenko (1995) and Katsoulacos and Takla (1995). The evidence reported in enterprise surveys should, however, be considered cautiously, especially if used to draw inferences about the relation between firm behaviour and systems of corporate control. Indeed, in many instances it is very difficult from the reported data to disentangle industry effects from corporate control effects.
5. The number has gone from 8453 to 4772 (see *Statistical Bulletin*). See also Hirschausen (1995a).
6. See OECD (1994b) and Hayri and McDermott (1995). The Czech privatization investment funds were established with a view to improving corporate control by preventing enormous dispersion of private ownership. Wijnbergen and Marcinin (1995) argue that where dominant investors emerged, the subsequent share price was above average. They suggest this may because the market expects better corporate control, but alternative explanations are also offered.
7. On competition in banking in central Europe, see Miklaszewska (1996).
8. Around the time of writing, two competing foreign car producers were vying to buy the Polish car producer, FSO, which is discussed below.
9. *Business Central Europe*, October 1995. We deal with several cases from the car industry below.
10. See also Baldwin (1994), who finds similar results. A gravity model postulates that trade is related to the reciprocal of the square root of the physical distance.
11. The common external tariff encourages such type of trade. For details, see Hoekman and Djankov (1996).
12. This assessment is in spite of survey evidence to the contrary. Belka *et al.* (1995) report a large increase in the proportion of firms which consider importers as major competitors.
13. These are concentration ratios at the level of production (not sales). However, for the EU productions and sales concentration data are very similar (see Davies and Lyons, 1996, for details).
14. Additional insights can be obtained from some enterprises surveys (see, for instance. Belka *et al.*, 1995, for Poland) where firms are asked about their market share. Firms tend to report relatively high market shares: as much as 40% of them report market shares in excess of 25% and 30% of them market shares in excess of 50%. It is hard, however, to interpret these figures as there is no control over the definition of the relevant product market (which may also vary a great deal across firms).
15. Indeed, some industry analysts have complained about a lax implementation of competition policy (Carlin, Van Reenen amd Wolfe, 1994; Zemplinerova, 1994; Flek, 1995).
16. This contrasts with common claims such as those of Elster (1994), who writes that 'In Eastern Europe, the main standing passions seem to be economic egalitarianism or even envy, and ethnic distrust or suspicion' (p.164). In support he cites experimental studies suggesting that 'although people dislike any type of inequality between themselves and others, they feel much more strongly about discrepancies that give the other party more than about those that give them more'. He also quotes 'a story I heard in several countries in the region [that] recounts how a farmer was told by a fairy that he could have anything he wanted, on the condition that whatever he got his neighbour would get twice as much. "Tear out one of my eyes", was his request"'. These pieces of evidence may indicate the presence of egalitarianism or envy, but do not show that such sentiments are any stronger in former planned economies than in Western societies.
17. This did not prevent subsequent electoral success for political parties linked to former Communists in Poland in 1993, and in Hungary and Slovakia in 1994, nor the election to the Polish presidency in December 1995 of Aleksander Kwasniewski, who had represented the Communist government in the round-table talks with Solidarity in 1989.
18. This is a more plausible resolution of the paradox than the claim that citizens of highly distorted economies are more likely to be temperamentally opposed to reforms. For one thing, first-hand experience of economic distortion should not be assumed to make its

effects more palatable. For another, Shiller, Boycko and Korobov (1991) show on the basis of survey evidence that there is little perceptible difference between Soviets and Americans in their willingness to favour rationing solutions to commodity shortages. They conclude that 'the strong opposition to price reform . . . that undoubtedly exists in the Soviet Union should not be attributed to peculiarities of national character; rather, the political and economic interests should be given more weight' (p. 390).

19. 'The government's efforts at a wide-ranging change of the economic elite have largely failed. Not even the assignment of government appointees to company councils could change this, after the repeated and forced confirmation votes [executives and company councils had been voted in June 1990 as part of the regular cycle, but the newly elected government demanded a re-vote by the end of September 1990] four fifths of company executives stayed in their previous positions. It is questionable whether such centrally designed campaign-like elite changes could result in systemic qualitative change' (Bayer, 1991, p. 246)

20. See, for example, the article by Gyorgyi Kocsis in the newspaper HVG (*Heti Vilaggazdasag*), 19 December 1992 in which he writes that the government has followed the principle that 'the owner does with his property as he pleases. The logic has nice closure: if state property belongs to the government, and the owner does as he pleases, the government can do as it pleases. SPA has clearly used the freedom given to the government by the coalition, and by the coalition to the SPA. According to the regulation already created on the basis of the new privatization law, "tenders are public, except if the board of directors of the SPA decides to organize a closed (invitational) tender"'.

21. See, for example, the interview with Peter Vadasz, deputy president of the Association of Hungarian Industrialists (MGYOSZ) in the newspaper HVG, who, the interviewer notes, 'can hardly be accused of siding with the opposition liberals'. Vadasz said, *inter alia*: 'I find it laughable – but most of all outrageous – that a person is placed at the head of one of the largest trading companies in the country, of whom no-one in the business had ever heard' (HVG, 28 March 1992, pp. 41–2.).

22. The case was complicated by two other factors. First, Minister Dlouhy was also a director of one of the firms (Unipetrol a.s.). Second, it is possible that higher taxes on unleaded fuel were intended by the government to prevent, not tax evasion, but imports from the main Slovak refinery Slovnaft, which according to press reports had been planning an expansion of exports to the Czech Republic (*Mlada Fronta Dnes*, 26 January 1996).

23. 'Today in Hungary over half a million people work for firms that, since 8th April, might be forced to file bankruptcy against themselves at any moment' (HVG, 11 April 1992).

24. For example, the 1990 economic program of the Hungarian Association of Young Democrats explicitly argued that consumer protection should be a right pursuable at law by individuals, precisely because consumers do not form an organized social group (*Hungarian Political Yearbook*, 1991). Individuals have the right to bring actions alleging breaches of the Hungarian constitution.

25. One of us (Seabright) was an adviser to the Polish government during 1990–1. The possibility that monopoly power might be responsible for the fact that initial price inflation in the first quarter of 1990 exceeded the government's expectations (Johnson and Kowalska, 1994, p. 202) was much discussed.

26. To the extent that pre-transition legal frameworks were merely a set of regulations that could be changed arbitrarily by the dominant Communist Party (see Hirschausen, 1995a), the state in Eastern and Central Europe and the former Soviet Union presumably suffered from a serious handicap in terms of legitimacy.

27. Public apologies are used as a penalty in Japan and the Republic of Korea. See Boner and Krueger (1991).

28. The citations here are all taken from the Polish Agreement. Identical clauses exist for the Agreements with the other three countries.

29. White Paper, Competition appendix, p. 58. The group exemptions and notices are 'secondary legislation' of the EC. They establish numerous rules. For example, group (or block) exemptions are provided because, under the EC system, exemption by the European Commission is required to establish the validity of agreements that have at least a minimal possibility of distorting competition. The group-exemption system allows auto-

matic exemption for contracts that fit a certain blueprint. Each regulation that creates a block exemption specifies lists of required clauses, permissible clauses, and prohibited clauses. The prohibited clauses do not always coincide with *de facto* harm to competition; the permissible clauses do not represent a full list of clauses that are pro-competitive or benign; and some permissible clauses may sometimes be anti-competitive. This over- and underinclusiveness is, perhaps, a necessary result of an attempt to regulate the most common forms of transactions, and to generalize sufficiently to create a block exemption. See Bermann *et al.* (1993) and supplement (1995), pp. 730–1. For regulations and notices generally, see Berman *et al.* (1993), Document Supplement, Part III. Accordingly, harmonization of details of law is both a large task and, in our view, not necessarily conducive to producing an optimal law (see Hawk, 1995). The Commission itself is conducting a study to re-examine its vertical restraint law. See Deacon (1996) regarding the Green Paper on vertical restraints.

3

The Design of Competition Policy: A Possible Framework

3.1   Conduct and Transactions

The main focus of this book is the rules that should govern behaviour and transactions of market actors; in other words, the set of problems addressed by Articles 85 and 86 of the EC Treaty of Rome and the EC Merger Regulation, and by Sections 1 and 2 of the US Sherman Act and Section 7 of the US Clayton Act. This set of problems is recognized throughout most of the industrialized world (where competitive markets are already established) as the centrepiece of competition policy. They also represent the aspect of competition policy where the four Visegrad countries took earliest legislative action, and the only one that has generated significant case law, so an evaluation of the role of competition policy in transition must inevitably focus on these problems if it is not to remain entirely theoretical.

Optimal rules for a nation must always begin with the nation's objectives. We try to encapsulate the goals of the Visegrad nations as expressed in their documents and by their officials, and to generalize those goals, as background for considering what kind of anti-trust rules would probably work most effectively in moving the nations toward their goals.

3.2   What Do the Visegrád Nations Want?

What, with respect to competition policy narrowly conceived, do the Visegrad nations want? The nations want to develop markets. They want their markets to work efficiently. They want businesses within their borders to be motivated to achieve efficiencies, in order to serve their businesses and citizens and to engage in external or world markets.

Also, the Visegrád nations want membership of the EU. Membership entails home markets that are in law and in fact open to businesses located in the EU and vice versa, and a functioning market system that will constitute a hospitable interface with markets in the EU.

3.2.1   Market Conditions

We have identified in Chapter 2 above the market and other realities in the Visegrád countries that are relevant to the design and application of appropriate competition rules. We noted that pressures from imports and foreign investment are not as strong as might have been expected. Capital markets are not yet working well and capable mangers are still in short supply, thus making entry and expansion of small and medium-sized firms difficult and sometimes doubtful. Numerous state-owned firms continue to exist and many do not behave responsively to buyers' needs and demands. Moreover, the performance and behaviour of firms restructured in connection with privatizations often show little change after restructuring.

These conditions indicate a need for strong and clear competition rules to prevent market actors and their trade associations from concerting to control markets, as by fixing prices, dividing markets, or setting standards to exclude competitors. Strong rules may be needed also to prevent dominant firms from blocking entry or growth of competition, and to prevent firms from eliminating important competition or potential competition by merger or joint venture.

Also, the conditions underscore a need for limits to anti-trust, lest anti-trust rules constrain firms from acting responsively to market needs and demands. This factor counsels against prohibitions that prevent firms from offering better, lower-priced products, from designing distribution systems that will get their product to market most efficiently, and, generally, from competing on the merits.

3.2.2   Institutional factors

Institutional factors also inform the shape of optimum competition rules.[1] Being new offices in an environment unaccustomed to competition, the competition offices need to gain credibility and respect. Thus, potential offenders must not only know the law but they must expect that the law will be enforced against violations. Moreover, one must take into account the facts that the competition offices are under resource constraints, and the available pool of competition-trained people to join their staffs is relatively small.

These needs underscore the merit of relatively simple law that is knowable and is brought home to those who might be violators; harsh penalties for egregious violations; clarity in defining egregious violations; transparency of rules of law and of decisions applying the law; a targeted enforcement policy focusing on the kinds of conduct or transactions that most seriously obstruct the working of markets; and as little bureaucracy and paperwork as possible consistent with carrying out the tasks of the office.

3.3 The Question of Transition

The designer of law must ask whether needs for a transitional period differ from those for the longer term. The considerations above focus on current conditions, and thus on the short term. We ask below whether circumstances suggest that longer-term rules should be different.

3.3.1 Options

The Visegrád countries have several options in designing both the substance and structure of competition rules addressed to conduct and transactions. Options include adopting only rules against cartels and market-blocking acts by dominant firms, adopting the US model, adopting the EC model, designing more interventionist law, creating new law responsive to the nation's special needs and norms, and combining parts of the foregoing.

The United States (being a common-law country) has minimal statutory law. Development of case law is based on a competition standard focused on consumer welfare. Except for cartel conduct, the law is hospitable to business freedom. No notification or filing requirements are imposed except for mergers that pass a threshold size. The principal statutory provision – Section 1 of the Sherman Act – prohibits 'restraints of trade,' but, as the US Supreme Court has said: '[That term] refers not to a particular list of agreements, but to a particular economic consequence [i.e. increase or use of market power at the expense of consumers], which may be produced by quite different sorts of agreements in varying times and circumstances.'[2] Agency guidelines explain analytical methodologies for determining whether and when transactions are in fact anti-competitive.[3]

The EC model is more rule-oriented. It is more interventionist. It is not focused on consumer welfare to the exclusion of other goals, but is concerned also with opportunities for small and medium-sized businesses and with fairness and inequalities, as well as with market integration. Exemptions are needed for many ordinary business transactions. Detailed block exemptions allow contracting parties to avoid the need to seek individual exemptions, but also they steer transactions into the form authorized by the block exemption, which contains lists of permissible and lists of impermissible clauses.

A law yet more interventionist than EC law might not only require notifications and clearances but could more closely regulate powerful firms and could redistribute power and wealth to firms that are less well off.

The Visegrad countries have accepted the challenge of the EU to approximate their laws to EC law as a price of being seriously considered for admission to the EU. Without this challenge, it was not inevitable that the Visegrad nations' laws would gravitate toward the EC model. The nations' goals, the realities of their markets, and administrative challenges and capabilities could recommend simpler law with a focus on serious market-wide problems capable of being deterred and remedied by competition authorities. For example, law could focus on cartel restraints and on dominant firm restraints that impose serious barriers to market entry and expansion. Ideally, the law would be sufficiently clear, simple and well publicized so that enterprises would know the law. Authorities would be able to ferret out and bring cases against virtually all significant violations and performance of the competition offices and deterrence from violations would be high.

3.3.2   A Focused Law

A variety of formulations for such a law can be suggested. As one attempts to formulate such a law, one appreciates the difficulty of achieving a formulation that will be simple and clear both to the users (businesses) and to the providers (the agencies) in countries that do not have deep experience with a market economy, much less with the complexities of anti-trust analysis. By one formulation, along US lines, the statement of the law can be simple but application of the law – beyond *per se* rules against hardcore cartels – has reference to economic concepts that must be understood; in particular, creation or increase of market power. By another formulation, along EU lines, the statement of the law is more complex; there are more rules and there is somewhat less economic analysis. Rules can produce more clarity. However, the rules are not always clear. Moreover, rules tend to be inflexible. When rules apply without regard to whether the market functions competitively, they are likely to be under-inclusive or over-inclusive. That is, they may fail to prohibit acts and transactions that harm market competition, and they may prohibit other acts and transactions that do not harm and may even improve competition.[4]

Whatever model is used, the adopting nation can anchor its law by having reference to the case law and practice of a developed model. Again, the adopting nation must choose between the greater clarity and simplicity entailed by 'swallowing' a system whole and the better 'fit' that would derive from choice and discrimination, which itself may require a degree of sophistication.

While these hard choices must be made by each nation, we present one possible formulation for a focused law.

The Rules

1. Competitors may not agree to rig bids, fix prices, allocate quotas, or divide markets or customers.
2. Competitors with market power may not agree to boycott competitors, buyers or suppliers; i.e. they may not concertedly refuse to deal to suppress competition.
3. Enterprises may not make agreements that substantially lessen competition, without offsetting gains in competition, efficiency, or technological progress.
4. Trade associations may not be used as a forum for formulating or carrying out any of the above agreements.
5. Dominant firms may not take action to block competitors' market access, where the action is not justified as a response to the market.
6. Mergers and acquisitions above a stated threshold must be pre-notified to the Anti-monopoly Office (AMO), along with specified information, and must observe a waiting period. The AMO must prohibit all mergers and acquisitions that create or enhance significant market power. [If the nation desires latitude for approval of anti-competitive mergers in the public interest, then:] For mergers that threaten to create or enhance significant market power, the AMO must recommend prohibition, and a specified minister [or body] must order the prohibition unless the minister finds with particularity that harm to competition is outbalanced by efficiencies, technological gains, or other specified economic advantages, all of which must be identified, quantified to the extent possible, and explained in a reasoned opinion.

Definitions

'Agreement' would include understandings, but not mere interdependent action. 'Competitors' would include potential competitors. 'Enterprises' would include all market actors, including entrepreneurs, corporations and incorporated entities, whether state or privately owned, except that state enterprises that perform public service duties could be permitted to justify their conduct to the extent necessary to carry out their public function, as under EC Treaty Article 90.

Commentary

Paragraphs 1 and 2 of the proposed law are directed towards horizontal restraints. Paragraph 3 would catch horizontal and vertical agreements, although horizontal agreements would be the primary concern. Paragraph 3 would cover exclusive purchasing and dealing contracts, tying contracts, and joint ventures and alliances that are the result of 'loose' cooperation rather than merger-like concentration. It would proscribe arrangements only when they harm market competition and not simply competitors. The proscription would therefore catch much less than Article 85(1) of the EC Treaty of Rome.

The paragraph 3 test would be a structured rule of reason. Only market-place considerations would be admissible; i.e. effects on competition, efficiency, and technological progress. Unless an agreement creates, maintains or increases market power in a market or directly interferes with the basic market mechanism, it would not be prohibited. Certain types of conduct or agreement might by their nature so directly interfere with the basic market mechanism as to be presumptively prohibited.

For the paragraph 3 rule of reason, in cases in which the proponent of a violation proves that market power is created, maintained or increased, the law might shift the burden to the respondent to prove outbalancing pro-competitive, efficiency, or technological benefits.

The law would not prohibit discrimination in treatment, which is often competition itself, unless the discrimination is caught by one of the specified rules.

What is not prohibited would be permitted, and much of what is permitted would be encouraged.

Newly established anti-trust agencies would need to work out, through case examples and over time, the analysis implied by paragraph 3 (contracts whose net effect is to harm competition), paragraph 5 (abuse of dominance) and paragraph 6 (anti-competitive mergers). Competition offices, Competition Councils and courts would naturally draw upon established bodies of law, bearing in mind a mandate to focus on making markets work; not on trying to equalize bargaining power or decreeing what is fair.

Nations might add or subtract from or refine the formulation, in view of the particular economic, social and political context. In particular, the nations might appropriately adopt a separate unfair competition law and separate laws regulating excessive pricing by natural monopoly firms, and conduct that is abusive but does not have a market impact. However, where enforcement of the law on unfair competition and abuses by natural monopoly firms conflicts with and undermines the effort of the competition law to make markets work, competition law would presumptively prevail unless the law states otherwise.

Enforcement

The principal enforcer would be the AMO. The AMO would be an independent agency, accountable to Parliament or other appropriate bodies. It would have the power and – in the best of worlds – practical ability to take even politically unpopular decisions. After hearings, with due process, the

AMO would have the power to enjoin violations and to impose fines. It would have the power and duty to impose large fines in cases of egregious violations that obstruct the workings of markets (e.g. bid rigging, cartels, and monopolistic imposition of barriers). In terms of accountability, all its decisions would be published and available. Appeal would lie to the courts.

To enhance enforcement and increase incentives to comply with the law, private parties in the line of injury from anti-competitive practices and transactions would have a right of complaint and could have a right to sue. In private actions the remedy would normally be compensatory damages and an injunction against anti-competitive conduct or transactions, with discretion of the judge to grant multiple damages in the case of bid rigging, cartels, and egregious cases of imposition of barriers by dominant firms.

3.4 Transition versus the Longer Term

Would changes be indicated for the longer term, once the transition has been accomplished? Since the proposed statute is geared towards making markets work, and well-functioning markets are both a short- and a long-term goal, little change would be indicated.

Over the longer term, the economic environment is likely to change in the direction of better functioning and more fluid markets and towards geographic markets that extend beyond a nation's borders. Such factual changes in the environment could indicate some differences in outcome simply because the facts have changed, and they could counsel some shifts in the application of the statutory principles. We note four situations:

1. The current poor functioning of some markets, the paucity of entrants and potential entrants, and the difficulties of successful re-entry by firms that may be squeezed from the market before they are able to reach efficient size could be relevant to the shape of rules on abuse of dominance, tying, and exclusive dealing during the transition. For example, nations in transition might sympathetically consider a price predation rule that does not require the enforcer to prove a clearly probable recoupment scenario (as does US law) when prices are set below marginal or average variable cost for the purpose and with the probable effect of destroying competitors. In a transition economy, the trade-offs between getting the benefits of the low-price competition of monopolists and preserving opportunities for potentially efficient smaller competitors may suggest a balance that leans less than does US law towards faith in the free market.
2. Sometimes potential competition is the main force relied on to keep firm behaviour responsive, because rivalrous competitors do not exist. The

transitional nation might appropriately be more sceptical than are well-developed systems about the strength of potential competition, and therefore more cautious about relying upon it to keep a market competitive (e.g. in the event of a merger of two major competitors).

3. Markets are likely to be geographically smaller and to be bounded by national borders in early stages than in years to come.

4. Post-Communist nations in early stages of transition must not only develop markets where none existed but also may need to dismantle firms vertically in order to open purchasing and distribution channels clogged as the result of command-and-control edicts. Accordingly, vertical integration law may properly be more interventionist in early stages of the law.

The above four points, though important for an informed perspective on the tasks of creating and facilitating competition in transitional economies, are relatively small ones in the scheme of things. The law may evolve to fit new market realities, or minor amendment may be indicated. However, the important point is that a focused approach is especially important for a newly created competition office in a post-command economy, and a focused approach is also a strong virtue in a mature economy.

3.5   Open Architecture for Market Integration

Is the simple statutory scheme sketched above hospitable to free trade and investment, so that the Visegrad countries would be well positioned for integration with Western Europe? The answer is yes.

Simple rules such as those set forth above do all that competition law can be expected to do to ensure that anti-competitive restraints do not block the flow of goods, services and factors of production across borders. As long as penalties and enforcement are credibly strong, such rules would ensure that anti-competitive private restraints do not replace public restraints after governmental trade barriers fall.

Trade-liberalizing competition policy is a small piece of competition policy. One would not write a comprehensive competition law if one's only objective were to remove blockages to trade and thereby move one economy along a path towards integration with another. Even a nationwide price-fixing cartel would not undermine trade objectives if the cartel were not accompanied by restraints against imports. Rather, the high cartel price would trigger a flow of trade. Anti-competitive exclusionary restraints do obstruct trade; and these are prohibited by the suggested rules.

For the above reasons, a simple competition law for formerly command economies would seem to have qualities superior to more regulatory law in facilitating competition and deterring market-obstructing behaviour, and it would be fully compatible with the goals of trade and market integration.

Notes

1. Related matters regarding the rule of law are discussed in Section 2.3 above.
2. *Business Electronics Corp.* v. *Sharp Electronics Corp*. (1988).
3. The guidelines are technically only expressions of government enforcement policy; however, they add an 'anchor' to interpretation of the law.
4. Dr Shyam Khemani has proposed similar rules. See Khemani (1996) and Khemani and Dutz (1996).

4

The Statutes

4.1   Introduction

We begin with the year 1989, which marked a social, political and economic turning point for Central and Eastern Europe. The report of the Polish Anti-monopoly Office (1990–3) well expresses the new state of political economy, in which competition policy would become a major foundation: 1989 signalled the beginning of a fundamental turn in Poland's political and economic system.

> The Constitution[al amendments] of December 29, 1989 proclaimed 'a democratic state of law realizing principles of social justice' (Article 1 of the Polish Constitution) and also gave constitutional status to 'economic freedom' (Article 6) and to the 'guarantee of ownership' (Article 7).

These constitutional changes paved the way for a market-oriented reform that was launched in January 1990 and whose goal was to liquidate the centrally planned economy and replace it with an economy dominated by private ownership, in which competition would be the catalyst for allocating productive factors and for compelling enterprises to become more efficient. The statutes of the countries are reproduced in Appendix 2 of this book.

4.2   The Statutes by Country

The preambles to the four nations' statutes indicate that the statutes were designed to facilitate the creation of competition, to preserve competition, and to protect economic entities and consumers from abusive practices of economically powerful firms. The statutes' description of goals is broad. The Hungarian statute, for example, protects 'freedom and fairness of competition.' The Polish Act, as noted, seeks to ensure development of competition, protection of consumers, and protection of firms from monopolistic practices. The Czech law would protect competition from 'restriction, distortion and elimination.' The Slovak statute specifically identifies efficiency and consumer interests as goals.

4.3　The Polish Statute

Poland was the first Central European nation to enact a competition law in the era of transformation from Communism. It adopted the Act on Countering Monopolistic Practices in 1990. The statute has since been modified by two amendments. The 1990 Act prohibited abuses – such as 'imposing onerous contract terms that yield undue benefits' – even by firms with no market power. By the second amendment, however, dominance became a necessary condition for an abuse offence. The 1990 Act created a presumption of dominance at a 30% market share. The first amendment raised the floor for dominance to 40% (Article 5).

The Act specifies practices that it characterizes as 'monopolistic.' These may be agreements or abuses of power. The Act then declares which monopolistic practices are flatly prohibited and which may be justified.

Under Article 4, monopolistic practices include in particular agreements fixing prices, dividing markets, limiting production, restricting market access, and eliminating economic actors who are strangers to the agreement, and competitors' agreements setting contract terms with third parties.

Under Article 5, monopolistic practices consist of abusing a dominant position, including:

1) counteracting the formation of conditions indispensable for the emergence or development of competition;
2) dividing the market according to criteria of territories, product groups, or entities;
3) selling commodities in a manner that leads to offering privileged status to certain economic entities or other entities;
4) refusing to sell or purchase commodities in a manner discriminating against certain economic entities when there are no alternative supply sources or outlets;
5) unfair influence on price formation, including setting resale prices and selling below costs of production in order to eliminate competitors;
6) imposing onerous contract terms that yield undue benefits to the economic entity that imposes them; and

7) making the conclusion of a contract contingent on having the other party accept or perform another service not connected with the object of the contract, which would not otherwise be accepted or performed if there were a choice.

Article 6 declares that monopolistic practices under Articles 4 and 5 'are prohibited unless they are objectively necessary from a technical or economic viewpoint to conduct an economic activity and do not result in a significant restraint of competition . . .'

Article 7 creates additional offences for economic entities in a monopolistic (as opposed to merely dominant) position; i.e. firms that do not encounter competition. These entities are prohibited from engaging in Article 4 and 5 practices and also from:

1) limiting the production, sale, or purchase of commodities, despite having adequate capacity, particularly when it leads to an increase in sales prices or a reduction in purchase prices;
2) refraining from the sale of commodities to increase prices;
3) charging excessively exorbitant prices.

When 'monopolistic practices' (under Articles 4, 5 or 7) lead to a price increase, the AMO may issue an order reducing prices for a specified period and may control conditions for price changes by the respondent during this period (Article 8).

A separate provision (Article 9) allows for examination and possible prohibition of agreements for product specialization or joint sales or purchase. The AMO may prohibit implementation of such an agreement when it 'prejudices the interests of other economic entities or consumers.' The AMO must prohibit the agreement 'when it leads to a significant restraint of competition or the conditions for its emergence in a given market, and yields no economic benefits' such as reducing costs or improving quality.

By the second amendment Poland adopted a merger control provision (Article 11, 11^1). Mergers with sales exceeding 5 million ECU must be notified to the AMO. The AMO 'may' prohibit the merger 'if as a consequence of the merger, the entities gained or consolidated a dominant position on the market.'

The merger control provision is part of a longer chapter entitled 'Influencing the shaping of structures of economic entities'. Also in this chapter is Article 12, which specifies that 'State enterprises, cooperatives, and companies under commercial law that have a dominant position on a market can be divided or liquidated if they permanently restrain competition or the conditions of its emergence'.

Remedies are separately provided for. The AMO may fine offenders as well as prohibit offending conduct or transactions. Fines may be imposed for amounts up to 15% of the revenues of the offending entity. Entities and their managers may be fined for failure of the entity to obey AMO orders. Managers' fines may be as high as 6 months of their salaries.

Moreover, among its various activities, the AMO must register economic entities whose share of the national market exceeds 80%.

Proceedings under the Anti-monopoly Act may be commenced by the AMO on its own initiative or at the request of authorized persons. The authorized persons are: economic entities whose interests may be prejudiced by the monopolistic practices, public bodies statutorily charged to protect consumers, and local and state governmental institutions.

4.4   The Hungarian Statute

Hungary was the second Central European country to adopt a competition law in the post-Communist era, which it did in November 1990. The law is administered by the Competition Agency, which is the successor to the price control agency. The law, which is called the Act on the Prohibition of Unfair Market Practices, is both a competition law and an unfair competition law. Part One has four chapters – Unfair Competition (e.g., misuse of business secrets, boycotts), Consumer Fraud, Agreements Restricting Competition, and Abuse of a Dominant Position. Part Two is the Merger Control law.

The Hungarian statute begins with this statement of its purposes.

Freedom and fairness of competition are basic preconditions to market competition that make for economic efficiency. In order to protect this freedom and fairness, forms of conduct that are contrary to fair market practices must be prohibited, and supervision over the merger of enterprises must be introduced through the creation of appropriate organizational forms   Accordingly, the public interest in competition, the interests of the participants of economic cooperation and, in connection with fair market conduct, the interests of consumers, shall be protected by law. In order to realize these goals, Parliament has enacted the following Act.

The section on prohibited agreements (Chapter 3) declares it to 'be unlawful for competitors to act in concert or reach an agreement that would result in the restriction or exclusion of competition . . .'. This clause applies 'particularly' to agreements that fix prices, allocate markets, exclude a class of consumers from purchasing or marketing goods, limit choice in purchasing or in marketing opportunities, restrict distribution, impede technological development, hinder market access, and disadvantage some market participants. Agreements to fix resale prices are illegal 'if competition could thereby be limited or excluded'. Unlike the law of the other

Visegrad countries, the resale price-fixing prohibition is the only specific restriction against vertical contract restraints, although other practices that constitute vertical restraints are picked up by the abuse of dominance prohibition, treated below. (A pending amendment would broaden prohibited agreements to include other vertical agreements.)

The statute provides that agreements that restrict or exclude competition are not unlawful, however, if they are 'aimed at stopping an abuse of dominance' or if they are of minor significance (defined as agreements of firms with a joint market share of not more than 10%). Moreover, restrictive agreements are to be exempted if the restriction or exclusion 'does not exceed the extent necessary to attain economically justified common goals' and 'the concomitant advantages outweigh the concomitant disadvantages.'[1] A market share of more than 30% is expressly to be counted as a disadvantage.

The Hungarian provision on dominance and its abuse (Chapter 4) presumes dominance at a 30% market share or more. Moreover, two or three firms that jointly occupy 50% of a market may be deemed to be dominant. The law states that it shall be an abuse of a dominant position to do the following things, among others (paragraph 20):

a) to stipulate unjustified and one-sided advantages or force the other party to accept disadvantageous conditions in contractual relations, including through the application of standard contractual terms;
b) to refuse to conclude a contract without justification;
c) to influence the economic decisions of the other party in order to gain unjustified advantages, including, in particular, by causing such other party to fail to enforce any legitimate contractual claims it may have;
d) to impede access to markets or hinder technical development; or
e) to create, without justification, disadvantageous market conditions for a competitor, or to influence a competitor's economic decisions in order to obtain any unjustified advantage.[2]

Further, the statute illustrates situations in which an unjustified and one-sided advantage exists (paragraph 22). Thus:

Situations in which an unjustified and one-sided advantage exist include, but are not limited to, those in which there is a considerable difference between the service rendered and the consideration tendered therefor under the contract. To establish the existence of such a difference, the following factors shall be considered:

- the conditions under which the contract was concluded,
- the contract taken in its entirety,
- prevailing market conditions,
- prevailing value relations,
- features of the transaction, and

- the manner by which the values of the service rendered and the consideration tendered were calculated.

As for mergers (Chapter 5), those that pass the market share threshold (30%) or revenue threshold may not be consummated without authorization. The supervising body may not authorize a merger 'that would have the effect of impeding the formation, development or continuation of competition'. Notwithstanding this mandate, mergers may be authorized if advantages to competition or foreign competitiveness outweigh the disadvantages to competition. Specifically the statute allows authorization if:

a) the totality of advantageous effects on competition outweigh the disadvantages;
b) the proposed transaction does not preclude competition with respect to the overall market for the goods in question;
c) it promotes transactions on foreign markets that are advantageous to the national economy.

The balancing clause (if advantages [to competition] outweigh disadvantages) appears to make the merger standard more permissive than the EC standard. EC law prohibits creation or strengthening of a dominant position as a result of which effective competition would be significantly impeded, and contains no clause that would allow competitive harm to be trumped by general advantages to the economy (EC Merger Regulation, Article 2). The Hungarian statute, and, as we will see, the statutes of the Czech and Slovak Republics, apparently allow consideration of a broad range of benefits, such as enhanced competitiveness in external markets.

The Hungarian Act's jurisdiction is specifically limited 'to economic activities of entrepreneurs on the territory of the Republic of Hungary' (paragraph 1) (except for prohibited agreements concluded offshore, paragraph 14). This provision has been interpreted to mean that foreign acquisitions are not subjected to merger control. A pending amendment would eliminate this restriction.

The Hungarian Act extends to anti-competitive state rulings. It provides: 'Should the ruling of some state administrative agency violate the freedom of competition, the [Competition Office] shall have the right to apply for redress.' The Competition Office may ask a court to review any such anti-competitive ruling.

The Hungarian Competition Office has the power to issue prohibition orders and fines. Fines must be in the amount of at least 30% but no more than 100% the value of the ill-gotten gains or the damage suffered by consumers and competitors; although lower fines may be assessed in 'special cases'.

While the Hungarian office may, of course, begin proceedings on its own initiative, a private party may petition the Competition Office, alleging a restrictive agreement, abuse of dominance, or prohibited merger. The party may move for an order establishing a violation, discontinuation of the violation, or rectification including damages. If the office establishes an abuse of dominance consisting of an unjustified refusal to conclude a contract, the party may petition the court to find a contract. 'In so finding, the court may establish its content under terms that are customary in the trade' (paragraphs 28 and 29).

The Competition Office has prepared amendments to cure certain perceived defects and to bring the Hungarian law more nearly into line with European Community competition law. The proposed amendments would adopt the language of EC Article 85(3) specifying the conditions for exemption of agreements (see note 1). The definition of dominance would be changed to include the firm's capability of acting independently from competitors (thus adopting the EC definition). The statute would be clarified to provide that anti-competitive intent is not a necessary condition for an abuse offence, and the examples of abuse of dominance would be expanded to include withdrawal of goods from the market and tying. The trigger for merger notification would be based solely on turnover; the market share threshold would be eliminated, and jurisdiction would be extended to foreign mergers.

4.5   The Czechoslovak Statute

In January 1991 the Federal Assembly of Czechoslovakia passed the Act on the Protection of Economic Competition. When Czechoslovakia was later reconstituted as two separate republics, the Act became law in each of the two states.

The 1991 Act, which was amended as we describe below, stated the following broad purpose:

> The purpose of this law is the protection of economic competition and the creation of favourable conditions for its further development and to prevent the rise and maintenance of monopolies or dominating positions of legal or natural persons, frustrating or hindering economic competition.

The Act prohibited 'cartel agreements,' defined as agreements between entrepreneurs (i.e. legal or natural persons) that 'can influence production, circulation of goods and services, [or] eliminate or restrict economic competition.' A procedure for exemption of certain agreements was provided. The Act required notification of a dominant position, defined as a 30% or larger market share, and prohibited abuse of dominance to the detriment of other entrepreneurs, consumers or the public interest. Abuse of dominance was defined as forcing unreasonable contract provisions on other parties, imposing tie-ins, discriminating against market participants, and limiting production.

The Act stated that mergers that may restrict competition were subject to approval. The Office was required to grant approval 'if the damage caused by restricting competition is outweighed by the economic advantages caused by the merger'. The danger of restricting competition was presumed if the merging firms' combined market share exceeded 30%.

4.5.1 The Czech Statute

The Czech Parliament passed amendments to the 1991 Act in October 1992 and November 1993. The first amendment related principally to the structure of the Office; the second amendment revised the substantive law. The second amendment states that the Act protects competition not competitors, clarifies that the Act covers vertical agreements, and incorporates various EC standards. As reformulated, the introductory paragraph now provides:

> The purpose of this law is the protection of economic competition in the market of products and services ('goods') against restriction, distortion and elimination of it ('disturbing competition').

Section 3 of the Act had been entitled 'Cartel Agreement's. This section was understood by the Office to be limited to agreements among competitors. The amendment changed the title of Section 3 to 'Agreements Disturbing Competition' to make clear that vertical agreements are covered. As amended, the prohibition on anti-competitive agreements begins as follows:[3]

> 1) All agreements between competitors, decisions of associations of entrepreneurs and behaviour of competitors in mutual agreement which lead, or can lead to a breach of economic competition on the market for goods, are prohibited and invalid, unless the Ministry of Economic Competition has allowed an exception.

The statute gives examples of prohibited agreements. The list more or less tracks the EC list of prohibited agreements, and adds: 'A commitment to restrict access to the market to competitors who are not parties to the agreement.'

The prohibitions of Section 3(1) expressly do not apply to customary agreements (other than customary price-fixing), rationalizations of economic activity by specialization that does not substantially restrict competition, and agreements wherein the collaborators hold less than 5% of the national market or 30% of local markets.

The Ministry may exempt agreements necessary in the public interest for production or technical or economic progress except that the exception may not 'exceed the limits necessary to pay special regard to the interests of consumers'. If the above conditions exist, the Ministry 'will allow an exception' if certain other conditions are also satisfied; e.g. the agreement contains no tying clause, and the agreement does not contradict 'the good manners of competition'.

Monopoly and dominant positions must be reported to the Ministry, under Section 9. A dominant position is one, acquired either alone or by agreement with other competitors, that 'is not exposed to substantial competition'. A firm is dominant position if it has 'at least 30% of deliveries of identical, comparable, or mutually replaceable goods'.

The statute states that a monopoly or dominant position may not be abused to the detriment of other competitors, consumers or the public interest. Abuse is:

a) the direct or indirect forcing of inappropriate conditions into contracts with other participants in the market, especially forcing accomplishments that are, at the time of finalizing a contract, in striking disparity to the counter-accomplishments provided,

b) making the finalization of the contract binding to the conditions that the second contractual partner will also take on other accomplishments which are not related to the required subject of the contract, nor factually according to business customs,

c) the application of various conditions with identical or comparable accomplishments towards individual participants in the market, which puts these participants in economic competition to a disadvantage.

d) ceasing or limiting the production, marketing or technical development of goods in order to gain unjustified economic benefit to the detriment of the buyers.

The examples are similar to the EC examples in Article 86 except that subsection (a) is more focused on protecting non-dominant market participants against one-sided bargains that they are 'forced' to make.

Mergers 'that disturb or can impair economic competition' are subject to authorization by the Ministry. A merger producing a market share in excess of 30% is regarded as disturbing competition. 'The Ministry will allow the merger if the participating competitors demonstrate that the detriment which can arise from impairing competition will be outweighed by the economic advantages which will be brought about by the merger.'

The prohibitions of the Act cover 'organs of state administration and organs of municipalities, as far as their activities which are directly related to economic competition is concerned'. This provision applies to states as economic actors.

A separate provision applies to states and municipalities in their governmental capacities. Section 18 states: 'The organs of state administration and the organs of municipalities may not, by their own measures, support or in other ways, restrict or exclude economic competition. The Ministry is charged with supervising this obligation, and may require correction.'

As for penalties against economic actors, the Ministry is authorized to fine enterprises that violate the Act in amounts up to 10% of net turnover. An enterprise must be fined at least the amount of its benefit from the violation.

4.5.2   The Slovak Statute

In 1994 the Slovak Assembly significantly revised the Act on the Protection of Economic Competition, inherited from Czechoslovakia. The Slovak Republic liberalized the law in some respects and aligned the substantive principles with those of the EU. The law was clarified to stress the purpose of promoting economic progress for the benefit of consumers. Thus, the statement of purpose was revised to read as follows:

> The purpose of this Act is to protect economic competition in the markets for products and services against prevention, restriction or distortion as well as to create conditions for its further development, in order to promote economic progress for the benefit of consumers.

The drafters of the 1994 law replaced the prohibition against 'cartel agreements' with a prohibition against 'agreements restricting competition', as had the Czech Republic, to make certain that the law was broad enough to cover vertical restraints. The list of prohibited agreements now includes 'in particular' virtually the same list as that contained in Article 85(1) of the EC Treaty of Rome (see note 1). The specified prohibitions are:

a) the direct or indirect fixing of prices;
b) a commitment to limit or control production, sales, technical development, or investment;
c) the division of the market or of sources of supply;
d) a commitment by the parties to the agreement that different conditions of trade, relating to the same subject matter of the contract will be applied to individual sellers or buyers that will disadvantage some of them in competition;
c) a commitment by at least one party to the agreement that contracts with buyers will require the purchase of other goods unrelated to the required goods either in substance or in commercial practice and custom.

The prohibition of restrictive agreements expressly does not apply to agreements that comply with four conditions – improving production and distribution or promoting technical or economic progress, allowing users a fair share of benefits, imposing no restrictive conditions unless they are indispensable, and not empowering the parties to eliminate competition substantially. These are the same four conditions necessary for an exemption under EC Article 85(3). The Slovak law differs in procedure from the EC law, however, in that the EC law requires an exemption to validated agreements that may have competition-restricting effects. In the Slovak Republic, agreements that comply with the four conditions are simply not illegal.

Slovakia's provision on abuse of a dominant position now codifies the EC case-law definition of dominance (not subject to substantial competition or able to act independently of competitors and customers). The statute states that a 40% market share establishes a rebuttable presumption of dominance. (Before amendment, the presumption arose at 30%.) The examples of abuse nearly track the list in EC Article 86. Instead of specifying as an abuse 'unfair trading conditions,' however, as does EC law, the Slovak law adopts the more sweeping Central European formulation of prohibiting 'enforcement of disproportionate conditions in contracts.'

Mergers and other concentrations in the Slovak Republic are subject to control if they exceed a monetary threshold or the partners' combined share of the market exceeds 20%. The substantive merger standard is:

> The Authority shall prohibit the concentration if it creates or strengthens a dominant position in the market unless the participants prove that the harm which results from the restriction on competition will be outweighed by overall economic advantages of the concentration.

The statute does not establish a market share of presumed invalidity, as did the statute of the former Czechoslovakia.

The merger standard of the Czech Republic is the same as that of Slovakia. Thus, general economic advantages may outweigh impairments to competition.

As under the Czech law, state administrative authorities and municipalities may not 'support or in any other way, restrict competition'; and if they should do so the competition authority may require correction (Article 18).

In general, the competition authority may bring proceedings on its own initiative or in response to a petition by an entrepreneur (Article 12). It may impose fines of up to 10% of turnover (Article 14).

Also, consumers or a legal person authorized to protect consumers may commence litigation under civil law. Other 'entitled persons' may join the proceedings as 'subsidiary participants.' After conclusion of the litigation, no suit by other entitled persons shall be permissible (Article 17).

4.6 Summary

The statutes of the four Visegrád countries are remarkably similar. Some are more detailed than others. The Polish statute is most detailed in listing examples of 'monopolistic practices'. The Slovak statute is least detailed and most like the EC Treaty of Rome, Articles 85 and 86. The statutory justifications for restrictive practices vary somewhat among the nations; the Slovak and Czech justifications are more closely aligned with the language of EC Article 85(3). The Hungarian justifications include industrial policy, that is, external competitiveness. In two of the nations a justified restrictive agreement must obtain the permission of the Ministry. In Poland and Slovakia, a restrictive agreement that satisfies the criteria for justification is automatically permitted.

For abuse of dominance two nations – the Czech Republic and Hungary – (rebuttably) presume dominance at 30% of the market; the other two nations place the threshold at 40%. All four prohibit dominant firms from imposing one-sided, disproportionate or onerous contract terms. Otherwise, the Czech and Slovak laws virtually track the EC examples of abuse. The Hungarian language is concerned somewhat more with dominant firms' gaining unjustified advantages over competitors, and the Polish language, while also expressing the Hungarian concerns, is more distinct and detailed and includes a ban against interference with emergence of competition and against selling below production costs to eliminate competitors. Poland alone allows the specified abuses of dominance to be justified, except that no justification is allowed if the firm is in a monopoly position as opposed to a merely dominant position.

All four nations have merger control. The Czech statute alone contains a market share presumption of illegality, which it sets at 30%. Poland and the Slovak Republic basically incorporate the EC standard: creation or strengthening of a dominant position. The Hungarian and Czech laws prohibit mergers that impair or impede competition (for the EC it is 'impedes' effective competition). In Hungary, the Czech Republic and the Slovak Republic, mergers that offend the standard must (as opposed to 'may') be prohibited or subjected to conditions, except that if economic advantages of the merger outweigh the harm to competition, the merger may be allowed. The Polish law gives the AMO the power but not the duty to prevent anti-competitive mergers, and makes no mention of advantages that may offset competitive harm. Similarities and differences are presented in Table 4.1.

Table 4.1 The statutes

Country	Restrictive agreements				
	Is prohibition virtually the same as EC Art. 85(1)?	Does it include vertical restraints?	Are factors for justification virtually the same as Article 85(3)?	Exemption by AMO needed?	Is there a market share presumption of dominance?
Czech Republic	Yes, plus: must not agree to restrict competitors' access	Yes	Yes	Yes	At least 30%
Hungary	Somewhat, plus: must not limit choices of competitors or consumers, restrict distribution, hinder market access, disadvantage market participants	Yes, prior to the current amendment, only RPM	No overbroad restriction of competition, and advantages outweigh disadvantages; factors: improvement in price, quality, distribution, technological development, external competitiveness	Yes	One firm has more than 30%, or three have more than 50%
Poland	Yes, plus: restricting market access, eliminating economic entities not party to agreement, setting terms of contracts with third parties	Yes, except RPM is illegal	Agreement must be objectively necessary and does not significantly restrain competition, or necessary to fulfil international obligations of Poland	No	40%
Slovakia	Yes	Yes	Yes	No	40%

Abuse of dominance			Mergers		
Prohibits			Standard		
One-sided contracts or disproportionate or onerous conditions	(Otherwise) exemplary list is virtually the same as Article 86	Justification available	Is there a market share presumption of illegality?	Creates or strengthens a dominant position	Unless competitive harm is outweighed by economic advantages
Yes	Yes, forcing inappropriate conditions into contracts in striking disparity to other party's benefits	No	30%	Disturb or impair economic competition	Yes
Yes	Must not: refuse to conclude agreement without justification, influence economic decisions to gain unjustified advantages, impede access, create disadvantageous conditions for competition w/o justification	No	No	Impeding competition	Yes if competitive harm outweighed by advantages to competition or foreign competitiveness
Yes	Similar, plus: must not interfere with emergence of competition, unfair influence on price including PRM and selling below production cost to eliminate competitors, discriminatory refusal to sell when there are no alternative sources. Additional constraint	Yes if firm dominant but not monopoly; some justifications for agreements	No	Yes	No, but AMO has no duty to prohibit
Yes	Yes	No	No	Yes	Yes

Substantively, the differences in language among the four statutes are largely unimportant. Though one might prefer certain formulations to others, the statutes have been interpreted to mean basically the same thing. Most of the law formation depends on the analysis of whether a firm is dominant and what interpretation is given to the terms 'anticompetitive' and 'abuse'. We shall consider these matters in detail in Chapter 4 below.[4]

Notes

1. The specified advantages are much like those listed in EC Article 85(3).
    Article 85(1) of the EC Treaty of Rome specifies as examples of competition – distorting agreements or concerted practices, those that:
    (a) directly or indirectly fix purchase or selling prices or any other trading conditions;
    (b) limit or control production, markets, technical development, or investment;
    (c) share markets or sources of supply;
    (d) apply dissimilar conditions to equivalent transactions with other trading parties, thereby placing them at a competitive disadvantage;
    (e) make the conclusion of contracts subject to acceptance by the other parties of supplementary obligations which, by their nature or according to commercial usage, have no connection with the subject of such contracts.
    While Article 85(2) declares such agreements void, Article 85(3) provides for an exemption procedure. Under this procedure a competition-distorting agreement or concerted practice may be allowed under Article 85(3) if it:
    contributes to improving the production or distribution of goods or to promoting technical or economic progress, while allowing consumers a fair share of the resulting benefit, and which does not:
    (a) impose on the undertakings concerned restrictions which are not indispensable to the attainment of these objectives;
    (b) afford such undertakings the possibility of eliminating competition in respect of a substantial part of the product in question.
2. As in Poland, the list is somewhat longer than that contained in EC Article 86 and somewhat more concerned with the dominant firm's taking advantage of trading parties or competitors.
    Under EC Article 86 an abuse includes:
    (a) directly or indirectly imposing unfair purchase or selling prices or other unfair trading conditions;
    (b) limiting production, markets or technical development to the prejudice of consumers;
    (c) applying dissimilar conditions to equivalent transactions with other trading parties, thereby placing them at a competitive disadvantage;
    (d) making the conclusion of contracts subject to acceptance by the other parties of supplementary obligations which, by their nature or according to commercial usage, have no connection with the subject of such contracts
3 The amendment replaced the word 'entrepreneurs' with the word 'competitors'; but 'competitors' means market participants and does not reflect a limitation of the section to horizontal agreements. Also, the amendment extended the Act to cover trade and professional associations. Further, the amendment deleted a prohibition (old (2)(g)) against contracts containing 'provisions excessively restricting the right of parties to withdraw from an agreement', and it deleted an exception from the ban against restrictive contracts (old (4)(c)): 'granting a rebate that is compensation for performance and not discriminatory'.

4 This is true generally of differences between other nations' and religions' competition laws; e.g. US law is compared with EC law. For example, much more turns on the meaning, accorded to the word 'anti-competitive' than differences in the wording of the Sherman Act and the EC Treaty of Rome. See Fox (1986).

5

Procedures and Institutions

5.1   Introduction

The implementation of competition law is undertaken in the first instance in many jurisdictions by administrative bodies rather than by courts. Examples include the European Commission's Directorate General for Competition (DGIV), the Competition Authority in Ireland and the Bundeskartellerant in Germany. In the United States, one of the two federal enforcers, the Federal Trade Commission, is an administrative agency. These bodies implement and enforce the law and, although powers, responsibilities and levels of independence vary greatly, each is ultimately constrained by the reviewing courts. The Visegrád countries have each adopted this administrative approach and established a dedicated competition office with the introduction of their competition legislation.

Before examining these offices in detail, it is useful to discuss the general question of using administrative bodies rather than the courts in the implementation of competition laws. While any law can be made effective by enforcement within the executive body (e.g. public prosecution) and by private rights of action in the courts, with incentives to sue, there are several reasons why competition policy may require dedicated institutions in addition to courts.

First, investigating competition cases requires technical and complex skills, and it is generally more efficient to delegate such tasks to special administrative bodies. This is done in other areas such as patents and regulation of safety standards. Second, there are economies of scale and scope across competition cases that a specialized body may be better able to exploit. An example is the establishment and publication of general guidelines and exemptions for particular types of business activities. Third, competition is an area where delays are particularly costly. An administrative body may be able to prioritize decisions according to commercial urgency. This is well illustrated by mergers, where their irreversibility makes it preferable to approve them in advance but where their value declines if they are not approved quickly. Finally, competition cases often affect many consumers or competitors so that the damage to any individual party may not be great relative to the total damage to all parties. In such a case, the incentive of the individual to pursue the matter in the courts may be very small, even though its pursual is socially worth while, and it may be optimal for the state to bear the costs of investigations and prosecutions. An administrative agency is one way of doing this. This centralization need not be at the expense of other mechanisms: the right of private action can remain. The need for centralization is particularly great with new legislation, where the requirement for and hence externalities associated with establishing precedent are greatest. At the same time, it is appropriate that the decisions of any administrative body be subject to judicial review so as to ensure the consistent and correct application of laws and procedures.

Where the implementation of competition law is delegated to an administrative body, certain powers and responsibilities are either laid down in law, or assumed by the body or they evolve over time. These include the ability to receive and investigate complaints, to initiate their own investigations, to collect information from a variety of sources, to make or recommend decisions,[1] to enforce these and to defend theses decisions in the courts if necessary. They may also have powers to impose financial or other penalties on firms, as damages as an example to other firms, and also specify what is prohibited by, for example, publishing guidelines or interpretations of the law.

In outlining the institutional approaches that have been adopted in the transition economies, we distinguish three broad characteristics. The first is *formal*, including characteristics of the competition office such as its physical size and resources, both financial and human, that determine the ability of the office to carry out its functions effectively. The second category of characteristics relate to the *function* of the offices: these include the powers given to, and responsibilities expected of, each office. Finally, we describe the *organizational* characteristics of the offices, namely their internal structure and management.

These characteristics vary, both in their exogeneity from the office itself and in their permanence. For example, the organizational characteristics are inherently within the control of the offices themselves and, as such, are capable of being changed more easily. On the other hand, the formal characteristics are exogenously determined by the legal statutes or parliaments. Aspects like financing can be changed in the short run, but the status of the office is relatively permanent. In between, the powers and responsibilities of competition offices tend to evolve over time, determined partly by the offices themselves and partly by external forces. The fact that the institutions can evolve in significantly different directions is best illustrated by the substantial differences that have been established between the Czech and Slovak offices, which share a common origin in the former Czechoslovakia.

This chapter also outlines the procedures used in considering competition cases, noting especially the interaction of the competition offices with the courts. Other institutions of the state, most notably the privatization agencies, the economic ministries responsible for trade, industry and agriculture, and local governments have a role in the determination of policy and the interplay between these various institutions is discussed in Chapter 7. Finally, the reader should note that this chapter merely describes the institutions and that an evaluation of how they have performed is presented in Chapter 8.

5.2   Formal Characteristics

5.2.1   Name and Location

The competition offices in the Visegrad countries were established at the same time as the legal statues were introduced in the early stages of transition and all were fully operational by the middle of 1991, except in Poland, where the law was passed in 1987 and the office established in 1990. The summary description of each office is outlined in Table 5.1. The differences in names and titles are not significant, except to note that the Czech office

Table 5.1   Formal characteristics of competition offices

	Czech Republic	Hungary	Poland	Slovakia
Legislation	January 1991	January 1991[a]	1990	March 1991[b]
Founded	May 1991[c]	January 1991	1990	Autumn 1990
First decision	October 1991	February 1991	1990	October 1991
Title	Ministry of Economic Competition (MEC)	Office for Economic Competition (OEC)	Anti-monopoly Office (AMO)	Anti-monopoly Office (AMO)
Location	Brno	Budapest	Warsaw	Bratislava
Title of Head	Minister	President	President	Chairman

Sources: Annual reports of competition offices and communications with competition offices.
Notes:
[a]Hungary had a similar legal statute since 1984, but without a merger regulation.
[b]Operated from July 1991 and became a Ministry from 31 October 1992.
[c]The new Slovak Act was passed in August 1994 but the legislation of the former Czechoslovakia applied.

is a Ministry, with the head of the office being a full (i.e. voting) Minister of the Government. It is the only competition office not located in the capital city and is the only Czech ministry located in Brno. This is not necessarily a bad signal: the Czech Supreme Court is similarly located.[2]

The near-simultaneous establishment of the offices with the passing of the legal statutes (noting the Polish exception) means that institutions were determined by the legal statutes rather than vice versa, although in some cases individuals responsible for the drafting of the statutes may have been destined to staff the offices. In other transition economies, offices have been established considerably in advance of the legislation and thus may have had a greater role in the drafting of the statutes. The generic term 'Competition Office' will be used to describe these bodies.

5.2.2 Funding

There are two aspects to the finances of the offices, namely the procedure by which the level of funding is determined and the actual level of funding. The funding of the office in each country is determined by an annual parliamentary vote, from the overall state budget. (In some of the Visegrad countries, this is the only opportunity for parliamentarians to comment on or influence competition policy.) This determines gross state expenditure on competition policy, because revenue earned from fines imposed by the offices is returned to the state budget.[3] Interestingly, the total revenue from fines has in some cases exceeded the total cost of running the office so that the net effect of operation of competition policy *on the state budget* has sometimes been positive. Differences in implicit or indirect state funding, such as free office accommodation or differential pension or social insurance contributions, also matter to the measurement of the actual budgets of the offices.

The level of funding of the offices in 1995 varied from 0.5 million ECU in Slovakia to 1.5 million in Poland (see Table 5.2). This funding must meet

Table 5.2 Funding of the competition offices

	Czech Republic	Hungary	Poland	Slovakia
Office budget (1995)[a]	0.75 million	1.32 million	1.43 million	0.47 million
GDP (1994)	30.3 billion	25.0 billion	63.5 billion	9.8 billion
Budget/GDP (index)	47	100	43	91
Total staff (1995)	74	115	159	63
Budget per staff member	10 135	11 478	8994	7460
Index of budget per staff	85	100	78	65
Staff cost/GDP per capita	3.4	4.9	5.5	4.1
Staff cost/GDP per worker	1.7	1.8	2.1	1.6

Sources: OECD and communications with competition offices.
Note:
[a] All monetary figures are expressed in ECU using October 1995 exchange rates.

all costs of the offices, including all payments to staff. It is reasonable to say that, given the number of staff they employ, the offices are not by any measure extravagantly funded. In general, the budgets have increased in nominal terms each year, but in several instances the real value of the budget has declined substantially since 1991. In Hungary, a fiscal crisis resulted in a uniform 10% reduction in fixed state receipts in 1995.

Comparing funding across countries is extremely difficult. Although larger economies, with higher levels of economic activity, are likely to place greater demands on competition policy, it is not obvious that constant returns to scale exist in the provision of competition policy services. Activities such as the issuing of block exemptions, commentaries on the law and guidelines for businesses are likely to involve fixed costs that do not vary with the size of the economy (and hence there are economies to scale, as may partially explain the EU approach and perhaps also the success of US competition policy).[4] Also, if consistent market definitions are adopted across countries, larger countries may not consider cases that smaller ones would examine (for *de minimis* type reasons). Table 5.2 reports both the total funding and the funding relative to GDP for each country. Although Poland receives the most in total, relative to GDP it appears poorly funded. This is consistent with modest returns to scale in the provision of competition policy. However, the discrepancy between the Czech and Hungarian figures are more significant, given that they are closer in size. By either measure, competition policy in Hungary is almost twice as well funded. If one believes the fixed costs are very important, then competition policy in Slovakia fares very badly, although doing almost as well as Hungary in terms of funding per GDP.

An alternative way to compare the funding of the offices, and one that throws light on the internal allocation of resources, is the budget per staff member. Here again, Hungary stands out with the highest figure, with the other countries ranked as the Czech Republic (85% of the Hungarian figure), Poland (78%) and Slovakia (65%). Hungary pays 15% and the Czech Republic 10% of its budget as office rental. To the extent that other countries do not pay office rent, the differences in net funding per staff member are less.

The previous comparison ignores differences in labour costs. The last two rows of Table 5.2 show the funding per staff member relative to the GDP per capita and the GDP per worker. This changes the ranking, with the Polish Office, faced with lower average salaries domestically, appearing to pay relatively more to its staff than other countries. Of course, the exercise ignores the fact that the balance chosen between labour and administrative costs is endogenous and may be different across the offices. Nevertheless, Table 5.2 indicates the trade-off faced in each office between the number of employees and the compensation per employee and other administrative costs.

It is not clear how these differences in funding matter for the offices and, in particular, whether they affect the quality of output. One explanation is that the offices are required or choose to fulfil more functions (we see below that Poland is) so that quality of output is not affected. Another is that offices that face greater political interference expend resources in rent-seeking A third is that the quality of decisions does not vary across offices because differences in efficiency compensate for differences in funding.

Although the staff numbers appear high (say, by the standards of the competition offices of some EU Member States), this does not mean that the offices are not constrained. Each office reported to us that it has just about adequate resources to fulfil its core legal obligations in terms of investigations, data collection, information technology and decision-making. However, resources are very limited outside this: for example, offices have not been able to collect market data in the absence of an investigations or undertake general market studies unless specifically requested by the government, as in Poland. Resources for staff training, publications and translating of material are certainly scarce, and there has even been some speculation that the current level of activity in these areas might have to be reduced. The offices may be constrained in the quality of new staff that they can attract either because they cannot offer adequate remuneration or because they cannot find appropriately and sufficiently skilled individuals. In this event, offices may be forced to substitute larger numbers of less qualified staff for a smaller number of more highly paid and better-qualified ones.

5.2.3 Human Resources

The total number of staff of the competition offices of the four Visegrad countries varies from 63 in Slovakia to 159 in Poland (see Table 5.3). The distribution of the staff follows the same pattern in each country, with a high proportion of professionals, the largest grouping being economists and then

Table 5.3 Human resources of competition offices

	Czech Republic	Hungary	Poland	Slovakia
Total staff (in 1995)	74[a]	115	159	63
Lawyers (%)	26	14	24	11
Economists (%)	46	31	37	54
Other professionals (%)	16	29	13	17
Total professionals (%)	88	74	74	83
Others (%)	12	26	26	17
Fluent in one EU language (%)	25	19	29	19

Sources: Communications with competition offices.
Notes:
[a]This excludes 12 people in the public procurement office so as to enable comparison.

lawyers, but with a surprisingly large (relative to Western standards) proportion of staff with technical or expert knowledge. The other staff include administrators, secretaries and drivers. Although the offices are new entities, many of the staff previously worked in price-control offices.[5]

The offices generally recruit trained staff, but considerable on-the-job training does occur. A minority of staff in each office is at any time continuing formal education or training, usually following a university or other course or obtaining a professional qualification (e.g., to practice as a lawyer). It is not clear to what extent the incentives for such training are motivated by career prospects *within* the office. Members of staff from each office have also participated in PHARE-assisted training programmes and in stagiaire programmes at DG IV of the European Commission and at EU member state-competition offices.

Salary scales in the offices are generally tied to public service pay, but there is some flexibility, and enhanced performance can be rewarded to some extent. There is little evidence of rent-seeking (e.g. for promotion) within the offices.

All countries share the major problem of recruiting high-quality professional staff, as public sector salaries are generally a small proportion of what can be earned in the private sector. The offices variously estimate the premium that an official could obtain in the private sector as between 1.5 and 5 times the salary paid by the competition offices, with the differential being greatest for lawyers. Nonetheless, competition offices generally have been lucky in attracting and especially in retaining the high-quality staff that have been with them since the foundation of the office. Staff turnover has been relatively low, and appears to be lowest in Hungary. It is plausible that many of the existing staff have become highly qualified over the last 5 years and that they could not be replaced by equivalently qualified personnel at their current salaries if they were to leave.

In summary, the similarities between the offices in regard to human resources are striking. They all have similar proportions of professional to non-professional staff and face the same constraints recruiting highly qualified staff in the face of strong demand from the private sector. There is no evidence of any one office being relatively overstaffed (as might be expected after central planning), but recruiting and retaining highly trained professionals will clearly be one of the major challenges of the offices in the coming years.

5.3   Functional Characteristics

The responsibilities and powers of the offices are determined largely by the statutes. They are also affected by each office's interpretation of these statutes and by court rulings. The core responsibilities of each office are broadly similar, but there is considerable variation in the supplemental functions assigned to different offices. It is more difficult to assess the powers the offices have, especially in the area of enforcement, where they have not yet been tested.

The main function and work of the competition offices concerns the investigation and determination of cases in the areas of abuse of dominance, mergers, cartels and restrictive agreements. Some functions are specifically required by law, but a voluntary dimension remains, with regard to both the rigour with which the legal requirements are met and the other voluntary functions that offices undertake without any legal requirement.

In the consideration of cases, the offices are *required*, either by competition law or by administrative law, and within specified time limits, to:

- Receive and reply to all complaints from consumers or firms relating to competition and notification of merger or acquisition agreements[6]
- Decide which cases merit detailed investigation and undertake investigations
- Make decisions on cases and publish these with reasoning
- Enforce decisions, including the right to defend them in the courts.

They have discretion as to whether to initiate investigations, known as *ex officio* proceedings. Only in Hungary is there a separation of prosecution and decision-making.

Each office also has responsibility for the drafting of changes to the competition law. This involves preparing an initial draft, circulating this to other government departments and agencies for their comments, and incorporating these comments, which are not binding, into the legislation as they see fit. The final draft is then prepared by the government's legal office before going to parliament.[7]

On the other side of this process, the competition office is required to comment, in what is known as a *standpoint*, on all draft legislation emanating from other government departments and agencies. This process enables the office to propose modifications to legislation which might damage competition, such as licensing or tariff changes. The standpoint is not binding, but the office may have subsequent options available to it (constitutional court action, break-up of a firm, etc.) if its advice is not heeded. These standpoints are written by the legal departments in consultation with relevant experts. This is a substantial workload: for example, the Polish office gave more than 500 opinions on draft legislation affecting competition between 1990 and 1995. Both the Czech and Slovak offices report that this is the major output of their legal departments, taking perhaps the equivalent of two to three full-time staff.

Table 5.4 Functions required of competition offices

Function	Czech Republic	Hungary	Poland	Slovakia
Annual report	Required	Required	Voluntary	Required
Publish decisions	Required	Required	Voluntary	Required
Market studies	Required	Voluntary	Required, of prices and concentration	Only if requested by government
Dominance register	No	No	Required if share above 80%	Voluntary
Other	Public procurement	Consumer fraud and unfair competition	Public utilities Investment law	None

Sources: Competition legislation, annual reports and communications with competition offices.

The offices, and individuals within them, voluntarily undertake several functions that are not required legally. These concern the promotion of competition in the wider economy and the international, usually academic, representation of the work of the office. In regard to the former, public lectures, educational campaigns, university courses, media appearances and other advocacy functions are undertaken by individuals and sometimes funded by the competition offices. In terms of international representation of their work, the offices translate annual reports and important cases into (usually) English and attend and present papers at international conferences on competition policy. Several such contributions have been published in international journals. Tasks such as the preparation for and representation of the government at international meetings on competition policy, such as those at the OECD and EU, are systematically undertaken and either are required by law or delegated by the government.

In addition to these core functions that all offices have in common, there are others that vary across offices. Table 5.4 indicates certain functions, whether they are legally required and, if not, whether they are undertaken voluntarily. For example, an annual report is required in two countries but is produced by all four. Only the Polish office is not legally required to publish its decisions (although it does). The Polish office has the greatest requirements with regard to maintaining a register of dominant firms and undertaking general studies of competition on markets. The other countries do this to varying degrees of formality and this is an area where the lack of resources has been considered significant. Offices have expressed a desire to be able to undertake more of this type of general market study: that which currently exists (in the other three countries) is either cross-subsidized or done voluntarily, and consequently is not as systematic.

The allocation of other functions such as price control and consumer protection is of significance insofar as it indicates how competition policy is perceived (or likely to be perceived) in its interaction with other policies. In general, competition policy has been separated from price control, consumer protection and other tasks, but some offices do have additional responsibilities that do not obviously need to be undertaken by competition agencies.

In Poland, the office has a role in the regulation of public utilities and the enforcement (of ownership aspects) of the investment laws.[8] Hungary has eschewed such a role, on the basis that it might allow the office to be perceived as being responsible for price control, an association that it wishes to avoid, especially as it is the successor to the price control office. The Slovak office has made (unsuccessful) recommendations to the government for a system of independent regulation along United Kingdom lines. No office has any explicit responsibility for price control, but it is understandable that the transition has seen price rises that consumers sometimes attribute to monopoly. This may explain why the Czech Ministry, because of its visibility as a Ministry, is overwhelmed by complaints about excessive pricing that it considers have little to do with competition.

The Hungarian office has a role in consumer protection if consumer choice is affected, without limiting the jurisdiction of the courts. Thus it does not becomes involved in consumer fraud cases, but issues like misleading advertising might get handled either by the office or by the courts. The Polish office may also be involved in consumer protection if an abuse of dominance is alleged. Otherwise, consumer protection is the responsibility of other agencies.[9] Unfair competition is dealt with by the courts, usually under separate legislation, but the competition offices often consider cases where fairness is at issue. In areas such as anti-dumping and public procurement, offices have been closely involved in the process of drafting new legislation but responsibility for these tasks has been allocated elsewhere (except in the Czech Republic).

In order to carry out the above functions, the offices have been given powers to collect information, impose fines, prevent certain activities and impose penalties in the event of non-compliance. Table 5.5 summarizes the various powers of the offices.

Broadly speaking, similar powers have been allocated to all offices and these powers are similar in general to those that prevail in established market economies, with the exception that the legal principles and expressions such as 'discovery' and 'injunction' either do not apply or have a different meaning. There are some notable differences, especially in Hungary, where powers appear somewhat weaker than elsewhere. In particular, the Hungarian office has no powers to break up firms or force divestitures.

Apart from the legal powers of the office, the level of political goodwill towards an office and its operation also affect its *de facto* powers. In

Table 5.5 Additional powers of competition offices

Powers to:	Czech Republic	Hungary	Poland	Slovakia
Collect data and evidence	Yes	Yes	Yes	Yes
Access unpublished national statistics	Yes	Yes	Yes	Yes
Access government files	Yes	Yes	Unclear	No
Enforce decisions	Unclear	Only via courts	Yes	Unclear
Impose penalties for non-compliance	Yes	Some[b]	Yes	Yes
Remedies				
Issue injunctions	Yes	Only via courts	No	Yes
Prohibit anti-competitive behaviour	Yes	Yes	Yes	Yes
Break up (dominant) firms	Yes	No	Yes	Yes
Impose exemplary fines	Yes	Yes[a]	Yes	Yes

Sources: Competition legislation, annual reports and communications with competition offices.
Notes:
[a]Where the Council can assess the loss or gain, the fine must lie between 130% and 200%. In the majority of cases where this is not possible, there is no limit to the level of the fine.
[b]If a firm refuses to supply data or information, there are no penalties. If it does not accept a decision, this can be pursued through the courts, but second fines may not be imposed on initial fines. The current legislative amendment proposes that fines be payable immediately, regardless of whether an appeal is being heard.

addition, it may be the case that having weak powers in some areas strengthens an office's hand in other areas, enabling it to exercise those powers it does have more fully. It might be argued, for example, that the Hungarian office is a case in point. This point is taken up in Section 8.1 below.

5.4　Organizational Characteristics

The abstract possibilities of organizing a competition office are myriad, but the main issues are whether internal divisions are organized along functional lines (e.g. merger department) or sectoral lines (agricultural department), whether management decisions are delegated, whether clear procedures exist for the exchange of information within the office, and the level of bureaucracy (especially important in offices inherited from a period of central planning).

In terms of the internal structure, all four Visegrad countries have chosen to organize themselves along both functional and sectoral lines, with a broadly similar pattern across the countries (see Table 5.6). There are three

Table 5.6 Departments within competition offices

Department	Czech Republic	Hungary	Poland	Slovakia
Executive 1	Energy, fuels, textiles transport, building communications, electrochemical	Industry	Industrial products	Oil, chemicals, textiles, agriculture
Executive 2	Gas, oil, chemicals, pharmaceuticals, health, housing	Commerce	Services and agricultural products	Energy, fuels, metals, engineering
Executive 3	Banking, printing, engineering, cars, tourism	Banking	Public utilities, local government, media and transport	Forestry, paper, printing, culture, building.
Executive 4	Agriculture, food, services education, retail	Services		Retail, banks, tourism, communications, insurance, media
Executive 5		Food processing		
Administrative	Office of Minister International Administration	Secretariat International Administration Office of competition policy	Office of President	Secretariat Administration
Specialist	Legal Analytical	Competition Council Database (IT)	Legal International	Methods and Legal Information

Sources: Annual reports of competition offices.

types of department, *executive* (collectively undertaking a single function divided along sectoral lines) and *administrative* and *specialist* (both organized according to function).

The executive departments undertake all the investigations (they are sometimes referred to as investigative departments). Each has responsibility for different sectors and sub-sectors of the economy, and the number of them varies from three in Poland to five in Hungary.[10] Indeed, the coherence of some of the groupings might question whether economies of scale and scope are fully exploited in all the offices. Each is staffed by a team of economists, industrial specialists (e.g. chemists, engineers) and lawyers. They undertake all investigations, collect evidence and make decisions. Although divisions are staffed by teams, investigations are often undertaken by individual professionals.

The executive divisions appear to enjoy considerable autonomy in that they are independent of each other and of the head of the office, in terms of the cases they investigate, the resources allocated to the case and their conclusions on cases. Coordination and information-sharing exists between the executive divisions, and support is provided by the specialist divisions. Several types of interdepartmental groupings exist in the office. In Hungary, a Board of Experts, chaired by a vice-president and made up of experts from each executive department, meets to discuss and tackle difficult methodological issues, and to decide on *ex officio* investigations. Such a grouping exists in the other offices, but is less formally constituted. The operation of an executive department may be affected by solicited or unsolicited advice, usually informal and unwritten, from the head of the office, although the precise extent and importance of this is difficult to gauge.

Each office has several administrative departments, one for core administration, another for liaison with international organizations such as the OECD and the EU and the authors of this study, and also a secretariat for the head of the office. The secretariat usually coordinates the competition advocacy role and represents the office with the government.

Specialist departments provide back-up services and support such as information technology, legal or methodological assistance to the executive departments. The use of specialist departments varies according to whether the tasks are assigned to each executive department or collected together.

Hungary uniquely has a separate division within its office known as the Competition Council, which is an entirely independent judicial body that decides on all cases. In the Czech Republic, the internal appeals committee (see below) is an interdepartmental group appointed by the Minister. The equivalent Slovak committee comprises both internal and external experts, also chosen by the head of the office, and is chaired by the Vice-Chairman of the office. These roles of these various bodies in the procedures are discussed further in Section 5.5 below. Interpretations of the law, in the first instance, are usually made by the decision-making body so that this function varies from country to country (the Competition Council in Hungary, and the heads of the Executive Departments with input from the Legal Department, in the Czech Republic, Poland and Slovakia).

The use of sub-offices varies in both extent and function. Poland has 9 with a total staff of 58 and Slovakia has 2 with a total staff of 6. These are regional satellite offices, undertaking local investigations and making decisions. In the Czech Republic, an office in Prague with a staff of 12 deals solely with public procurement. The Hungarian Office has no sub-offices.

The head of each office wears several executive hats, as an internal manager, as the spokesperson for competition policy in domestic policy-making fora, and as the international representative of the country in competition policy fora.

By far the least contentious of these, and the one in which the countries are most similar, is that of international representative of domestic competition policy. Membership of the EU and the OECD has long been an ambition[11] for these countries and one that attracts a high degree of internal consensus. As both international organizations have placed a strong emphasis on competition policy issues (perhaps in different ways), the head of the competition offices have and continue to play an important role in outlining the progress to date with domestic competition policy.

The role of the head of the office as internal manager also differs little across countries. This involves deciding on appointments, promotions and financial decisions. Most of these functions are fully delegated to the head of the relevant department, and the head of the office only becomes involved if a decision is not routine or controversial, although the head of the office retains ultimate responsibility. The role of the head of the office in deciding on cases varies from Hungary (no involvement) to the Czech and Slovak Republics (strong powers in regard to appeals).

The role of the head of the office in domestic policy-making matters centrally to the politicization of the offices (see Section 8.1 below) and can be best understood by considering the terms on which the head of the office is appointed and his or her interaction with the government. The head of each office is appointed, in effect, by the government or prime minister (or by the head of state on the advice of one of these) and can be dismissed at any time. Other details are summarized in Table 5.7. The major contrast is between the Czech head, who is a Minister, and the Hungarian head, who plays the least formal role in government decisions. The fact that the Slovak and Polish heads do not vote at the government means that they are not affected by the burden of collective responsibility in the same way as the Czech Minister. We return to this issue later.

Table 5.7   Status of heads of the competition offices

	Czech Republic	Hungary	Poland	Slovak
Term of office	Indefinite [a]	6 years	Indefinite	Indefinite
Answerable to	Prime minister	Economic or Plenary Committee of Parliament	Prime minister	Prime minister
Government member	Full voting minister	No, sits without a vote at the economic cabinet	Attends without a vote[b]	Attends without a vote
Number to date	1[c]	1	2	6

Sources: Annual reports, communication with offices.

Notes:

[a]Synchronized with the electoral cycle.

[b]This is an informal practice. The first President, Anna Fornalczyk, was invited to attend and the practice has persisted. Some government meetings exclude all but full ministers.

[c]At the time of writing, there has just been an election in the Czech Republic and it is not clear whether the current Minister (or even the Ministry itself) will continue.

5.5 Decision-making and Procedures

The procedures by which cases are processed and decided matters greatly, both to the effective enforcement of policy and to the parallel costs that policy imposes on enterprises. Good procedures may enable the offices to narrow the margin of error by focusing on the worst abuses, and may enable relatively quick decisions. For example, if competition cases are resolved quickly and efficiently, the threat to take a competition action may be more credible. In terms of procedures, we are interested in how cases get chosen, how they are decided, what information is taken into consideration and how it is collected, what rights of representation and reply the parties have and what time limits are imposed.

5.5.1 Selection of Cases

Cases generally arise because the competition offices receive complaints by consumers and competitors or notifications of agreements from competitors (mergers are considered below). Each offices is obliged to reply to complaints within 30 days (in Hungary 45 days for cartels and 60 otherwise; in Poland 60 days for some cases), with the possibility for extensions to double or more of this limit. This obligation to reply does not mean that a case must be fully investigated. In some cases the reply may say that the issue does not come under competition law or that there is no obvious breach of the law.[12] A *de minimis* rule applies in some countries, but in effect is applied in all, with typically a higher threshold on local markets than on national markets. The selection of cases, therefore, depends on an external demand for investigation and on the competition office deciding to carry out an investigation. Within the competition offices, the prioritization of cases is determined by the heads of the executive divisions, although consultation across divisions or with senior officials sometime occurs in difficult cases. The decentralization of decision-making within the office suggests that there may occasionally be a mismatch of workload if a disproportionate number of complaints arises in one area.

Offices may also initiate their own (*ex officio*) investigations, but this has been relatively rare, except in Poland, and even there it has been decreasing. This might cause concern if one believed that intimidation or fear or commercial or other reprisal prevented complainants from coming forward, or if one worries that the office would busy itself handling complaints that have no market impact. The rarity of *ex officio* investigations is explained by a number of factors. The most obvious is that the number of complaints that require a reply has been large and this may have forced offices to investigate relatively trivial matters while more important matters were ignored because no complaint was received. In fact, in Hungary it is proposed to change the law so that the Office will use *ex officio* investigations as a mechanism for having discretion over which complaints to follow up.[13] The second reason *ex officio* investigations are infrequent is that competition offices often lack the information required to initiate an investigation or, in the case of Hungary, the mandate to acquire information until after a formal investigation is started. As a result, sufficient information may not be available to warrant an *ex officio* investigation. Third, given the background of price and other controls, offices might be reluctant to be perceived as interfering, without invitation, in the workings of the market. Such self-restraint would be greater if, because information is poor, some investigations subsequently reveal little basis for concern about competition.

5.5.2 Deciding Cases

Investigations are always conducted within the relevant executive department. The investigation may draw on specialist legal or industrial skills within the office, and this happens in difficult or contentious cases. Parties directly involved are consulted and given an opportunity to present evidence. Third-party involvement only occurs if the third party has a clear interest in the matter, as in merger cases if competitors are asked to submit information. Investigators have powers to compel parties to provide information and have access to other sources such as unpublished national statistics; however, there is no *discovery* procedure as practised in common law.[14] There is no right of cross-examination, rather the investigator informs the parties of each other's arguments and assertions, except for any trade or business secrets that either party does not want released.[15] At the end of the process a conclusion is reached by the investigator handling the case.

In the Czech Republic and Slovakia, this conclusion is communicated to the parties, who are allowed to make further points. In Poland, the parties have a right of consultation under the Administrative Code. Then the investigator publishes the conclusion as a decision of the office.[16] Thus, in these three countries, there is no separation of prosecution and decision-making. In Hungary, the investigator's conclusion is presented to a committee of the Competition Council which hears representations from both sides before making a formal decision. The Competition Council, although part of the AMO, is subordinate only to the law in making its decisions.[17] Hungary thus has separation of prosecution and decision-making, albeit within the same institution.

Hearings tend to be closed to the public except for abuse of dominance cases in Hungary (unless parties present convincing reasons for a closed hearing). The head of the Office may not intervene after a decision has been signed and presented to the parties. However, the extent to which informal or indirect advice from the head of the office may affect the initial decision of the investigator is not clear, although we have no evidence that this has indeed occurred, nor of any external influence being brought to bear.

The procedures governing mergers and acquisitions differ slightly, in terms of the notification requirements, the information acquired and the time limits on decisions. These are summarized in Table 5.8.

5.5.3   Appeals

Two-stage appeals are possible in all four Visegrad countries, but with some fundamental differences in approach (see Table 5.9). In the Czech and Slovak Republics, the initial appeal is internal with considerable discretion for the head of the office. In particular, the head of the office appoints the appeals body and decides whether to allow the appeal and whether to uphold the decision of the appeals body. In practice, neither of the powers to block an appeal or to vitiate an appeals decision has been used: all appeals have been permitted and the decision of the appeals body upheld.[18]

In Hungary and Poland, the initial appeal is to an external court, independent of the competition offices. In Hungary this body is a branch of the regular courts, the Capital Court of Budapest (where cross-examination is allowed), whereas in Poland the appeal is heard by the Anti-monopoly Court.[19] In all countries, subsequent appeal on both substantive and procedural grounds to the Supreme Court is possible, except that in Poland this must be an Extraordinary Appeal on the consistency of the law by the Minister for Justice or the Human Rights Commissioner. Short time limits apply for the submission appeals, but there is no limit on the time within which an appeal decision must be handed down. In practice, appeals sometimes take several years. The experience to date suggests that more defendants than complainants appeal and that the rate of appeal of decisions is increasing in all countries.[20]

5.6   Assessment

The institutional approaches adopted by the four Visegrad countries are broadly similar at a general level but they differ importantly in their detail. In terms of the general similarities, each country has chosen to use an administrative agency that is accountable to parliament and that is reviewed by the courts. Each of these agencies specializes in investigating and deciding on competition cases, although other (semi-related) functions have additionally been allocated to some of them. With regard to their competition function, they have similar responsibilities, powers and procedures.

Table 5.8 Procedures for mergers and acquisitions

	Czech Republic	Hungary	Poland	Slovakia
Threshold				
Market share	30% national or local	30%	None	20%
Turnover	None	54 million ECU	50 million ECU for merger, 2.5 million ECU for acquisitions	7.8 million ECU with at least two parties with 2.6 million
Notification fee	290 ECU	540 ECU	None	390 ECU (< 26 million ECU), 1300 ECU (>26 million ECU)
Notification				
Mergers	In advance	In advance	In advance	In advance
Acquisitions	1 week[a]	1 week	14 days	15 days
Time limit	30 days	90 days	2 months 2 weeks for banks	1 month
Extension	30 days[b]	6 months	No mention	3 months[c]
Tacit approval if no action[d]	No	Not in Act	Yes	Yes
Procedure				
Published	No	Newspapers	No	No
Questionnaires	To both parties, rarely to competitors	To parties, important suppliers, customers and competitors	To parties, important suppliers, customers and competitors	
Remedies	Not used, seen as extreme solution	No[e]	Not clear	Yes, but not used

Sources: Communications with competition offices, legal statutes.
Notes:
All financial thresholds in local currencies have been converted to ECU (at June 1996 exchange rates) for comparative purposes.
[a] National Property Agency acquisitions are exempt for 12 months in the Czech Republic.
[b] Further extension if written reasons given by Minister or Chairman.
[c] The 3-month rule applies if a preliminary ruling against the concentration has been made within 1 month.
[d] No mergers have been implicitly approved because a competition office has not replied in time.
[e] Can force divestiture only if merger was not notified and is illegal: no cases to date.

Table 5.9 Procedures for appeals of competition office decisions

	Czech Republic	Hungary	Poland	Slovak
Appeal within:	15 days	30 days	15 days	
Appeal to:	Minister[a]	Capital Court of Budapest	Anti-monopoly Court	Chairman[a]
Appeal body is	Internal Appeals	External	External	Internal appeals Commission
Right of hearing at appeal	Yes	Yes	Yes	Yes, in public
Appeal binding on competition office	No (always upheld)	Yes	Yes	No (always upheld)
Higher appeal	Yes	Yes, within 15 days	Extraordinary appeal[b]	Yes

Sources: Legal statutes and communications with competition offices.
Notes:
[a]The head has discretion in whether the appeal is heard, but so far all appeals have been admitted.
[b]An appeal of a decision by the Anti-monopoly Court to the Supreme court cannot be taken directly, but rather by the Minister of Justice, the Attorney General or the Ombudsman. This is expected to change as legal procedures are being revised.

The differences between the countries largely turn on the political status of the office (and its head) and the separation of prosecution and decision-making. The Czech Ministry, at one extreme, is wholly integrated into government, whereas the Hungarian Office, at the other, is formally relatively politically independent. The separation of prosecution and decision-making prevails only in Hungary and Poland, and in different forms. In the other countries, the procedures in this regard leave some cause for concern.

Comparisons with the competition offices of EU Member States or other Western economies are difficult to make, because of the different tasks and constraints facing the Visegrad competition offices. Without wishing to pretend to a systematic comparison, it does appear that the Visegrad offices have greater staff numbers than comparable offices in the EU and that they are more or less formally politically independent.

Notes

1. It is not necessary, and some would argue not wise, to combine the prosecutorial and decision-making function within a single organization. Therefore some prefer the US Department of Justice model to the Federal Trade Commission model.
2. The Czech Republic consists of two regions, Bohemia to the west and Moravia (in which Brno is located) to the east. At the time the Ministry was established, the Moravian independence movement was relatively strong.
3. The Slovak Office was allocated a portion of revenue from fines until last year. This

funding was marked training and information technology and, in 1994, amounted to a total of 2.435 million CZK (64000 ECU) or almost 14% of its budget.

4. The use of exemptions varies. Individual exemptions have been used in the Czech Republic. In Hungary, an exemption is permitted under Article 15 if it prevents abuse of dominance or is of minor importance and an individual exemption is permitted under Article 17. By contrast, Poland and Slovakia have no exemptions but in Poland a rule of reason Article 6 may be used for the exemption of practices prohibited under Articles 5 and 6. All offices do issue guidelines.

5. The Polish office, however, was formed from the previous anti-monopoly division of the department of finance.

6. This has a strong form and a weak form. The strong form is that the competition office must issue a formal decision (only Hungary, but formerly in Poland). The weak form is that the office must formally inform the complainant what action is being taken on the case.

7. The draft is subject to revision by the legal office of the government and amendments can follow in parliament.

8. Laid down in the Act on Public Trading of Securities and Trust Funds (22 March 1991), the Act on Ownership of State Enterprises (5 February 1993) and the Act on National Investment Funds (16 April 1993).

9. In the Czech Republic it is the Ministry of Industry and Trade under Act 634/1992. In Poland, the ministry with the same name oversees consumer protection and a Consumer Protection Act is being prepared. In Slovakia, there is a special law and implementation is by the Ministry of Economy.

10. Until the end of 1995, the Polish executive departments were arranged along functional lines, with executive departments responsible (very loosely) for structural issues, behavioural issues, and public utilities.

11. Both the Czech Republic and Hungary recently became full members of the OECD.

12. In Hungary, all cases that come under the law must be investigated but the investigator may quickly decide that the complaint has no merit and recommend accordingly to the Competition Council. This is the strong form indicated in note 6.

13. This is in the amendment before the Parliament at the time of writing.

14. In no country does the investigator or the parties have the right of discovery of confidential government files, although this has not hitherto been seen by any office as a constraint. Laws on state secrecy may also inhibit the ability of the competition offices to access government files.

15. It is not clear that the offices all have clear criteria for the omission of business secrets. In Poland, at one stage the administrative court gave all parties rights to see all documents.

16. In Poland, it is formally the President of the Office who makes decisions but in practice this task is delegated, except in important cases where decisions have been made and signed by the President, vice-president or Director General.

17. It is chaired by a vice-president of the Office and sits in a group of three with a lawyer in the chair. The members of the Competition Council do not have other tasks within the office.

18. The Slovak Commission has found in favour of about 20% of appellants.

19. This Court is established especially under the law to consider appeals to decisions of the Competition Office. It is entirely judicially independent of the Office. To some extent, the role of the Anti-monopoly Court in Poland is not so different from that of the Competition Council in Hungary. Both are specialized and the main difference is that the Polish Court hears only the contentious cases.

20. In Slovakia, no appeals were filed in 1991 or 1992 but, since January 1995, 90% of cases have been appealed, with appeals by 100% of losing defendants in abuse of dominance cases.

6

The Caseload and the Case Law

6.1 Caseload of the Competition Offices

This chapter investigates the detailed standards of competition determined in the Visegrád countries by examining their case law. Before we undertake this exercise, it is useful to outline and assess the overall caseload of the competition offices, examining the pressures under which they operate and the general proportions and qualitative features of their output.[1]

The first decisions were issued in 1990, and since 1991 there has been a steady and uninterrupted flow of investigations and decisions in all countries. As we saw in the previous chapter, each office is obliged to reply to all complaints, regardless of whether that complaint results in a full investigation and decision. Table 6.1 summarizes the total matters coming to the attention of the competition offices. The number of matters arising is

Table 6.1 All issues considered by competition offices, 1992–5

	Czech Republic[a]	Hungary	Poland[b]	Slovakia	All
1995	285	87	155	141	668
1994	290	55	143	143	631
1993	114	58	136	117	425
1992	78	75	101	111	365
Total	767	275	535	512	2089

Sources: Competition offices.
Notes:
[a]The Czech Ministry receives hundreds of complaints each year that may not all be included here. In particular, the 1995 figure should be adjusted to include 362 applications of minor importance that include irrelevant complaints.
[b]The Polish figures relate only to decisions issued: information on all matters coming before the AMO was not available.

Table 6.2 Decisions of competition offices, 1992–5

	Czech Republic	Hungary[a]		Poland	Slovakia	All	
1995	119	152	(75)	155	29	455	(378)
1994	64	105	(33)	153	47	369	(297)
1993	72	96	(33)	150	48	366	(303)
1992	62	91	(44)	110	39	302	(255)
Total	317	444	(185)	568	163	1492	(1233)
Staff	74	115		159	63	411	
Total per staff member	4.3	3.9		3.6	2.6	3.6	

Sources: Competition offices.
Note:
[a]For Hungary, we use the total output of the office for comparative purposes. This includes consumer fraud cases for which the office is responsible, and the figures in parentheses are competition cases. This is also reflected in the totals.

increasing steadily over time, rising from 365 in 1992 to 668 in 1995. By far the largest number of complaints is received by the Czech Office, perhaps reflecting higher public awareness because of its status as a Ministry. In fact, the reported numbers for the Czech Republic do not include very large numbers of complaints that had no bearing on competition policy, indicating that greater awareness of the existence of a competition office does not equate to a clearer understanding of the purpose of competition rules.

The decisions of the competition offices are summarized in Table 6.2. The output has been increasing generally over time, although there has been a recent decline in Slovakia. The Hungarian data are complicated by the fact the office has responsibility for consumer protection and consumer fraud cases, so the figures in parentheses represent competition cases. Given this caveat, the statistics suggest that the Polish Office has been most prolific, followed by Hungary, the Czech Republic and Slovakia. Considering the relative sizes of the economies, this is not surprising. The fact that the Hungarian Office is obliged to make a decision on all complaints that come under the law and are correctly made probably explains why it makes a decision in the highest proportion of cases.[2]

Comparing the number of decisions by staff member, albeit a crude measure of productivity, suggests reasonable regularity across the offices, with the Czech Republic slightly more prolific, followed by Hungary and Poland and with the Slovak office lagging a little distance behind. The overall figure of less than one decision per staff member per year suggests that not all staff are involved in taking decisions. Given the strict time limits on decisions, it may even suggest that the competition offices (are constrained or obliged to) employ substantial numbers of staff that are not suitably qualified. In any event, the countries are broadly similar in this regard, suggesting that all offices face similar constraints.

Comparisons between the countries should be treated with caution. Some offices have more functions to perform than others; for example, the Polish Office probably faces a greater burden in terms of restructuring during privatization. The balance of cases is also important in that cartels, for example, may be more costly to investigate so that a higher proportion of cartels would conceal greater productivity. Decisions are not the only output of the offices: for example, the Czech Ministry must devote time to dealing with irrelevant complaints.

We now turn to the actual detail of the caseload, and in particular to the source of investigations and how they have been resolved, in aggregate terms. The source of the complaints and matters arising sheds light on the perception of policy and state of information about competition in the economy and the pressures under which the competition offices must operate. These statistics are reported in Table 6.3.[3]

Over half (765 out of 1413) of all cases result from complaints from producers, with about a quarter coming from consumers. This is particularly driven by complaints in single-firm (abuse of dominance) cases where complaints by parties to an agreement figure highly, especially in Poland. Most merger and acquisition cases arise from voluntary notification, although in Slovakia, where the majority arises from complaints, the notification procedure may not work well. The vast majority of cases (and of decisions as reported in Table 6.4) concern single-firm issues, and in many instances these concern vertical relations, as indicated by the high number of complaints by parties to an agreement.

Cartel agreements are investigated mostly by *ex officio* actions by the competition offices, suggesting that information to pursue cartel investigations is not forthcoming from consumers or competitors. The use of *ex officio* investigations varies, with over 80% of all such investigation occurring in two countries, Poland and Slovakia. In fact, there have been only seven such investigations in Hungary. There are several possible explanations for why *ex officio* investigations have not been used. First, the complaint system may work unusually well, but this is unlikely given that the law is relatively new. Second, the offices may be fully occupied dealing with existing complaints and may not have time to undertake 'extra' work. If so, the obligation of the offices to respond to all complaints could result in investigations of relatively trivial matters where information is readily available from external sources (i.e. complaints) and neglect of very important cases simply because no complaint has been made. Third, given the greater burden of information required in taking an *ex officio* case (e.g. monitoring markets and collecting price data), the offices may be able to devote resources to this, especially if they are being evaluated on quantitative measures such as cases per year. It will not be surprising to find that future changes allow all offices to discriminate more in the cases they consider

Table 6.3   Source of investigations, 1992–5

	Czech Republic	Hungary	Poland	Slovakia	All
Single firm	187	222	481	138	1028
Complaint by consumer	145	78	0	39	262
Complaint by party to agreement or competitor	36	136	400	59	631
Ex officio by AMO	5	3	54	22	84
Other	1	5	27	18	51
Mergers and acquisitions	70	38	21	68	197
Voluntary notification	70	37	10	14	131
Complaint by competitor	0	0	0	49	49
Ex officio by AMO	0	1	9	4	14
Other	0	0	2	1	3
Cartel agreements	7	8	16	18	49
Voluntary notification	0	1	0	4	5
Complaint (consumer, competitor or party, government)	1	4	7	5	17
Ex officio by AMO	6	3	9	9	27
Other agreements	26	8	17	88	139
Voluntary notification	2	5	0	7	14
Complaint by consumer	7	0	0	3	10
Complaint by party to agreement or competitor	3	3	10	56	72
Ex officio by AMO	13	0	5	15	33
Other	1	0	2	7	10
All decisions	290	276	535	312	1413
Voluntary notification	73	44	10	25	152
Complaint by consumer	153	78	0	43	274
Complaint by party to agreement or competitor	39	143	417	166	765
Ex officio by AMO	24	7	77	50	158
Other (includes government requests)	1	4	31	28	64

Sources: Competition offices.
Notes:
For the Czech Republic these data are for 1994 only. For some countries, these data are only for cases where decisions resulted. This means that they do not always correspond to the figures in Tables 6.1 and 6.2.
Cartel agreements may include all horizontal agreements.

(along the lines already proposed by the Hungarian Office), so that *ex officio* cases may rise considerably. This would be a welcome move if it allowed offices to prioritize better which cases should be investigated.

The evidence from complaints received suggests that some of the offices have faced much stronger pressure than their counterparts in market economies in two areas: price control and vertical relations between firms. The Czech offices in particular have faced large numbers of complaints about price increases and a corresponding pressure to act as a price con-

Table 6.4 Nature of decisions issued by competition offices, 1992–5

	Czech Republic[a]	Hungary	Poland	Slovakia	All
Single firm	65	132	512	90	799
Violation found	3	32	247	33	315
No violation found	13	100	265	57	435
Mergers and acquisitions	178	38	21	30	267
Violation found	11	1	18	16	46
No violation found	76	37	3	12	128
Allowed subject to conditions	11	0	0	2	13
Cartel agreements	49	7	16	10	82
Violation found	4	3	10	7	24
No violation found	2	4	6	3	15
Other agreements	25	8	19	30	82
Violation found	10	3	7	18	38
No violation found	6	4	12	12	34
Allowed subject to conditions	0	1	0	0	1
All decisions	317	185	568	160	1230
Violation found	28	39	282	74	423
No violation found	97	145	286	84	612
Allowed subject to conditions	11	1	0	2	14

Sources: Competition offices.
Note:
[a]For the Czech Republic the data on violations are only for 1993 and 1994.

troller of last resort. Similar pressures have been observed in Poland, with the AMO in an uneasy intermediate position of trying to intervene in pricing behaviour while simultaneously trying to bring about conditions that would make such intervention unnecessary.[4] This view is backed up by the detailed discussion of the case law below, and the figures here serve to indicate the relative magnitude of the problem.

The field of vertical restraints provides some interesting evidence. In general, competition offices receive two kinds of complaint about vertical restraints: from one of the parties involved complaining that the terms are unduly onerous, and from third parties complaining that the contract concluded between two consenting firms has adverse external effects on competition in the market as a whole (for instance, by foreclosing the market to competitors and/or raising prices for consumers). Although policy in market economies is often inconsistent, there is a general tendency to accept that the latter provide a more secure foundation for legitimate intervention by the offices, who should not normally intervene in free contractual bargaining between the parties purely to strengthen the bargaining position of one against the other (see Seabright, 1995). Vertical agreements also typically take up much less of a competition agency's time in a established market economy than do horizontal agreements. Although interpreting the evidence is difficult since many offices do not explicitly classify agreements into horizontal and vertical, such evidence as we have gathered strongly suggests that in Poland:

1. Vertical relations take up a very much larger proportion of the AMO's time and resources
2. There is much more pressure to intervene in vertical relations because one party directly is perceived to be damaged (i.e. fairness) than because of concern about effects on competition in the market as a whole.

Such striking evidence is to be found in the early experience of the Polish AMO. Fornalczyk (1993) writes:

> Most of the decisions of the Office [in 1991] concerned counteracting anti-competitive practices defined in Art. 4.1.1 of the Act as imposing onerous terms of contracts that yield undue benefits to the economic entity imposing them (50 decisions [out of 113]). Another 18 decisions concerned Art. 4.1.2, which prohibits making the conclusion of a contract contingent on forcing the other party to accept or perform another service not connected with the object of the contract. In an additional 16 cases, the decision finding or not finding a violation was based on both of these articles (pp. 32–3).

This means that no fewer than 84 of 113 decisions (74%) involved the AMO essentially in intervening to strengthen one party's arm in a bargain with another, without any appeal to possible adverse effects on third parties. This has not diminished in subsequent years, with 85%, 72% and 75% of cases in 1992, 1993 and 1994 respectively issuing from complaints by one party to an agreement. This evidence contrasts with that from Hungary where the law has no *per se* prohibition of vertical restraints, although Hungary is under strong pressure from the EU to introduce such a prohibition (along with the apparatus of block exemptions on the model of Article 85 of the Treaty of Rome), and at time of writing has a draft amendment to the competition legislation along these lines. Nevertheless, the majority of cases in Hungary concern complaints about a firm made by competitors rather than contractual partners.

An important part of the explanation for the dominance of vertical issues in the workload of the Polish AMO is the fact that its mandate includes the regulation of naturally monopolistic network industries, for which there has been no independent regulatory provision. Many of the cases cited above (especially those involving 'onerous contract terms') involved a network industry such as electricity or telecommunications. Of 129 judgments of the Polish Anti-monopoly Court between 1990 and 1994, 35 concerned network industries while a further 27 related to vertical issues in other industries, 17 of the latter appealing to excessive pricing or 'onerous contract terms' (Skoczny, 1995, Appendix 3). This suggests that the decision to pool the powers of general competition policy and the regulation of natural monopolies in the hands of a single agency may have had a cost, in leading to a great regulatory control over the terms of individual contracts, even outside the network industries, than would otherwise have been desirable.

Table 6.4 summarizes the qualitative nature of the decisions issued in aggregate form. As already noted, single-firm cases make up the majority of all decisions, but this is driven by Poland and, to a lesser extent, Hungary. In the Czech Republic, most decisions concern mergers and acquisitions (although these data are the least reliable). In general, violations are found about 35% of the time, but this varies by type of case. For cartels, most investigations result in a violation being found, whereas the opposite is true for mergers. The data on violations in the case of mergers may be exaggerated due to reporting problems. If so, a much more permissive attitude to mergers prevails in all countries than that indicated by in Table 6.4.

Although Table 6.4 indicates that powers that competition offices have to prohibit behaviour have been widely exercised, their powers to alter market structure by breaking up firms or forcing divestiture (which exist in the Czech Republic, Slovakia and Poland) have only been used in Poland, and there exclusively in privatization cases. A few mergers have been prohibited, but these are small relative to the total notifications. Thus it is fair to conclude that the offices have little direct effect on market structure except in Poland. This might cause some concern if de-monopolization of the economy was desirable.

Data-collection powers have sometimes been used fully, particularly for cases involving abuse of dominance in Slovakia and cartels in Hungary. In the Czech Republic, the existence of non-compliance penalties has meant that information has been more readily forthcoming. In all four Visegrad countries, information is systematically collected from the complainant and defendant or notifying parties, as appropriate. For merger notifications, this is done by issuing questionnaires to the parties, and in Hungary and Poland to all competitors, requesting information on sales, prices, products and other relevant information.[5] Unannounced visits (sometimes known as dawn raids) have been carried out in two cases in Hungary (one consumer-fraud and one cartel case[6]), and in Slovakia (cartels).

The use of fines varies (see Table 6.5), with Hungary imposing fines in the highest proportion of cases (apparently all where a violation is found: see Table 6.4) and Poland lying at the opposite extreme. We do not have systematic data on the absolute size of fines or their size relative to either the maximum allowed or the damage.[7] What data we have suggest that if exemplary fines are imposed, then this is only in Hungary where the maximum fine was imposed in at least one case.[8] In Poland, fines have been imposed at less than 5% of the damage, despite an allowable limit of 15%. We

Table 6.5   Fines imposed, 1992–5

	Czech Republic[a]	Hungary	Poland	Slovakia	All
Single firm	25	32	15	7	79
Cartels	3	3	0	3	9
Other agreements	0	3	0	1	4
Total	28	38	15	11	92

Sources: Competition offices.
Note:
[a]For the Czech Republic these data do not include 1995. Moreover, the data are not consistent in the sense that more fines than violations were reported.

understand the Polish AMO did not impose fines at the maximum level because it considered that enterprises were still learning about the market and the fines were intended to be educational rather than exemplary.[9] Although Table 6.5 would appear to indicate that fines are imposed most frequently in single-firm cases (86%), this is solely because of the high incidence of single-firm decisions (84% of the relevant violations), and is not due to a higher rate of imposition of fines in such cases. The power to impose penalties for non-compliance has rarely been invoked.

The ownership of the firms involved in decisions of the competition offices is reported in Table 6.6. The numbers under 'State' refer to instances where only state-owned firms were involved and those under 'Private' where only privately owned firms were involved. The balance is for cases where there was a mixture of state and privately owned firms.

The overall picture is that the majority of decisions involve state-owned firms, either in whole or in part (the totals are weighted by the relevant numbers). This statistic is particularly driven by Poland and Slovakia, and a different scenario prevails in the Czech Republic and Hungary. The proportion of decisions involving state-owned companies is rising somewhat over time. In all headings, it is clear that the offices tackle issues involving both private and state-owned enterprises.

6.2   Detailed Case Law

The case law very well reflects the tenor of the statutes (outlined in Chapter 4 and reproduced in Appendix 2), which seek to advance equity, efficiency and sometimes industrial policy, even without recognizing tensions among these goals.

Before beginning to analyse the case law of each of the nations, we set forth premises of our approach and several concerns and lines of inquiry:

1. The most important role competition can serve in the CEECs is to establish the foundational environment likely to facilitate market entry and

Table 6.6 Ownership of respondent firms

	Czech Republic		Hungary		Poland		Slovakia		All countries	
	State	Private	State	Private	State	Private	State	Private	State	Private
All (%)	4	51	30	58	76	19	15	16	42	29
By year										
1995			21	0.59	89	11	43	45	64	29
1994	2	69	33	58	81	16	0	0	49	39
1993	6	38	30	67	61	30	0	0	30	31
1992			41	50	73	22			32	16
By type										
Single firm	20	63	42	54	80	19	27	17	60	27
Mergers	0	41	0	58	52	19	2	13	6	34
Cartels	0	83	0	100	56	19	36	36	33	48
Other	0	76	0	88	47	13	5	13	9	27

Sources: Competition offices.

Notes:
The remaining cases are those where there is a mixture of private and public firms.
For the Czech Republic and Slovakia, these data do not include 1995.
In some cases, the statistics reported are for all matters arising rather than decisions, and this may bias the weights used in obtaining totals.

growth and to produce business behaviour that responds to demand. It is vital to create an environment likely to produce business that is efficient and competitive and that can serve consumers and business buyers at home and, where possible, abroad. The most important competition law tool to aid in this task is the law against hardcore cartels,[10] combined with the law against competitors' boycotts and similar action by competitors or dominant firms to erect artificial road blocks to competition. We are, therefore, particularly interested in cartel cases, and in 'road block' cases where the conduct cannot be explained as a response to demand.

2. The law against 'abusive' and 'excessively one-sided' action is, one observes, very important in the CEECs, principally, it seems, to establish fair rules of the marketplace and to limit powerful firms, unleashed by removal of price controls, from taking unfair advantage of others. We know from our own experiences how difficult it is to reconcile the value of hard competition – which tends to make businesses responsive to the marketplace – with the value of fairness. Rules of fairness may sometimes handicap firms, lest they hurt their rivals; and such rules can impose significant costs. Since handicaps may hurt the competitiveness of the dominant firm and the functioning of the market, we paid particular attention to the fairness violations.

3. Abuse of dominance law may also prevent excessively high pricing. This is another area where the cure for one problem might create another potentially worse problem. For example, prices may appear high for exogenous reasons – e.g. the lifting of price controls; and a finding of excessive prices might lead to (a) pushing prices down to a level too low to attract capital to the business and to finance R&D functions, and (b) the need for government surveillance that amounts to reinstituted price control and that ends up preventing the pricing mechanism from working. Therefore we paid special attention to excessive pricing violations.

4. The law on restrictive contracts is a complex area. If the animus behind, say, an exclusive dealing contract is clearly to exclude and thereby to gain or retain monopoly power, the dangers to competition are clear. But normally there is no bright-line indicia of whether a contract is helpful or harmful to competition. For example, the contract might be important to induce entry and investment by a distributor. Such a contract would not normally tend to harm competition unless certain structural conditions are present, and even then it could have net pro-competitive effects depending on many market facts. Firms that find themselves 'excluded' from the chance to distribute a certain producer's product may complain to the competition agency. Because of the complexity of these cases, the difficulties of analysis, and the costs of error

in mislabelling a pro-competitive contract unduly restrictive, we also gave special regard to these cases.

5. Merger control law is normally used to prohibit mergers that produce or increase dominance and harm competition. Nations sometimes have incentives, however, to approve anti-competitive mergers when the office believes that the merger is nonetheless good for the country – to preserve jobs or to create a national champion. There is a risk that predictions (e.g. that an anti-competitive merger will save jobs) may be wrong. Moreover, anti-competitive mergers may have spill-over effects beyond the nation's borders, and therefore neighbours may have an interest in their prohibition. In reviewing the merger law, we were particularly interested in whether the law was being used for competition policy alone or for industrial policy.

6. We are also interested in the analytical soundness of market definition and the identification of dominance; two concepts often crucial to case-law outcomes. We have not covered this subject in detail, but make some comments on points.

With these concerns in mind, we turn to the case law of each of the four Visegrád countries. We have tried to draw from a representative sampling of the cases. In some cases we had available to us the case reports. In others we had only the summaries in the annual reports of the competition offices.

6.3   Poland

In the past six years, Poland has developed a large body of case law. Except for the Polish merger law, which has seldom been used, the Polish Anti-monopoly Office has been an active enforcer.

As construed by the Anti-monopoly Court, the Polish Act protects 'freedom of economic entities in taking actions to organize their activity'[11] and 'freedom of entities to participate in market trade on equal terms'.[12] In particular, according to the Court, the Act protects the freedom of economic activity that is threatened by excessive concentration, monopoly or group action, and the right of individuals and entities to shape the terms of their contracts free from compulsion to accept terms less favourable than a competitive market would provide.[13]

The aim of protecting economic freedom could be read as equivalent to protecting competitors' rights, and the aim of empowering parties to participate in trade on equal terms could be read as advancing fairness above efficiency. Professor Tadeuz Skoczny (1995, p. 201), however, a principal scholar of the Polish competition law, construes these objectives as tantamount to protecting competition, especially its development.[14]

The principal prohibition of the Polish Act is the prohibition against monopolistic practices. Such practices include restrictive agreements, abuse of a dominant position, and abuse of a monopolistic position.

The Anti-monopoly Court has stated the following to be the essence of 'monopolistic practices':

> The essence of monopolistic practice lies in restricting the freedom of contractors, competitors and consumers, compelling them to participate in trade on terms which are less favourable than those of an unrestricted competitive environment, by an economic entity or a group or combination of economic entities, and as a result of unlawful abuse of market power derived from their position occupied on a given market.[15]

According to this definition, Professor Skoczny observes, there are three necessary constituent elements of the offence:

a) the activity of the economic entity or combination (in the case of individual actions) or a group of economic entities (in the case of agreements) must cause limitation of freedom of other entities (contractors, competitors and consumers), deteriorating their position in the market;
b) the said limitation of freedom to make decision[s] must be a consequence of abuse of market power by an entity or few entities, based on their market position;
c) the said abuse of market power must be illegal, i.e., must fulfil one or more prerequisites specified in the Anti-monopoly Act and cannot be permitted by virtue of this Act or any other statutory act.

The annual reports of the AMO present statistics and summarize selected important cases. According to the annual reports, the most frequently reported monopolistic practices are imposing unfavourable contract terms and tied selling. A significant number of cases concern restricting access to distribution networks, price discrimination, excessive pricing, and predatory pricing. Cartel cases are relatively few; only one price-fixing case (artificial fertilizers) is noted in the Annual Report for 1995.

In the report for 1995, the AMO reports the following statistics. A monopolistic practice was found in 78 cases. Of these, 69 of the proceedings were initiated by complainants and 9 by the Office. In 54 cases initiated, no monopolistic practice was found. Of these 54 cases, 50 were initiated by complainants and 4 by the Office. The Office undertook 433 exploratory investigations. Of these, 416 investigations were triggered by complainants. Seven agreements were presented to the AMO for its approval, and all were approved. The AMO opposed no mergers.

We summarize below some of the enforcement activity and case law, first in the area of single-firm Acts, then in the area of agreements, and finally in the area of mergers.

6.3.1   Abuse of Dominance

Poland's law on dominance and monopolization falls into two categories; abuse of a dominant position (dominance being presumed from a market share in excess of 40%) and abuse of a monopolistic position. A firm in a monopolistic position is one that encounters no competition. This category applies predominantly to monopolies such as gas and water supplies.

A firm in a dominant but not a monopolistic position may justify its conduct. The challenged practice may be justified if objectively necessary and if either the conduct does not significantly restrain competition or is necessary to fulfil Poland's international obligations. A 'rule of reason' is applied to determine if the justification is proved.

It has been held many times that monopolistic firms – especially natural monopolies – violated the prohibition against excessive pricing. In 1993, according to the Annual Report, excessive pricing was the subject of 29 cases. The AMO proved excessive pricing violations against three enterprises, which included the local water and sewage provider, Polish Telecom, and a local funeral monopolist. In two cases in 1993 the AMO found that the monopolist PZZ illegally refrained from the sale of grain plants in the fat industry, causing a price rise. The AMO found also that the car company FSO had illegally ceased production of the FSO 1500 and the Polonez cars, causing a price rise; but its decision was reversed in court for lack of proof of FSO's monopolistic position.

Cases regarded by the AMO as most significant abuse of dominance offences have included excessive pricing and imposing other onerous contract terms, refusals to deal, price discriminating, and acting to prevent the appearance and development of competition. Recent cases tend to focus on onerous contract terms. For example, in Katowice, the Batory Housing Cooperative built additional heating equipment on property owned by Heating Utility Enterprise (HUC). HUC refused to help pay for the equipment. The refusal was held to constitute imposition of onerous contractual conditions. In Wrocaw, the Lower Silesia Regional Gas Utility Company had contracts with gas customers. It charged the customers a 'participation' fee, and a charge for partially financing installation costs of a heating system, and for unrelated financing of technical improvements. Imposition of these charges was held to violate the act. Likewise, the Cracow Municipal Cemetery Administration was held liable for charging excessively high cemetery fees in order to ensure funds for cemetery-related investments, for imposing a clause stating that a fee would be required for future disposal of graves, and for ceasing to sell permits for graves until after a price rise.[16]

Only one abuse case summarized in the 1995 Report unambiguously appeared to have marketwide as opposed to fairness (redistributive) effects. This is the case against Telekomunikcaja Polska SA (TP SA). TP SA had refused to provide access to underground telephone lines in Swidnik. Access was apparently necessary in order for Lublin to serve Swidnik. The AMO required that TP SA grant access, contingent upon Lublin's co-financing the local network (1995 Report, pp. 18–19).

A series of typical cases have involved Ruch, a distributor of newspapers and magazines, which was found to have at least 60% of the market; some of these cases focused on abuse of dominance and others on restrictive contracts. Ruch required its independent kiosk operators to buy their press goods exclusively from it or to pay a penalty, and it required them to display only the titles distributed by Ruch; thus, not the goods of competitors. The AMO found that the exclusive purchase contracts impeded market entry. Also, Ruch charged rent for kiosks calculated as a percentage of sales, rather than the usual basis (square metres). The AMO found the pricing mechanism to be an onerous contract term, yielding undue benefits to Ruch. The Anti-monopoly Court agreed, defining 'onerous contract terms' as 'such a provision of the contract, which is unfavourable for the contractor of the entity with market power in comparison to other contracts of a given kind'.[17]

Also typical is a series of dairy cooperative cases against the Spomlek milk cooperative. Spomlek offered different purchase prices for milk depending on whether the supplier was a member of the cooperative. The AMO found the price discrimination to be an illegal monopolistic practice. It called the conduct 'especially dangerous', characterizing it, as did the Supreme Court on appeal, as a 'division of the markets according to criteria of entities'.[18]

While the Office purports to examine market power and apply a rule of reason in abuse of dominance cases, we are not always convinced that markets and market power are fully analysed, or that pro-competitive and pro-efficiency effects are fully credited. For example, in *Ruch*, where exclusive dealing was condemned, it was not clear why competing suppliers of press goods could not develop their own distribution outlets; and Ruch's rental terms, which were held onerous because they were based in part on turnover, could have been a risk-sharing device. In *Spomlek*, where price discrimination was condemned, it seemed plausible that members of the cooperative would have made investments or otherwise taken risks that entitled them to a lower price.

6.3.2   *Restrictive Agreements*

Restrictive agreement offences include price fixing, market division, and restricting market access. Though cartels are clearly restrictive contracts within the meaning of the statute, as of the January 1994 report the Office had investigated only six price cartel cases. In only one – the *Sugar* case – did it find an illegal hardcore price-fixing agreement.[19] In another case (not characterized as hardcore), insurance companies were found to have agreed on maximum commissions for insurance agents and minimum rates on fire risks, and the agreement was declared illegal.[20]

A case against the Pharmacists' Council demonstrated the AMO's willingness to challenge professional cartels.[21] The Pharmacists' Council controlled the granting of applications for pharmacy licences. It held back licences when competitors occupied the territory. The AMO found that the Council's activity constituted an illegal agreement to divide markets according to territorial criteria.[22]

The cartel law is perceptive and modern. The Anti-monopoly Court has held that 'agreement' can be proved by circumstantial evidence, such as evidence of parallel activity that cannot be explained except on the basis of a prior understanding. Further, the Court has held that a price-fixing agreement is in itself illegal; defendants may not justify by proof that the agreement was not carried out or that it had no effect.[23]

Cartel cases are especially worthy subjects for enforcement. One would expect (if fines were sufficiently high) that the above-described enforcement actions saved consumers substantial amounts of money in buying necessities – sugar, insurance, and pharmaceutical products.

In many other cases against restrictive contracts, however, the enforcement may have hurt rather than helped consumers. For example, the Polish National Insurance Company (PZU) offered insurance to car owners for collision damage. It entered into contracts with service stations that repaired damaged vehicles. These contracting service stations agreed with PZU that they would pay low wages and that they would accept payment for their services at not more than specified prices. PZU, in turn, agreed to insure at the full repair price. The AMO found that these agreements illegally limited access to the market by service stations that had not signed agreements with PZU. The Anti-monopoly Court agreed (though it reversed on other grounds). The Court said that PZU's arrangement:

> forced the said service stations to make a choice either to 'be pushed out from the market' or to accept unlawful conditions imposed upon them by PZU. Concluding such contracts by the said service stations and fixing wage rates below the level to which market mechanisms would have led was attained under the pressure exerted by PZU . . .[24]

The Court declared that the contracts illegally deprived non-contracting service stations of freedom of market activity.

In 1990, the AMO prohibited a contract granting Mostostal Export an exclusive right to import Wartburg cars – a low-priced German model.[25] The Anti-monopoly Court affirmed. It noted that the car producer FSO had 70% of the market and therefore the remainder of the market was small. The Court said:

> [S]anctioning . . . the exclusivity of import would not only result in limitation of the number of sellers in the market, but also create advantageous conditions for setting the margins on unreasonably high levels by sellers, at the costs of buyers.

Both decisions could harm consumers. The insurance company had the incentive to provide a low-priced service for its clients; it had no incentive to exclude good repair service providers or (much less) to raise the cost of repairs. As for Mostostal, the Wartburg car was one of many; its producers had no market power. The exclusivity clause may have had efficiency benefits, and it did not and could not block sales by competing car companies.

After the *Mostostal* case the AMO relaxed its aggressive approach to exclusive car distributorships, citing the appearance of many car dealers on the market. The response of the AMO, though placed on grounds of a changing market, may reflect the AMO's growing appreciation of the fact that exclusive contracts may be adopted to compete rather than to restrain competition. Foreclosure (e.g. from the opportunity to distribute Wartburg cars) does not in itself more signal competitive harm.

6.3.3   Mergers

The Polish law was not applied to mergers before the 1995 amendment, which introduced merger control along the lines of the EC model. Under the amendment, filing is required for mergers above a threshold, and the AMO is empowered to prohibit mergers that would create or enhance a dominant position. As of 30 November, 1995, 134 mergers were considered by the AMO. The AMO reports that it prohibited no mergers in 1995. Also, as Professor Skoczny (1995, p. 179) reports, the AMO prohibited no mergers before 1995. Some mergers, however, have been allowed only after the parties accepted modification of the transaction.

6.3.4   Conclusion

The Polish law against abuse of dominance and restrictive contracts is broadly applied, and in many cases freedom of competitors is protected at the expense of freedom of efficient firms to choose their marketing strategies. Relatively few cartel cases seem to be found, but where they have been, the AMO has strictly applied the law. Merger law in Poland is still in its infancy.

6.4   Hungary

The Annual Report of Hungary reports that in 1995 the Competition Council decided 5 cases on restrictive agreements, 44 cases on abuse of dominant position, and 24 merger cases. The number of merger cases were eight times the number of merger cases decided the year before.

Few cartel cases have been decided in any year since the formation of the Office of Economic Competition. According to the 1994 Report, deep restructuring of the economy in 1993 had led companies to 'consider that they can survive only to the detriment of each other on the markets; thus, that they were pressured to compete'. The report implies that for this reason cartel conduct was not prevalent and states that as the market situation became more stable, monitoring by the Office for cartels became more important.[26]

6.4.1   Abuse of Dominance

Most of the cases in Hungary concern abuse of dominance, and most of the case law concerns imposition of one-sided advantages in contractual relations or refusing or threatening to refuse to deal.

A typical example is the *CATV* case. A cable-operating company, which provided cable reception service and also controlled the line on which HBO delivered a film channel, cut off both services (because it could not cut off one alone without access to the customer's home) when the customer was momentarily in default to HBO. The default had been caused in part by the ineptitude of the HBO collector. The cable operator refused to restore service without payment of a reconnection fee, the customer complained, and the OEC brought proceedings. The Competition Council determined that the cable operator had a dominant position, though another larger cable operator (also 'dominant') also supplied the market. It found that the CATV company had abused its dominance, stating:

> Naturally, a dominant firm is no more required to perform its obligations without consideration than any other party to a contract. However, due to its dominant position, which enables it to conduct its business independent of the market influences or the needs of customers, it has to take special care, like in the present case, to observe the basic requirement of fair business conduct, i.e. to respect the reasonable interest of consumers. The Competition Council considers that any conduct is unfair, thus violates the Competition Act, where in an existing business relationship the dominant firm, by the unilateral interpretation of the contract, or in any other way, including a breach of contract, forces, or attempts to force, its partner, who is in a partly or wholly helpless position due to the market characteristics, to accept terms which are advantageous for the dominant firm only, and disadvantageous for the partner.[27]

This principle seems quite sweeping. Recognizing that not all exercises of bargaining power or disregard for customers create competition problems, the Competition Council attempted to draw a line. When a gas works company inadvertently failed to take note of the fact that its bill had been paid and wrote a letter to the customer threatening suit if the customer did not pay, the Competition Council dismissed the customer's abuse of dominance complaint. The Council reasoned: 'It could not be stated that the letter sent, requesting payment, would affect market competition. Competition law is namely a field of law dealing with effects of the market mechanism on the economy.'[28]

Typical other abuse cases concern price discrimination. In the *Salami* case, Szalamigyar, a large salami maker, accounted for 70% of the purchases of hogs produced by the small hog producers of Csongrad County. Szalamigyar paid a lower unit price to the small producers than to the large producers, noting that the hogs of the small producers contained a larger fat content than those of the large producers and that demand for the higher-fat product had declined. The Competition Council rejected Szalamigyar's justification. While accepting that there was lower demand for high-fat hogs than low-fat ones, it found that the extent of the lower demand did not justify so large a price difference.[29] It said: 'Abusing its dominant position, Szalamigyar forced the acceptance of disadvantageous conditions in the contractual relations when it reduced the purchase price to small producers to a significantly greater extent than to large producers.'

Other typical cases involve exclusive contracts and refusals to deal. In one case a publisher of gossip newspapers and novels refused to take on two small firms as distributors.[30] In another the Hungarian State Railways sought to replace small food and drink sellers operating from kiosks with a single seller of food and drinks at all railway terminals.[31] In both cases respondents gave quality and efficiency justifications for their business decisions; and in both cases respondents' incentive seemed to be to serve consumers better. In both cases the Competition Council, having first found dominance, found that dominance had been abused. The Council said, in the first case:

> Concluding a deal [with the two small distributors who sought distribution contracts] can give the consumer different benefits (supply speed-ups, up to now unprovided areas can obtain goods under better conditions).[32]

Other cases involve pricing behaviour. In the *Cereol* case[33] the respondent, a monopsonist, was charged with substantially reducing the price it would pay for sunflower seeds from the price paid in the previous year. The Competition Council found no violation, holding that deteriorating market conditions justified the lower price. But it said nonetheless that imposing an excessively low price would be illegal, and added:

[A] dominant firm must not use its position to significantly increase its profits at the cost of others. This is especially true if there is a significant change in the distribution of profits between the participants of a related production chain.

The above cases indicate a high degree of market intervention. The *CATV* case suggests that the OEC might intervene in matters that – viewed from the point of view of the functioning of markets – seem trivial. The *Salami* case and the *Cereol* dictum suggest second-guessing in matters of price. The exclusive dealing cases raise the concern that the Council may be banning efficient contracts that serve consumers; that it may protect the economic opportunity of small dealers at the expense of consumer interests.

In an important price-predation case, however, the Competition Council showed itself to be a protector of hard competition. The subject was the Alkali War.[34] The respondent, Borsod-Chem plc, occupied 70% of the market for caustic soda and chlorine. Budapest Chemical Works plc and Nitrokemia plc were the only other significant participants in the market. Borsod-Chem began to offer its product at prices so low that Budapest Chemical Works could not compete except by suffering 'considerable losses'. Budapest Chemical Works complained that Borsod-Chem was abusing its dominance.

The facts revealed that the demand for the alkali products had fallen sharply. Moreover, due to Hungarian trade liberalization, Romanian, Slovak, Polish and Czech caustic soda was flooding the market. The import price was sometimes two thirds or less of Budapest Chemical's production cost. Borsod-Chem was not shown to be selling below its own production cost. 'It could be stated only that Borsod-Chem was able to produce the affected product at a lower cost level than the applicant.'

The Competition Council dismissed the complaint. In doing so it specified the conditions for a predatory pricing violation by a dominant firm: The predator must reduce prices below its average production cost. It must suffer temporary losses while the competitors disappear from the market. The strategy must be en route to charging monopolistic prices, by which the loss can be recouped and extra profit realized. For the strategy to be successful, the predator must have much more financial power than its competitors, and the barriers to entry into the market must be so high as to make 'improbable the quick market entry of a new operator even in a case of increased prices'.

The Competition Council further said (as summarized by the Office of Economic Competition):

Price competition is a part of market competition. In most cases price reduction to production costs coincides with the fair competition. In the present case the price charged by the party involved in the price competition which price was lower than the price of the competitors but higher than its own production cost cannot be regarded unfair even if this is disadvantageous for the competitors because it contributes to enforcing the purpose of economic competition, i.e. economic efficiency, that's why it's pro-competitive.

Thus, the Hungarian rule on price predation, far from being protective of small or inefficient competitors, favours hard competition on the merits. Indeed, it goes farther in this direction than even the EC rule, which does not require proof of probable recoupment.[35]

6.4.2   Cartels

While cartel cases seem to be few, two particular cases are illustrative of the work of the Office and Competition Council. One is the *Sugar* cartel,[36] and the other is the *Coffee* cartel.[37] Both present the universal problem. When can concert of action be inferred from identical or nearly identical conduct combined with circumstantial evidence?

In the *Sugar* case, eleven sugar-processing plants in Hungary raised their list prices by about the same amounts at about the same times despite decreasing demand. Their list prices increased by almost 50% in a year, and their revenues increased 25% over the previous year. The Competition Council reviewed three different periods of practically identical price rises. While it found insufficient evidence of concert in the first period, it found sufficient evidence in the second and third. During these periods, discussions took place at trade association meetings; members had expressly stated that they were 'trying to find solutions to their common problems'. Also, given the market conditions in the second and third periods, the Council found that the price increases could not have been sustained unless the firms had assured one another that each would follow suit.

In the *Coffee* case, five companies had 97% of the market. Through their trade association they induced the government to reduce consumer taxes and keep out 'black imports' (low-priced and possibly 'dumped' goods). They then raised their prices by approximately 100% in three stages, largely on identical dates. They did so despite the fact that the five firms' cost and capacity situations were quite different, and their products were different; they used different proportions of cheap to expensive beans.

The coffee companies denied cooperation. They tried to explain the coincidences by the considerable increase in the commodity exchange coffee price, the devaluation of the Hungarian currency, and the structure of the market, which, they said, produced a leadership/followership model. The Competition Council found an infringement and imposed fines. It reasoned that the firms' different costs and other conditions of competitiveness, the enormity of the price increases (averaging about 33%), the identical dates of increase, and the role of the trade association and the opportunities it offered for regular meetings and information exchanges pointed to cooperation, not mere market leadership.

A very different price-agreement case concerned three competitors or potential competitors who underwrote customs duty fees for livestock at border crossings. They all charged the same fee of 60 DEM. Then one and, a few hours later, a second reduced the fee to 15 DEM. In the face of these low prices, Hidfo, the third, complained of a conspiracy by its two competitors to eliminate it from the market. The Council upheld Hidfo's complaint. It found concerted action by the two competitors to charge a fee so low that it – the low price – could have had no purpose except to eliminate Hidfo from the market. The Council found that the firms violated the law that prohibits competitor agreements that put market participants at a disadvantage.[38]

While the *Sugar* and *Coffee cartel* cases are exemplary and the enforcement undoubtedly protected the public against high sugar and coffee prices, the competitors' conduct in *Hidfo* may well have been mischaracterized by the Council. This might have been a case not of concert but of competition itself. If we treat *Hidfo* as an outlier, the cartel and low-pricing case law in Hungary is insightful.

6.4.3 Mergers

Merger cases in Hungary were few until the past year. The paucity of mergers in need of approval may in part be attributable to the Act's failure to cover mergers by foreign firms. This gap is expected to be closed by the pending proposed amendment.

We report here several merger cases. The first two involve high concentration and a permissive government policy.

In *Tiszamenti Vegyimuvek (TVM)*, TVM, a state-owned company, had a 40% share of the detergent market but was in financial difficulties. Over the prior four years, TVM had cooperated with Henkel Hungary, and Henkel had invested capital in the modernization and expansion of TVM. TVM wished to acquire control of Henkel Hungary, and the proposal was approved by the State Property Agency. In the consolidation, which was to operate as a joint venture, Henkel Hungary was to receive the detergent plant of TVM.

Both TVM and Henkel Hungary were major producers of chemical products including detergents. Henkel had been distributing the TOMI detergent line produced by TVM since October 1992, at which time TVM had ceased to market this detergent.

The detergent market in Hungary was highly concentrated. Economies of scale appeared to require large size. The significant participants in the market, in addition to the merger partners, were Unilever Hungary and Egyesult Vegyimuvek. There were four or five smaller producers, but they made an inferior product. Imports from more than three high-quality foreign producers played a role, though the amount of imports was limited. There were numerous buyers, including many trading companies.

The Competition Council concluded that the consolidation would have no negative effect on competition. Despite the high concentration, the Council said, the manufacturers competed keenly for customers. The diversified and ample supply that came on the market was seen as 'a fundamental obstacle to restricting the continuation or development of competition, even if market shares are relatively large'.[39] The Council approved the merger.

Also, in the *Ceramic Brick* acquisition, the acquiring and acquired parties together had very large market shares. In categories of burnt structural bricks their joint shares ranged from 58% to 89%. However, 'only' acquisition of control was contemplated; not corporate consolidation. The Competition Council noted that the purchase would not change the number of participants in the market; that under the Hungarian competition law market participants owned by the same company may not coordinate their policies in an anti-competitive manner, though common ownership could make it practically impossible to detect such coordinations. Also, entry into the speciality-brick markets was easy for several other Hungarian brick makers, competition from non-brick construction methods could play a role in constraining exercises of power, and the acquisition furthered the privatization programme (the seller was a state-owned company). The Competition Council permitted the acquisition and noted that the Competition Office would monitor the firms' market practices.

In three more recent cases in which mergers were approved, it seemed that the market was competitive and there was no case at all to be made that there would be a lessening of competition. Either the market was not concentrated and the merger partners' shares were not significant[40] or the merger partners were neither competitors nor potential competitors.[41] Nonetheless the Competition Council approached the cases as if good justifications were important for approval, and it counted favourably the support of the Ministry of Industry and Trade and the lack of opposition from competitors.

The merger cases as a whole leave the impression of a lack of precision by the Competition Council in defining what is a merger that creates or strengthens a dominant position. The case reports do not contain sufficient market facts to enable the reader to understand the merger's effects on competition. They quickly turn to 'advantages' of the merger, and, confusingly, they consider as a benefit the support of ministries and competitors. In doing so, the cases do not distinguish (in weight or importance) efficiency and market effects from political support for the merger. This methodology for decision-making could create a high risk of industrial policy without transparency, which in turn could entail both hidden political influence and a missed opportunity to give guidance to business.

In short, the decisions, together, suggest a leniency in Hungary's merger policy, even while Hungary conducts a rather interventionist policy in cases of abuse of dominance. These tendencies seems to be followed also by the other Visegrád countries, as we see below.

6.5 The Czech Republic

In 1994 the Czech Ministry of Economic Competition (MEC) issued 15 rulings on restrictive agreements, 16 on abuses of dominance, and 36 on merger control. All the mergers were approved, and all of these except one was approved without limitation.

More than 40% of the complaints made to the MEC concerned abuse of a dominant position. More than half of these were dismissed as unfounded. Most cases investigated by the MEC for abuse of dominance concerned 'alleged inappropriate price increases by undertakings with a dominant position' (Annual Report for 1993, paragraph 62). 'A smaller category of cases concerns refusal to supply and efforts on [the] part of dominant undertakings to determine minimum volume of supplies' (paragraph 63).

6.5.1 Abuse of Dominance

The Ministry of Economic Competition regarded as the most important cases situations in which the car company Skoda and, separately, the Czech Insurance Company, raised or threatened to raise prices. In the Skoda matter, in 1993, the Ministry of Economic Competition asked the Ministry of Finance to investigate (under the Price Act) whether Skoda's price increase did or did not reflect increases in cost as a result of improvements in equipment. The Ministry of Finance found that the price rise was cost-justified; it did not find a violation of the Price Act. Skoda continued to increase prices. The Ministry of Economic Competition regarded the price rises as problematic in view of Skoda's high share of the Czech market, and suggested resolving the problem by removing trade barriers to the Czech market. By decision of the Council of Ministers and in keeping with the then Interim Europe Agreement, the government offices gradually reduced duties on cars imported from EU Member States, thus using a free market remedy rather than a regulatory remedy to deal with the sensitive problem of high pricing.

A second pricing problem involved the Czech Insurance Company's prices for third-party car insurance. The insurance company – though regarded as dominant because of its market share – was suffering losses. It announced a price increase. The Ministry of Economic Competition proceeded to examine whether the company's prices were too high. It did so by trying to determine whether its costs could have been lower. To make this determination, it evaluated principles 'expected to bring success on the traditional insurance markets in the EC Member States', and it evaluated approaches employed by other third-party car insurance companies. It found that the respondent insurance company could significantly reduce its losses by employing some of the methodologies used by others. It noted that the insurance company 'failed to prove . . . that it had exhausted all alternatives of prevention of losses'. These factors pointed in the direction of an abuse-of-dominance violation. However, since the Czech Insurance Company did not, after all, increase its prices, and it announced an intention to introduce cost-saving changes systematically, the MEC closed the proceedings. As further support for closing the file, the Ministry noted that the responsible authorities were in the process of granting licences to other insurance companies in connection with the transformation of the economy, and that new entry was eliminating the monopoly position of the respondent (Annual Report for 1993, paragraphs 68–73).

The *Czech Insurance* case reflects the Ministry's readiness to presume dominance from market share alone, to give close scrutiny to announced price rises by firms with large market shares, and to become involved in micro-management issues surrounding the efficiency of the large firm's performance.

A number of abuse of dominance cases also concern refusals to supply. The MEC follows the law of the European Community in distinguishing between cut-offs of regular customers and not supplying others. A dominant firm's cut-off of a regular customer is illegal unless justified.

6.5.2 Restrictive Agreements

The 1994 Annual Report identifies as the most common and the most serious violations price cartels and agreements to limit competitors' access to the market. Price cartels that were detected and found illegal included a coffee cartel (which included two of the same players that participated in the Hungarian coffee cartel – Tchibo and Douwe Egberts). The administrative procedure was triggered by a notice in the press published by *Cesky Kavovy Svaz* 'inviting all coffee producers to increase their prices gradually by 10% monthly because of a sharp increase of prices of the green coffee beans in the world markets' (Annual Report for 1994, paragraph 65). The coffee prices were increased in July and August, apparently in response to the 'invitation'.

Also, an association of taxi cab drivers was found to have taken a decision to maintain uniform rates. The Minister prohibited fulfilment of the decision and ordered fines.

The Annual Report of 1994 reports as '[o]ne of the most significant cases' (paragraph 71) proceedings against the Czech Chamber of Pharmaceutical Chemists. The Chamber imposed the following charges, for a two-year licence to run a pharmacy: 1000 Czech crowns if the establishment was to be run by a pharmaceutical chemist, and 1 million Czech crowns if the establishment was to be run by others (e.g. a legal entity comprising a pharmaceutical chemist and a physician). Challenging this restrictive action, which was apparently designed to keep out competition rather than to safeguard standards, the Ministry noted that the decision of the Chamber 'limited the access of possible competitors to the market of pharmaceutical services'.

Other cases involved an exclusivity arrangement for which an exemption was granted, another exclusivity case where an infringement was found (exclusive sale of Scholler ice cream products at petrol stations), and a supplier's contract with a favoured buyer to treat other buyers less well. The last was found to be an illegal contract to discriminate.

Thus, the restrictive contract cases range from important cartels cases where the violation apparently has significant price-raising effects across the market, including cases against professional associations bent on keeping out the competition, to vertical contracts that are, at the least, ambiguous in their effects.

6.5.3 Mergers

Under the statute, mergers are said to threaten or harm economic competition when the partners' market share exceeds 30%, and only such mergers (market share in excess of 30%) are subject to merger control. The MEC is directed to approve a merger when its economic advantages outweigh its harm to competition.

Most of the merger applications involve acquisitions by foreign firms. All or nearly all applications are approved; some (but few) are approved with conditions.

Apparently, the 30% market share carries with it the presumption that the merger will harm competition, for the analysis focuses on whether the economic benefits of these mergers outweigh their harm. The Annual Report for 1993 categorizes the arguments of economic benefit that the

Table 6.7 Arguments of economic benefit of mergers, Czech Republic

Argument offered	Frequency
Investments into reconstruction and modernization of production for new technologies	20 times
Increase of exports including facilitation of entry into foreign markets	11 times
Upgrading of the quality of products which will reflect itself by an increased competitiveness on the domestic market	9 times
Maintenance of employment following its rationalisation up to the European standard and creation of new jobs, including the maintenance of the existing social conditions for a period of 2–3 years, etc.	9 times
Provisions of know-how in technology	7 times
Provision of know-how concerning company management (introduction of marketing, implementation of the total quality control system)	7 times

Source: 1993 Czech Annual Report.

foreign investors made (see Table 6.7). Each of these economic benefits – from increasing exports to maintaining jobs to upgrading quality – was accepted by the Ministry as admissible in principle. While not listed in Table 6.7, improvement of the environmental characteristics of the relevant product has also been treated as a benefit tending to justify a merger.

The approved consolidations include the acquisition by Tchibo Freisch-Roest-Kaffee Gmb of the majority of the stock of Balírny Jihlava, leading to a 'dominant position' of Tchibo on the Czech coffee market. The Ministry found that the acquisition would not have a negative effect on competition because the market behaved competitively and efforts were being made by other companies to penetrate the market. Moreover, the Ministry found that the acquisition would ensure modernization of buildings, it would increase jobs in an area of high unemployment, and it would help to stabilize the Balírny Jihlava by an infusion of capital. Despite finding no harm to competition in the marketplace, the Ministry attached conditions to its grant of approval. The conditions required Tchibo to place emphasis 'on utilization of domestic sources of production and respect of interests of the end consumer'.[42]

The Ministry's assessment that the merger would not harm competition seems to have been wrong. After the merger the Ministry discovered a coffee price-fixing cartel, and parties to the merger were parties to the cartel (see above). A similar cartel was the subject of successful proceedings in Hungary (see above). A merger producing a dominant (or oligopolistic)[43] position would tend to create conditions that make cartelization possible and attractive, and perhaps this merger did so. (One cartel member made the 'mistake' of publishing a notice in the press (see above) and thereby calling attention to itself.) This evidence leads one to query. On what factual basis did the Ministry find that, despite the merger's creation of a dominant position, 'the market behaved competitively and efforts [presumably assessed as likely to succeed] were being made by other companies to penetrate the market'? (Annual Report for 1993, paragraph 82). How thorough was the factual and economic assessment of the circumstances?

The Ministry also approved Ford's acquisition of Autopal Novy Jacín, with conditions. The conditions required Ford to invest in technology and equipment, to train employees in specialized activities and management, and to maintain existing jobs for two years.

Another approved acquisition was by Rieber a.s., one of the largest food-processing companies in Norway, which bought Vitana, a leading Czech producer of dehydrated soups, consommé, and pastry mixes. As for benefits of the merger, the Ministry cited Rieber's intent to improve quality and to export to all markets in which the Vitana mark is protected, and it made the positive findings 'that traditional domestic production will develop and the domestic sources and the Vitana trademark will obtain a better position on European markets'. The Ministry approved the consolidation subject to Vitana's promise not to reduce production of the relevant products without prior approval for five years, not to 'change its production programme or trading strategy in such a manner that the Czech Republic would have to resort to importing the products in question', and 'to give preference to sources offered by the Czech market for all its production and other activities' (paragraphs 84, 88).

The Annual Report for 1994 reports several other 'significant' merger cases approved by the Ministry. One case involved sale of two plants that produce electrical car accessories, by PAL to the German firm VDO Adolf Schindling AD. The plants produced almost 100% of electrical car accessories in and for the Czech market. The Ministry stated that the merger would not change this market share because Schindling did not previously act on the Czech market. The Ministry welcomed the merger in view of 'the plans of the merging companies to improve the quality and range of its products, so as to be able to enter into foreign markets and to improve the competitive edge of their products' (paragraph 85).

No information is provided in the case report about whether the plants were, separately, of efficient size and whether Schindling was a potential competitor that would have entered the Czech market *de novo* or even by purchase of one plant if the two plants were not available as a package. If so, an opportunity for increased competition was foregone. But, on the other hand, if barriers to entry including sales into the Czech Republic were virtually non-existent, if the two plants had synergies with one another and if separately each was below efficient scale, and if Schindling's management was likely to make the enterprise efficient and competitive, the balance would tip the other way. Unless the last scenario was true, the merger was probably anti-competitive.

Other approved mergers reported had similar characteristics. Karosa, a maker of buses and coaches for the Czech market, had a 'highly dominant' position. In a privatization proceeding, it was bought by Renault and the European Bank for Reconstruction and Development. The acquisition 'would not change the competitive environment' apparently because Karosa was already highly dominant. The acquisition was hoped 'to increase [Karosa's] competitive edge on world markets' (paragraph 86). But, one wishes to know, did Renault's purchase entrench the dominance of Karosa? How was Karosa able to remain dominant? Were there government procurement barriers or other barriers to entry or expansion that allowed Karosa to remain dominant and might usefully have been dismantled?

In connection with the privatization of MEZ, Siemens AG entered both the Czech and the Slovak markets. In the Czech Republic, the Ministry observed, the MEZ plants accounted for the production and sale of almost 90% of electric motors for various uses. Siemens made electric motors of different applications. The Ministry's investigation concluded that the costs of Siemens' introducing interchangeable motors 'would be prohibitively high' and it apparently concluded that Siemens was not a potential competitor. (The Slovak Office had a different view of competitive effects in the Slovak Republic. See below.) Moreover, Siemens committed itself 'to complementing and improving the range of products for the foreign markets'. It would help adapt the Czech products to international standards, transfer know-how, upgrade production technology, and 'give MEZ products a considerable additional competitive edge' (paragraph 88).

Finally, in a joint tenure between Nutricia of the Netherlands and Rekord, the dominant firm in the Czech Republic in the market for non-milk-based baby food, the Ministry also found economic advantages. The advantages included not only prospective improvements in quality but also greater usage of local raw materials. The latter prospects 'outweigh the possible negative effects in the infringement of economic competition' (paragraph 89). Whether there were indeed negative effects of the joint venture on competition was not clear; but if there were, one wonders, how and on what record did the Ministry balance the prospective national benefits of the injunction to 'buy local' against the losses to competition?

The merger cases tend to assume harm to competition from acquisitions of competitors that produce a market share of more than 30%, and they reflect a readiness to take the occasion of merger approval to serve industrial policy goals such as jobs, domestic production and exports.

6.6 Slovakia

The law of the Slovak Republic was liberalized in August 1994. Most of the available statistics reflect experience before the last amendment; but since the law did have and still has prohibitions against abuse of dominance, restrictive contracts, and mergers to dominance, the pre-1994 case law remains meaningful.

In 1994 the Anti-monopoly Office resolved 60 cases, of which 32 related to abuse of a dominant position, 17 to agreements restraining competition, and 6 to mergers and other concentrations. Complaints on abuse of dominance largely involved forcing unreasonable conditions in contracts, tying extraneous obligations to fulfilment of deliveries, and applying dissimilar conditions for equivalent transactions (discrimination).

From 1991 to 1994, the Office evaluated 123 concentrations. In 35 of these cases it issued decisions. In two cases the concentration was not approved; in three it was conditionally approved. Three merger cases were dismissed as not requiring approval and in one case a preliminary measure was issued. In the remaining 26 cases the Office approved the concentration without conditions. All but two of the mergers approved were acquisitions by foreign firms.

On 1994, as noted, the statute was amended. It was thought, according to competition official Milan Banas, that the pre-existing system posed obstacles to the freedom of business to engage in efficient transactions. According to Mr. Banas in an explanatory statement announcing the amendment, the new law made clear that consumer welfare 'in the sense [of] society welfare' is the overriding goal. Mr. Banas pointed also to a 'subordinate objective of the law – a control of the economic power of the dominant firms against its exploitative abuse.' Mr Barns defined abuse of dominance under the Slovak law as follows:

The abuse of dominant position is unilateral conduct to the detriment of competition. It means 'exclusionary' practice, such as predatory pricing, discrimination or refusal to deal which harm competition in particular in upstream or downstream markets. It is prohibited the exploitation of dominant position in the way which harms consumers' interest (e.g. enforcement of excessive trading conditions, or tying). However, the extent to which the 'exploitative' abuse should be prosecuted is narrow and it will depend on the situation in the relevant market (e.g. where high barriers to entry exist, there is no potential competition) (Barns, page 4).

6.6.1 Abuse of Dominance

Application of the abuse of dominance prohibition can be seen from several examples. A customer of an electric power supplier had acquired in a privatization sale most of the assets of a state-owned firm and the state-owned firm had not paid its electric bill. The power company threatened to cut off the customer's service unless the customer paid the debt of the firm whose assets it bought. The Competition Office held this threat to constitute abuse of dominance.

Other common abuses have involved discrimination and tying, other situations of forcing unreasonable conditions, and foreclosing access to distribution systems. An example of the last is the case of a dominant producer of candy, which entered into an exclusive distributorship contract with a wholesaler. As a result of the exclusive contract, retailers were unable to obtain supplies directly from the producer and 'had difficulties in their own entrepreneurial activities.' They complained to the Competition Office. The Competition Office made a 'complex analysis of the potential advantages and/or disadvantages [of the exclusivity clause] to retailers, [for] one of the priorities was also the public interest (i.e. promotion of small business . . .).'[44] The Office found that the exclusivity did not increase quality of services or extend the assortment of sales, as the candy producer had hoped it would. In view of the perceived harm to retailers, the Office found an abuse of dominance.

Here, again, is an example of a decision that protects market opportunities for small business more than efficiency in distribution, and the competition offices do not grapple with the trade-offs.

6.6.2   Cartels

Cartel enforcement in Slovakia has recently involved a hardcore cartel in the cement industry, where the significant issue was proof of concert. The cement companies in Slovakia exchanged essential information, including data on output, cost, exports, inventories and profit. The data were compiled monthly and consolidated, and the consolidated information was circulated to the directors of the cement companies. At the same time a 'mutually established' consulting firm prepared documents stating in detail how to divide the market geographically among the factories, and it described orderly market devices that could be used in lieu of quotas. The Competition Office found that a cartel did indeed exist, and, in 1994, assessed the highest penalty yet imposed.

Another price cartel case involved the two dominant fuel distributors. The two fuel distributors had considered merging during the process of privatization. Their merger plan aborted but their cooperation continued. The Office charged certain individuals in the firms with fixing prices. In defence, they argued that they had only exchanged information concerning the prices that they planned to set, but that they did not and could not set prices without authorization of their boards of directors. The Competition Office rejected the defence. It noted the very high concentration in the market, the close collaboration of the companies, and the fact that the individuals had no reason to exchange the price information other than to fix prices. The Competition Office said:

> The most important fact that demonstrate[s] the cartel agreement is the exchange of information on prices that the participants will charge in the future. Also, the way the information was exchanged – personal meeting – creates [the] condition for prompt reaction to each other which supports our conclusion about [a] cartel agreement.[45]

The Office determined that there was a cartel agreement, and they banned the cartel. The analysis in both cartel opinions is modern and sensitive.

6.6.3 Mergers

As for mergers and joint ventures, the Slovak policy is liberal and the Office usually grants approval. The cases subject to approval are those in which the merger or joint venture creates or strengthens a dominant position without outbalancing benefits. Approval may be based on net economic advantages to the Slovak Republic.

Among others, the Office dealt with the plan of the Czech Post & Telecom, Slovak Telecom, and the Dutch firm Atlantic West BV to establish a joint venture named Eurotel to provide cellular radio/telephone and data network services. The joint venturers agreed not to compete with the joint venture. Slovak Telecom, which alone provided radio/telephone services in the Slovak market, was a potential competitor in data services, as was Atlantic West, though it currently did no business in the Slovak market.

The Office found that the joint venture led to a monopolistic position of Eurotel in the market. It found that both services provided by the joint venture – cellular and data – are 'indispensable for the overall development of the economy and it is necessary to promote them as quickly as possible. To do so, investments, know-how and connections to the single telecommunication network, which is a state monopoly, are needed. It was not possible to arrange for these services in any other way.' Balancing the economic advantages against the disadvantage of forming a monopolistic position, the Office found net advantages, and it gave its approval.

Mergers, like joint ventures, are often conglomerate. For example, a Slovak firm may have a dominant position and an acquiring foreign firm may be thought to strengthen that position by bringing capital and technology to the market. An example is the case of the state-owned MEZ Michalovce (a counterpart to the Czech MEZ cases). MEZ produced electric motors for washing machines and commercial electric motors for other uses. It was divided into four companies pursuant to a programme of restructuring and privatization. Siemens AG acquired a 25% interest in the resulting company that planned to produce electric motors for washing machines. '[T]he Office was aware of the strengthening of the market power of MEZ . . . and therefore the possibility of fixing the price of the product in future years . . . On the other side, the economic advantages of the merger outweighed the potential damage. . . .' The economic advantages were catalogued as: a positive effect on revenues, reduction of production costs as production is increased, an opportunity to improve MEZ's quality because of the high innovative ability of Siemens, a resulting guarantee of no delay in delivery of the product, and 'a strengthening of a competitive ability on foreign markets by using the image of the foreign partners.'[46]

Siemens acquired a 75% interest in a second company resulting from the division of MEZ. This company was intended to develop, produce and sell electrotechnical systems and components for appliances and cars. 'Such product market had no representation in Slovakia before and [the Office said] it is very likely the new company will reach a dominant position.' The Office determined, however, that there were weighty advantages of the acquisition; namely increased revenues, sales to markets with convertible currency, contributing to foreign exchange for the Slovak economy, the possibility of entering the Ukrainian market, Siemens' investment in development and modernization of production, and bringing new products on the market.[47] The Office found a restriction of competition (though in another jurisdiction this new entry might have been seen as an introduction of competition to the market and not a restriction of it), but that the advantages outweighed the harm.

Perhaps the most dramatic use of Slovak merger control to carry out non-competition ends is the case of the monopolistic acquisition of petrol filling stations by Slovnaft a.s., the largest oil refiner in Slovakia. Slovnaft owned some 100 petrol stations in Slovakia. Benzinol, the state-owned gas distributor, owned some 200 stations. The state was in the process of privatizing Benzinol through the offer for sale of 51% of its stock. It offered the shares only in a block, and, despite bids by Agip of Italy and OMV of Austria, awarded the sale to Slovnaft, which would gain an 80% share of the market. Zdenko Kovac, the Director of the Anti-monopoly Office, publicly questioned the legality of the acquisition and expressed concern about its impact on competition. This is believed to be the reason for his departure from office.[48]

6.7 Assessment of the Case Law

6.7.1 Goals

To assess the state of any country's competition law, one first must ask what the country is trying to achieve and how well the law is suited to this task. For this purpose we treat the laws of all four countries together, for, as we have seen, the countries' stated goals regarding competition are quite similar, if not identical.

By their competition laws, the Visegrád nations are trying to achieve a range of objectives. They are attempting to create markets where none existed, to develop an environment hospitable to entrepreneurship and thus to help produce a healthy and growing small and medium-sized business sector, and to protect the people and entrepreneurs against unfair advantage-taking – a particular concern in economies marked by state-owned monopolies and only recently experiencing privatization and the lifting of government controls. Each country is trying to create a healthy economy and one attractive to trade and investment, and thus to strengthen the nation's economic condition. To accomplish these several tasks the countries are availing themselves of a number of tools and strategies, in addition to unleashing and preserving competition itself by proscribing cartels and monopolistic exclusions. These include trade tools (lowering barriers to trade and investment), industrial policy tools (buy-national mandates), and applying an analytical framework in which regard is given to the treatment of small firms and in which competition losses may be offset by export and 'competitiveness' gains.

No one model or formula is equally well suited to assessing the three substantive areas examined in this chapter – abuse, restrictive agreements, and concentrations. Hence, we deal separately with each segment of the law.

6.7.2   *Abuse of Dominance*

The abuse offence in the Visegrád nations seems predominantly to concern either pricing too high or too low, refusing to grant distribution contracts, or abusing bargaining power. Especially when the complaint is abuse of a power relationship in contracting, exercise of dominant market power in a well-defined economic market does not seem to be the essence of the offence. Therefore, not surprisingly, the nations' anti-monopoly offices have taken some liberties in concluding that dominance does in fact exist for purposes of finding that an entity imposed onerous contract terms. For example, in abuse cases, the authorities may define the market from the perspective of the person claimed to be abused rather than from the perspective of all buyers of the product, and may presume dominance from a 30% or 40% market share without serious inquiry into the strength of remaining competition, barriers to entry, and potential competition.[49] In later cases, however, some authorities show increased sophistication and increased attention to the particular market facts.

The scope of the abuse offence in the laws of all four countries is broad. This may be explained by three facts or objectives – the removal of price controls, an unease about business freedom when outcomes might be unfair, and the mission to facilitate the emergence of a critical mass of entrepreneurial enterprises. In all the Visegrád nations, price and other direct controls were removed at the start of the transition, and consumers and entrepreneurs were seen to exist at the will of monopolistic state-owned firms and other firms with new-found power. Control over the unleashed monopolists' 'taking of advantage' was one of the major purposes of the Visegrád competition laws. Concern also existed that small firms would be victims of discriminatory treatment, and that they would be unfairly blocked from opportunities to enter markets and grow. Thus, the market and fairness questions became inextricably intertwined.

At the same time, from the statistics and also from the thrust of most of the case law, one might suspect that significant market problems (e.g., cartels, and monopolistic acquisitions) may proceed undetected or unrestrained. Given the size of the anti-monopoly office staffs, the amount of resources available to them, and the fact that the public is invited to lodge complaints with the offices, it is not surprising that most proceedings in the Visegrád countries are abuse of dominance proceedings, and that most of these proceedings raise unfairness questions rather than problems whose solution would produce pro-competitive marketwide effects. Although a very large number of complaints are dismissed, the resources devoted to unfairness (abuse) claims overwhelm the resources devoted to other prohibited practices such as cartels. This appears to signal an imbalance that should be corrected over time.

6.7.3 Restrictive Contracts

The restrictive contract offence has at least two objectives. First, hardcore cartels are prohibited.[50] A near *per se* rule against hardcore cartels seems to be developing, though, as noted, one might suspect, from the few cartels prosecuted and the very few cartelists heavily fined, that serious problems remain with detection and proof. The competition offices are working towards distinguishing productive, synergistic combinations from cartels, and they normally allow the former, as does the law of the EC, United States and most other nations; but it seems to us that not enough hardcore cartels are discovered. It is something of a disappointment that more resources are not devoted to the area of hardcore cartel detection.

Second, the restrictive contract law is aimed and used to protect opportunities for entrepreneurs and small firms. This objective applies to restraints that foreclose or shift significant opportunities away from strangers to a deal, as well as to restraints imposed on parties to a bargain (though the latter are more likely to be handled under the abuse-of-dominance proscription). Most often, we find, the authorities and courts implicitly assume that helping the entrepreneur will help the market to work and that it will help the consumer to get a better deal including a more acceptable range of choice. The assumption that law that helps small competitors helps competition once dominated US law, but is now rejected by US law (see Fox and Sullivan, 1987). The assumption is more credible in the Visegrád countries in view of the long lack of choice and lack of a developed medium-sized business community. Understandably there is a current view in the Visegrád countries that government should be proactive to help small business begin operations, put down their roots, and survive.

Even if there is a frequent compatibility of entrepreneurial and consumer interests in the CEECs, however, the interests of the two groups are frequently in tension. Visegrád authorities and courts might find it useful to identify and address the trade-offs more systematically, especially by giving attention to the possible costs to consumers that may stem from protecting entrepreneurial opportunities. The Visegrád nations might begin to develop a jurisprudence that focuses not only on harm to 'excluded' retailers, dealers, and other sellers but also on the benefits to competition and efficiency that might come from allowing firms (i.e. the purportedly excluding firms) to devise and employ strategies to compete, even though as a by-product the strategies may have the effect of a refusal to deal.

For abuse of dominance and restrictive contract cases we believe that the competition offices need more focus on activities likely to have significant impact on their economies, and that more refined statistical data-keeping could help. For example, the currently used category 'restrictive contract cases' gives little information, whereas a 'hardcore cartel' category would give significant information. So, too, categories that separate onerous contract cases from monopolistic abuses that block market entry and growth would be informative. For each of the more specific categories, and at least for cartels and monopolistic exclusions with serious market effects, annual reports could usefully provide information such as:

- Number of investigations
- Number of proceedings
- Number of findings of infringement
- Aggregate fines, other punishment
- Average fine
- Median fine

The statistical reporting should be designed in a manner likely to reveal the percentage of suits with significant market impact and the percentage with little or no market impact.

6.7.4 Merger Control

The third area of law we address is merger control.[51] In general, the Visegrád nations allow and approve mergers whose economic benefits outweigh their competitive harms. The focus of merger policy is, in general:

What is good for the country? Mergers that make domestic firms stronger, e.g. by infusions of needed capital and transfers of technology, are favoured. Mergers that promise to increase exports and to increase competitiveness in foreign markets are especially favoured. The role of a merger in facilitating a privatization is also counted favourably. At least in one CEEC country, the competition authority uses the occasion of merger approval to impose buy-national conditions that are unrelated to any competitive aspects of the merger but are apparently thought useful to shore up demand for domestic sellers.

To assess the Visegrád countries' merger analysis, we focus first on harm to competition and then on the industrial policy offset.

Harm to Competition

The authorities seem often to presume harm to competition from the fact that the merged firm has or is likely to gain a 30% or 40% share of the market. In these cases the focus of the inquiry is on the merger's economic benefits, which are to be weighed against the presumed harm. Analysis to support the conclusion of competitive harm is complex, and is usually missing in the case law. More systematic economic analysis to understand when competition is lessened might improve the nations' merger jurisprudence.

Industrial Policy

In a number of cases in which a Visegrád competition authority has used industrial policy to justify a merger, it is not clear that a justification was needed. The merger may not have created or strengthened a dominant position. Indeed, the merger may have increased competition. Especially where the country did not employ trade barriers and where foreign competitors could freely enter the market, the merged firm may simply have become a better competitor.

In some instances the industrial policy considerations invoked fit nicely with competition policy. For example, it is likely to be the case that technologically strong foreign acquirers will bring significant improvements to a domestic firm and thus to the domestic market. These improvements might offset short-term losses in competitive rivalry, depending on the facts.

But the nations are also prone to applying *ad hoc* industrial policy where it is not apparent that the policy serves the nations' purposes in strengthening their economies. For example, in connection with buy-national clauses, when a newly merged firm must buy from domestic sources it is handicapped by not being able to choose the best deal for itself. Moreover, if a merger is anti-competitive, worker interests favouring the merger would be in tension with the interests of consumers and intermediate buyers.

Merger policy would be strengthened by separate analysis of each of the following effects: (1) competitive harms in the home market, (2) efficiency and technological gains, (3) greater competitiveness of the merged firm in foreign markets, and (4) other specified advantages, including those expected to flow from buy-local obligations. Merger guidelines that specify how anti-competitive effects are predicted and what offsets will be allowed under what circumstances would be helpful. Moreover, the competition agencies could usefully monitor the firms and the market after permitted mergers, especially those with anti-competitive properties, and track the agency's predictions of competitive effects and 'economic advantages'.

6.7.5   Approximation of Law

Thus far we have considered the nations' needs and wants without regard to their desire to join the EU. As noted earlier, to be eligible for membership, which appears to be an important objective of the Visegrád nations, they are obliged to approximate EC competition law.

Approximating EC competition law at a general level should be beneficial; also it should be a natural by-product of the evolution of Visegrád nations' competition law. EC competition law is intended to preserve open markets, to facilitate market integration, to eliminate abuses of power, and to control creation of power. So, too, are the Visegrád nations' competition laws intended to achieve these objectives. Therefore approximation at a general level constitutes harmonization of the law of equal trading partners towards commonly embraced principles. Also, approximation at this level is well under way.

To the extent, however, that the Visegrád nations must approximate the detail of EC law, there may be costs both to the EU (in its desire to promote economic readiness for membership) and to the Visegrád nations. The costs derive from the fact that, for any one nation, its own choice of law, legal system, and pace of law formation may be better for it than EC rules and methodologies. Therefore freedom of each nation to tailor its law to its context may set it on a faster, firmer track to a strong economy and may hasten its real economic readiness for EU membership and engagement in the European and world trading systems.

The task to approximate to detail thus presents tensions. It also creates opportunities, however; for, all other things being equal, uniform law is more conducive to foreign investment, competition and trade than multiple sets of rules. The challenge for the European Commission is to accept breathing space for CEEC autonomy, while the challenge for each Visegrád nation is to identify areas in which EC law does not fit well with its needs or vision and to show that there is a more productive way to meet the shared goals – a more robust economy, an open economy, and economic readiness for membership in the EU.

Meanwhile, each of the Visegrád nations has achieved a creditable degree of convergence towards EC law with regard to the development and application of the substantive principles in the three areas of law treated in this chapter. The abuse of dominance law is very similar to the law under Article 86. The laws prohibit abusive restraints that clog entry channels. They protect small and medium-sized firms from abuses that make it hard to compete. The principal difference between Visegrád law and Article 86 can be found in the greater tendency of the Visegrád authorities to attempt to correct imbalances in bargaining power. Since many of these interventions are against natural monopolists, and especially state-owned monopolists, this difference might tend to disappear as regulation of natural monopoly and as privatization proceed.

The law against restrictive contracts is also quite similar to the law under Article 85. The Visegrád counties, like the EC, seem to be developing a near *per se* rule against cartels. They could usefully devote more resources to the cartel offence, but so too could the European Commission. The Visegrád competition offices might too freely conclude that exclusive dealing is anti-competitive, but EC law, also, has tendencies in this direction. The EC has a large body of law concerned with keeping markets open to parallel imports (cross-border intra-brand competition) regardless of the strength of inter-brand competition (*Consten and Grundig*[52] and its progeny). This line of EC law is currently a subject of re-examination,[53] and law in possible flux is not ideal as a model towards which the law of other nations should converge.

The merger law standard of illegality is virtually the same in the Visegrád countries as in the EU, except that the laws of two of the Visegrád countries – the Czech Republic and Hungary – are more progressive in that they fill the 'oligopoly' loophole that might exist in EC law.[54] However, three Visegrád countries allow industrial policy to override harm to competition. This is a difference that should be revisited. Indeed, such an industrial policy trump is prohibited by the Europe Agreements if a Member State of the EU is a victim of the condoned anti-competitive effects. As a practical matter, such effects probably have not occurred; it would rarely be the case that a merger in a Visegrád country created a national champion with dominant market power extending beyond the national borders; but rarity of the case should not excuse reform.

While noting a high degree of approximation, we add a closing caveat. Even complete convergence of substantive law, as it is written in the statutes and case reports, cannot be equated with effective competition policy. Effectiveness of competition policy requires that the law be known in the business community, that it be enforced, and that, against the most heinous offences, it be aggressively enforced and attended with substantial punishment. Only a focused enforcement policy, applied even-handedly and free from political influence, and a credible threat of enforcement, can be expected to elicit compliance and thus to be a real spur to competition.

That being said, we would add that the progress of the Visegrád competition authorities over the short time span of six years is remarkable. The anti-monopoly officials deserve enormous credit for their pioneering efforts and deep commitment to create robust competition policies in the wake of command economies.

Notes

1. The collection of these data emphasized their comparative natures, so that they may differ from figures reported in publications of the competition offices. For several reasons, unavoidable inaccuracies and omissions remain.
2. This appears to be the case for Poland, but only because the data in Table 6.1 refer to decisions, as indicated in the footnote there. However, until June 1991 when the law was amended the Polish offices were similarly obliged to issue a formal decision on every complaint received (Fornalczyk, 1993, p.38). Now only a formal reply is required.
3. Because of differences in reporting, they do not correspond precisely either to the total number of matters arising or to the total number of investigations.
4. The Polish Office also reports that most complaints from competitors concern barriers to entry.
5. In Vj-109/93, the prices had to be checked directly in a misleading advertising case.
6. In the *Coffee* case (Vj-185/1994, see below) identical dawn raids were carried out simultaneously at five companies, and the case resulted in a fine of 388 million HUF (2.1 million ECU at the June 1996 exchange rate).
7. The total fines issued to the end of 1995 in Hungary was 1.6 billion HUF (approximately 9.5 million ECU). Comparable information is not available for the other countries.
8. Even for Hungary, it is difficult to say whether a fine is exemplary as it is not possible to measure the damage.
9. The expression used in conversation was that small children should not be beaten too hard.
10. Hardcore cartels are agreements among competitors – usually in the form of price-fixing or market division – designed only to eliminate competition and not to respond to buyers.
11. PRP in P, judgment of Anti-monopoly Court of 5 December 1991 (XVII Amr 14/91).
12. Power plant ZE in Cz., gas plant KOZG in T., judgments of Anti-monopoly Court of 4 October 1993 (XVII Amr 8/93 and 29/93).
13. Ruch, branch in Lodz (II), judgment of Anti-monopoly Court of 12 February 1993 (XVII Amr 33/92); Gas plant ZG in Lodz, judgment of Anti-monopoly Court, 27 October 1992 (XVII Amr 20/92).
14. The importance of the distinction between protecting competition for the benefit of consumers and protecting rights of and fairness towards market participants can be seen by comparing the US law of the 1960s and early 1970s with the US law of the 1990s. US Supreme Court case law of the 1960s contained many statements on protection of freedom that are very similar to the referenced statements of the Anti-monopoly Court. Moreover, like the Anti-monopoly Court, the US Supreme Court in the 1960s conceptualized antitrust law as multi-valued; as designed to protect, at the same time, opportunity for small firms, autonomy for distributors, freedom from coercion, and consumers' interests (e.g. *United States* v. *Topco Associates, Inc.*, 405 US 596, 610 (1972); *Fortner Enterprises, Inc.* v. *United States Steel Corp.*, 394 US 495, 498–9 (1969).

The freedom standard, however, cannot be absolute, because one person's freedom (e.g. a distributor's freedom to distribute the product of another) is another person's limitation of freedom (e.g. a producer's freedom to choose the most effective means to get to market). Therefore either some other guiding principle is needed or decisions will be subjective within a large range.

In the United States in the late 1970s, the uncertainty of the 'freedom' standard and the wide breadth of the resulting enforcement were eventually thought to undermine both clarity and efficiency, and the law evolved towards a consumer welfare standard. See Fox and Sullivan (1987).

This does not mean that the countries studied should adopt the US model. The United States has a mature economy and in the United States markets work quite well. Nations that must develop competition, both in the sense of developing markets where none existed and in the symbiotic sense of instilling the competitive ethic in business people who were born into a society that condemned profit-making, face a much more daunting task. They might appropriately decide that the US approach is too narrow and too outcome-oriented and does not sufficiently focus on the creation of markets. Nonetheless, the contradiction inherent in the freedom standard remains, and should counsel dealing face-to-face with trade-offs and developing clear principles for decision-making.

15. Housing cooperative SM in S. W., judgment of 10 May 1993, XVII Amr 6/93.
16. Poland, Report on Activity of Anti-monopoly Office in 1995, pp. 19–20.
17. Ruch, judgment of the Anti-monopoly Court of 8 November 1993 (XVII Amr 39/93). See also decision of the Anti-monopoly Office of 30 September, 1993; Report on Competition Law and Policy in Poland (1990–3), paragraphs 56, 58, 60, 63. 'Imposing onerous contract terms' was originally a restrictive agreement offence. By the first amendment, this prohibition was moved from restrictive agreements to abuse of dominance, so that a dominant market position would be a necessary condition of the offence.
18. Spomlek, decision of the Anti-monopoly Office of 5 May 1992, reviewed by Anti-monopoly Court, 16 December 1992, reviewed by Supreme Court, 23 June 1993; Report on Competition Law and Policy in Poland (1990–3), paragraph 57.
19. An additional hardcore price-fixing case – artificial fertilizers – is noted in the report for 1995.
20. Report on Competition Law and Policy in Poland (1990–1993), paragraph 73.
21. Though some nations favour professional self-regulation, this can result in considerable exploitation of the public. Exploitative conduct by the pharmaceuticals industry, made possible by exclusionary restraints not justified by quality, has been the subject of cases in more than one Central European nation. (See below.)
22. Judgment of the Anti-monopoly Court of 6 July 1994 (XVII) Amr 8/94.
23. *Sugar* case, Judgment of the Anti-monopoly Court of 1 March 1993 (XVII Amr 37/92).
24. PZU, judgment of Anti-monopoly Court of 5 Sept. 1991 (XVII Amr 7/91).
25. Competition Law and Policy Report for 1990–3, paragraph 77.
26. 1994 Annual Report, paragraph 29. The opposite could be true, however; incentives to form a cartel may increase when demand falls.
27. *CATV* case, Case no. Vj-94 1993.
28. *Gas Default* case, Case no. Vj-125/1994.
29. Case no. Vj-16/1992; summary by Office of Economic Competition.
30. *Axel-Springer* case, Case no. Vj-139/1993; case study by Office of Economic Competition.
31. *MAV* case, Case No. Vj-72/1993/40.
32. See 30 note above. Some more recent cases have avoided the problem by finding no dominance. For example, Renault Hungary was held not to be in a dominant position and therefore not answerable to a disappointed dealer who wanted to be a principal wholesaler. Szabóki és Társa Ltd – Renault Hungaria Ltd, Renault Baumgartner Ltd, Case no. Vj-130/1995/20.
33. Case no. Vj-72/1993/40.
34. Case no. Vj-211/1993; summary prepared by Office of Economic Competition.
35. See *Tetra Pak International SA* v. *Commission*, Case T-83/91, [1995] ECR II- (CFI) (6 October 1994).
36. *Sugar* case, March 1993. See Annual Report on 1992 activities, paragraphs 78–80.

37. *Coffee* case, Case no. Vj-185/1994.
38. Case No. Vj-167/1992.
39. Case No. Vj-205/1992/9.
40. Unilver Magyarország Beruházási Ltd – Bajai Hûtôipari Ltd, Case no. Vj-219/1995/9; Mezôbank-Agrobank, Case. no. Vj-124/1995/21.
41. Dunapack Joint Stock Co. – Halaspack Joint Stock Co., Case no. Vj-27/1996/11.
42. Annual Report for 1993, paragraph 82.
43. Since dominance may be found at 30% market share, the line between merger to dominance and merger to tight oligopoly is blurred.
44. Case study prepared for the OECD, November 1992.
45. Case study prepared for the OECD, April 1993.
46. National Reports, report by Alena Cernejová, [1994] 4 ECLR R-125.
47. *Ibid.* The last two improvements – modernizing production and bringing new products on the market – are likely to be helpful to competition and efficiency in the Slovak Republic. Indeed, foreign acquirers are often best positioned to bring such structural advancements to the domestic market.
48. Almost immediately after expressing his views, Kovac was dismissed from his post. Kovac contended that his dismissal was politically motivated ('Slovak refiner will have dominance in gasoline filling stations', *Bureau of National Affairs Antitrust and Trade Regulation Report*, 15 June 1995, vol. 68, p.797).
49. See e.g., the *CATV* case (Hungary) on page 123, the *Ruch* case (Poland) on page 120 and the *Czech Insurance* case on page 130.
50. See note 14 for a definition.
51. Our sample does not include Polish cases, reports of which were not available to us.
52. Cases 56, 58/64 [1966] ECR 299. *Consten and Grundig* and its progeny stand for the proposition that the law must protect intra-band competition in the form of parallel imports across Member State lines regardless of the strength of inter-brand competition and of the need for (e.g.) protection against free riders in the interests of efficiency. The protection of parallel imports is deemed essential to increase market integration.
53. A Green Paper on Vertical Restraints, European Commission, is expected in 1996.
54. The EC Merger Regulation expressly addresses only 'dominance'. While the Commission has held that the Merger Regulation covers merger to oligopoly that impairs competition (Nestlé/Perrier, Kali + Salz, Impala Platinum (Gencor)/Lurcho), this principle is being contested in the Court of First Instance and the Court of Justice.

7

The Coverage of Policy

To the extent that external and internal market pressures for competition may be weak in transition economies, policies to encourage and set standards for competition are all the more necessary. In the context of transition, it is especially important that the scope of policy be broad, covering all sectors of the economy, and that a credible and internally consistent policy emerges.

Competition policy rarely applies to all sectors of the economy uniformly and consistently, usually because of conflicts with other policy objectives, concerns about safety or political factors. In various jurisdictions, any of agriculture, banking, printing currency, state-owned enterprises, professional services, taxis, etc. may not come under the aegis of the competition agency. The exemption may be legal, possibly with a different agency responsible, or may arise *de facto* because of lack of effective powers. Even if a different agency is responsible for competition, say in banking, it is not always clear whether the same standard of competition is being applied, and even less clear what is the reason if not.

In transition economies, the set of possible conflicts may be greater, because competition policy may often be perceived to be in conflict with some aspect of transition itself. For example, industrial policy arguments about national champions, i.e. building domestic firms large enough to be world players, are likely to be encountered in transition economies at least as much as in established market economies. Even more likely are arguments that firms need trade protection while they restructure and become efficient and competitive. A typical consequence of such an argument being accepted is the creation of a trade barrier or the exemption of a company (or industry) from competition policy. Another example might be the privatization process. In any economy, there is a trade-off between privatizing firms into competitive markets and privatizing them into monopolistic markets and earning increased revenues from the sell-off. In transition economies, there is more privatization to be undertaken and greater fiscal pressure to raise revenue so that the consequences for competition could be a whole order of magnitude greater if a different point on the trade-off is chosen.

7.1   Exemptions and Special Treatment

Sectors or activities may be partially or wholly exempt from competition policy, either by separate legislative or institutional arrangements or as a result of a competition agency's decisions. Such exemptions generally reflect the priority given to policy objectives other than competition. In some cases unrestricted competition may be unworkable for safety or organizational reasons (e.g., broadcasting, banking, medical services) and in others it may be workable but considered undesirable because other objectives, such as employment or equity, are more important (e.g. heavy industry, agriculture). The granting of any exemptions may create incentives for enterprises or sectors to engage in wasteful rent-seeking activities, especially if the criteria by which sectors or activities are exempt are not clear.

Exemptions or special rules for specific sectors or activities exist in all Visegrád countries, although there is some variation in their magnitude and effect. The broad features, and individual treatments, are as follows:[1]

1. Agricultural production, but not downstream distribution, may not come under the competition offices by virtue of being overseen by the relevant ministry.[2] No other sectors are similarly exempt *qua* sector. In Hungary, the Ministry of Agriculture is authorized to foster workable markets for agricultural products, taking account of the provisions of the anti-monopoly law. Thus it must take into account the same considerations that the competition office would have done when it sets quotas or prices, although this does not ensure consistency of treatment. In the Czech Republic, decisions have been made against beet and oilseed producers in particularly blatant cases of horizontal price-setting and in Poland agricultural cooperatives cases have featured.
2. The competition offices appear to have limited power in preventing national and local government from issuing licences that restrict entry and competition, that is, in controlling regulatory barriers to entry.[3] There have been incidents where decisions on licences for taxis (several countries), importation (Hungary and Slovakia) and foreign exchange trading (Slovakia) have been considered to be anti-competitive. In the area of broadcasting, licencing decisions are currently been taken and it is not clear what role, if any, competition offices have in such decisions. In all countries, the office can require the state administrative body to change a decision, but this requirement is not binding on the body.[4]

3. In each country, separate legislation exists enabling chambers and professional associations to organize. Although this legislation does not enable overt anti-competitive behaviour such as fixing prices or dividing markets, safety requirements or qualification standards could consciously be tailored to create barriers to entry.[5] Given the possible conflict between laws, powers of competition offices in this area may be inadequate.

4. Patents exempt the holder from competition policy purview, although the effect of a patent on competition may be examined.[6] More generally, procedures for the protection of intellectual property and trademarks and the exemption of research joint ventures in competition policy are less well developed, although guidelines and new legislation are being prepared in most countries.

5. Companies are not exempt by virtue of their ownership, so that the law applies equally to public and private enterprises. It is not possible to say whether state-owned enterprises still face soft budget constraints or other subtle state aids which may not be challenged by the competition offices. The use of a *de minimis* rule on national and local geographical markets indicates a uniformly consistent approach across all markets regardless of sector or size.

6. Individual markets or enterprises have occasionally been exempt from competition policy in some cases on an individual basis. Car production has been particularly prone to such exemptions. The most notable case is that of Skoda, where a foreign investor, Volkswagen, negotiated trade protection with the government as a precondition for investment. This resulted in a dominant position for Skoda in both the Czech and Slovak Republics, as there was a free-trade agreement between them.[7] It is sometimes argued that domestic firms need to be protected from competition from more efficient firms from abroad in order to invest, restructure and become more efficient. To the extent that this argument is valid, there is a trade-off between short- and long-run competition.

7. There is no evidence of exemptions resulting from self-restraint or neglect by the competition agencies. If anything, the greatest pressure against exemptions in general would appear to emanate from the competition offices and conflicts between competition offices and governments have been observed in all four countries. It is less clear from the case law considered above that the investigative efforts have always been directed towards the worst abuses of competition.

8. Exceptionally, in Hungary, the Office has no control over mergers involving foreign-registered firms.[8] This is based on the view that market structure is not affected by the sale of a firm to a foreign registered firm, although there could be an adverse effect if the foreign firm already was

owned by or owned a major competitor. This policy may also impede contestability in the sense that the alternative of buying a smaller existing firm might result in greater competition. This feature of the Hungarian legislation is currently under review.

In addition to exemptions, some sectors and activities may be partially protected from competition by tariffs and other trade barriers. In both Hungary and Slovakia, tariffs or surcharges have increased, thereby changing the relevant markets from international to national and, in some cases, creating dominance on the newly defined national market. A good example of the problem that this presents for competition offices is given by the FSO (passenger cars) case in Poland (see above).

The precise degree of exemption depends on whether competition offices have powers to intervene *ex ante* or *ex post*. *Ex ante* powers vary considerably and the ability of the competition office to have its views prevail in the drafting of such legislation is variable. Intervention before the relevant decision usually takes the form of a standpoint on the draft legislation and this is not binding in any way on the legislature, although it is an effective mechanism for alerting the competition office to potential trouble spots. In Hungary, the Office had considerable input in the legislation on professional chambers, and no problems have yet arisen, but has had its standpoints ignored in many other instances (see below). In Slovakia, proposals on changing the legislation on professional chambers and on the regulation of public utilities have not been heeded.[9] In all four countries, but especially the Czech Republic, the input from the heads of competition offices to new legislation, even before the drafting stage, is not observable as it takes place at high-level closed meetings. With regard to *ex post* powers, there are broadly three avenues for the competition office to take if it perceives a problem with competition. First, it may be able to apply the law in the usual way. Second, it may be able to challenge the government decision in the courts. Third, it may be able to mount a political campaign, either publicly or by discrete lobbying for a change in the policy.

Where the legislation creates a barrier to entry or restriction of supply, the application of the law in the usual way may not be effective.[10] There may be little the competition office can do without finding itself in the position of regulating prices, especially if other legislation appears to condone the activity. For example, if a state body decides that two licences are sufficient to serve a particular market, competitive conduct may still enable monopoly rents to be earned and the competition office would be powerless. The office may monitor such markets more closely than others and take action if they consider that conduct is clearly anti-competitive. In some cases, for example where dominance is increased by tariffs, this may work, although it is clearly second-best relative to the possibility of increased import competition. The Skoda experience in the Czech Republic supports this point.

In terms of legal action, the decision may be challenged in the courts. In Hungary, the Competition Office has right of action according to the administrative code under the competition legislation.[11] In two cases such action has been successful, one directly and the other indirectly. The direct case concerned a government proposal to authorize local authorities to restrict the number of taxi licenses and to impose other (e.g. price) regulations. The Competition Office argued that it was not necessary to restrain entry because the other regulations would suffice. This advice was rejected by the parliament but a subsequent Constitutional Court ruling effected the Competition Office advice.

The indirect case involved competition between private news vendors and the post office (which previously had a monopoly in this activity). A local authority had imposed charges for street space on the private firms but not on the post-office vendors. This was allowed by the Postal Act, so the Office initiated a constitutional case to determine the legality of the Postal Act. Meanwhile, the government revised the Postal Act, removing the protecting provisions, and this avoided the constitutional court case. In the other countries, an equivalent right does not appear to exist.

There is a legal time limit of six months within which the Hungarian Office can challenge the decision of state administrative bodies, and the Office may not challenge formal decisions of the government. No other office has challenged exemptions in such a way, although legal routes may be available for use in the future. In Slovakia, private action under Article 55 of the constitution is possible (see Chapter 2) but no action has yet been brought.

On the political side, the competition office may engage in public criticism of or debate on a government policy. This has happened in several cases, most notably when there have been proposals to increase tariffs, either in general or on specific goods. The Slovak and Hungarian offices argued vigorously, publicly and unsuccessfully against general tariff or surcharge increases.[12] Where a decision of the government is perceived to affect *fair* competition and where the fiscal consequences are not great, the competition offices may have more success in the public debate.[13] The Slovak Office challenged subsidies for firms purchasing inputs from specific suppliers, and this led to a public debate in the media which was supportive of the competition office position.

Lobbying the government quietly may be a more effective political weapon, and is less observable. Advice from the Slovak Competition Office regarding taxi licensing has not been heeded and Competition Office objections in 1994 to 10% surcharges against imports from the Czech Republic (see above) were not accepted. This is a common phenomenon. Direct negotiation with the relevant authority has also worked: the Czech Minister successfully negotiated with several municipal authorities concerning taxi licences.

7.2   Regulation of Natural Monopoly

Natural monopoly is a special case where an industry may be exempt from competition policy or subject to a different standard of competition.[14] In network industries (e.g. utilities such as telephony, gas, electricity, railways) of the transition economies, both the networks and the service providers are owned[15] and regulated by the state. Only Hungary has a clear and transparent regulatory rule whereby prices are allowed to increase exactly with the industrial price index of the previous year. Otherwise regulation is implicit, with 'special rules' on the development of the industries. It is not clear that the special rules for these industries prioritize competition policy concerns (e.g. access, excessive pricing, tied-selling, etc.) so that there is no consistency of treatment with other industries or, where appropriate, similarity[16] of treatment with other firms.

Competition offices can and do intervene in markets where there is natural monopoly. Uniquely in Poland the Office plays a major role in regulating public utilities. In particular, it can prohibit practices it considers undesirable, force price reductions (in either access or final prices),[17] restructure companies or force divestitures and impose fines.

In the other countries, natural monopoly cases only arise in the event of a complaint of abuse of dominance. In the absence of explicit regulation, competition offices have been relatively vigilant in this area and there are many cases of abuse of dominance against public utilities. Cases involving state monopolies (which include natural monopolies) have been running at approximately 5 to 10 per year in each of the Visegrád countries (Table 7.1).

Table 7.1   Statutory monopoly cases before competition offices

	Czech Republic	Hungary	Poland	Slovakia
Cases since 1991	35[a]	51	256	33
Decisions	2	17	256	33
No violation	na	3	136	23
Violation	na	14	120	10
Action of competition office	Cease abuse	Cease abuse	Cease abuse	na
Action upheld	na	3	45[b]	na

Sources: Annual reports and communications with competition offices.
Notes:
This category includes at least postal services, telecommunications, gas, electricity, railways and sewage disposal.
[a]For 1994 only.
[b]From 73 appealed decisions.

Typical markets involved have been those for energy generation, postal services, telecommunications and railways. The issues have concerned excessive pricing and restriction of entry into downstream markets by, for example, tied-selling of appliances. However, the offices are in a weak position and even in Poland, where the brief of the Competition Office explicitly includes regulating the conduct of public utilities, the *de facto* powers of the Office are weak.[18] In Slovakia, for example, the Office has not been able to prevent the tied selling of telephones and electrical appliances despite wishing to do so.

Plans to introduce explicit independent regulation of natural monopoly are as yet undeveloped. A proposal to develop a system of independent regulators along United Kingdom lines was presented to the Slovak Government in 1994, but was rejected. This proposal and the existence of price-cap regulation in Hungary suggests that the United Kingdom model may be a likely future development. Janínski (1995) has proposed a system of regulation that would have anti-monopoly offices regulate both final prices and access charges for service providers. However, competition offices may, with some justification, shy away from regulation of natural monopoly during the transition period so as to limit any possible identification as price control offices. A central question to be addressed is whether, in the event of a system of independent regulators, competition law will apply additionally to regulated enterprises.

7.3   Privatization

Privatization decisions may adversely affect competition in several ways. First, a dominant or monopoly enterprise may be privatized without being restructured horizontally (i.e. broken up) even though this is feasible, resulting in the persistence of concentration. Second, a non-dominant enterprise may be sold to its main competitor, thereby increasing concentration. In both cases, the receipts for the privatization agency will be higher, the more concentrated the market is after privatization, especially if potential entry and import competition were weak. The agency may also face pressures from other policy objectives, such as the arguments about national champions or the managed development of strategic or declining industries.[19]

In each country the competition office has a role in offering opinions on the effects of privatization on competition, but in no country can it overrule the decision of the privatization agency although the Polish Office has the power to order a restructuring if annual sales exceed 5 million ECU (there was no limit before April 1995). With the exception of Hungary, competition offices are routinely involved in approving privatization decisions, usually being asked for their opinion if the *ex post* market share

Table 7.2 Competition office opinions on privatizations

	Czech Republic	Poland	Slovakia
Opinions since 1991	2000	1500	2500
Approved	1900	1200	90%
Opposed	100	300	10%
Opinion accepted where opposed	100	Mostly[a]	Not known

Sources: Annual reports and communications with competition offices.
Notes:
In Poland and Slovakia, the interaction between competition offices and privatization agencies procedure is confidential.
[a]There have been very few cases where the AMO's opinion has not been accepted, although these cases may have had a high profile.

would exceed some critical value (e.g. 30% in the Czech Republic). As the data in Table 7.2 indicate, each of these three offices has dealt with a very large number of privatization cases, especially in comparison with the other work.

The overwhelming majority of privatizations has been approved by the competition offices (see Table 7.2). The criteria by which they are approved are not discernible, as the opinions are not published, but all claim that market concentration is always the motivating factor. However, it is not possible to evaluate the standard or consistency of approvals. The Polish Office has objected to more privatizations and has advocated further restructuring.

Where a privatization is opposed, enforcement of the competition office's viewpoint varies. The Polish considers it has been effective in achieving restructuring that is beneficial to competition prior to privatization: almost all oppositions have been successful, but in a few cases the order was not complied with or was complied with after the time limit imposed. The fact that the Polish Office also has the power to break-up firms after privatization may strengthen its hand *ex ante* in getting its recommendations accepted. In the Czech Republic, disputed cases generally go to the government, and the resolution of the trade-off is not explicitly observed. In Slovakia, the proceedings of the National Property Fund are not published and it is not known to what extent the opinions of the Competition Office are taken on board.

In Hungary, the institutional situation is completely different. In the framing of competition policy, a deliberate decision was taken not to give the Competition Office a role in privatizations in order to increase political consensus over the role of competition policy. Only privatization cases which are captured by the merger thresholds must be notified to the Competition Office for formal approval. In this way, the Competition Office is involved only in cases where concentration is strictly increased, rather than just being maintained. The privatization board is required more generally to have regard to competition policy legislation and this is formalized by inviting a representative of the Competition Office to sit on the privatization board.

Only 11 privatization cases have arisen and only in one was the merger prohibited.[20] In about 70 other cases, the informal opinion of the Competition Office has been offered and, in the vast majority of these, the opinion has been that there is no great effect on competition. In one case the Competition Office was unhappy with the procedure used in a privatization where a competitor was the successful bidder but the Competition Office was obliged to accept the outcome, given the procedure used. As a result, it has recommended that closed tenders be used in the privatization process to exclude firms with a strong position in the market from bidding.[21]

Generally, the privatization board appears to have a good understanding of the trade-off between allocating a company to the highest bidder and fostering competition and usually take this into consideration in deciding whether to accept the highest bid. There is no evidence that growing fiscal pressure in Hungary has altered this trade-off. The major criticism of the Hungarian system is the fact that foreign firms buying domestic ones are not considered to have any effect on competition if market concentration is unchanged.[22] It is proposed to repeal this part of the legislation, however, in the light of the evidence that entrants have been weak in challenging incumbents. It seems false to presume that a foreign firm buying a domestic firm has no effect on competition if concentration is not effected. It might be desirable instead to 'encourage' foreign firms to invest in non-dominant firms.

7.4   Industrial Policy

Another reason competition policy may not apply is if the government gives priority to industrial policy objectives that conflict with competition policy. Generally industrial policy targets specific industries (or firms) for special treatment with the intention of encouraging the growth of that industry. Typical policy instruments include advantageous tax rates (known as fiscal privilege), direct subsidies, tariff protection and exemption from competition policy (or other regulation).

The case law indicates that industrial policy objectives creep into competition policy decisions, as with mergers being approved subject to meeting certain employment objectives. Explicit industrial policy is less developed by Western standards and industry lobbies are still only forming. That which does occur is idiosyncratic and non-recurring. It is also argued that financial constraints and the memory of central planning makes industrial policy unfeasible and politically unpopular.[23]

In Hungary, industrial policy is largely directed towards crisis management and industries with specific structural problems like coal and railways. The main planks of industrial policy are a ten-year tax holiday for car manufacturers, a substantial direct and indirect subsidy to the steel industry and a system of free ports that exempts certain trades from taxation.[24] No industrial policy arguments have successfully been put forward for differential surcharges or tariffs. In Poland, industrial policy is applied in several industries, namely electric power, mining, metallurgy, armaments, rail transport and agriculture.

7.5   Other Areas

7.5.1   Public Procurement

Legislation on public procurement exists in all four Visegrád countries. Only in the Czech Republic does the office implement this legislation. The existence of low thresholds means that the workload of the office is great, although there are proposals to increase these thresholds.[25] In Slovakia, the law dates from 1993 and is implemented by the Ministry of Transport. The Competition Office had a central role in preparing the legislation but has no role in implementing it. The Hungarian law dates from 1995 and established a Council on Public Procurement under the aegis of the Ministry for Industry and Trade.[26] This Council is now operating and one member is an expert from the Competition Office. The Competition Office has a direct role if there is bid rigging or collusion. The Polish Office has no role under the Procurement Act 1994 and there have been no cases under the new Article 4 of the Anti-monopoly Act.

7.5.2   State Aids

In terms of state aids, all four countries are in the process of developing rules to implement a state-aid regime and in each case it is expected to be the Ministry of Finance, rather than the competition office, which will have the responsibility for making decisions and reports to the EU as required under the Association Agreements. It is expected that competition offices will be able to comment on state aids where these distort competition, but the extent to which any such comments will be binding is not yet clear.

7.5.3   Anti-dumping

The state of anti-dumping legislation (i.e. covering cross-border competition) varies. Both Hungary and Poland have enacted legislation and the Czech and Slovak Republics are currently preparing legislation and the competition offices have an advisory role. Implementation is external to the competition offices (Ministry of Industry and Trade in Hungary, Ministry of International Economic Competition and Ministry of Finance in Slovakia), although the Polish Office does participate in decisions and refers to its price-predation law as anti-dumping. Anti-dumping provisions have not yet been much used and it has been suggested to us informally that investigations of dumping claims tend to take a very long time to be completed. If true, this suggests that the rigour of implementation, rather than the actual legislation itself, is the most important determining aspect of anti-dumping provisions. This contrasts with the very rigorous approach of the EU.[27]

7.6   Assessment

How good is the coverage of competition policy in transition economies? The answer is very mixed. In some areas it conforms very well, in others it conforms less well but not so differently from many established market economies, and in others there are problems specific to transition economies that have yet to be resolved.

The picture is best in terms of the general applicability of the competition legislation to most sectors of the economy and to most enterprises (regardless of ownership), the exemption of research joint ventures and the rules on public procurement. The rigour with which competition offices seek to apply the law to all sectors and with which most of them advocate competition wherever possible suggests that competition policy, in practice, reaches all the sectors and activities that it can and that gaps in coverage are formal rather than implicit. In areas such as public utilities and state aids, policy is still developing but there is no reason to believe that sectors will be excluded.

In some areas, the full force of competition law does not apply because separate legislation or regulations designed for safety or organizational objectives (such as licensing and professional associations) are susceptible to 'capture' by the regulated groups. Although this is not very different from the situation that prevails in many industrialized economies it is undesirable, and enabling the competition offices to have greater powers in these areas would be a welcome development in improving the coverage and uniformity of policy.

With privatization, the competition offices play a secondary role of official observer, aware of potential problems but without the power to prevent them, suggesting that competition policy itself is of secondary importance in this area. Although conflicts have been relatively rare, those that have occurred tend to be extremely politically or economically sensitive. If competition and other policies facilitate entry into markets and foster competition more generally, or if competition offices have strong *ex post* powers (such as those to break up firms), this may be less of a problem. However, where the privatization process does not give priority to demonopolization, with the exception of Poland, the competition offices lack adequate powers to deal with this problem either at the time of the privatization or subsequently. Indeed, it may not even be possible for them to raise the issue in the public domain.

Regulatory barriers to entry are also a concern, and while the offices have tried to challenge professional organizations and local government, their overall success in the area has been mixed. Their powers would be considerably enhanced if regulations that might create barriers to entry had first to have competition office approval, via a transparent procedure.

The greatest difficulty for competition policy would appear to be the potential conflict with industrial and trade policies. Although trade liberalization has generally assisted competition, there have been cases where general or specific increases in tariffs or surcharges have increased dominance. Protection for specific industries (either by trade measures or exemption from competition policy) is especially worrying because of the rent (and rent-seeking) that it creates, and there is evidence that it may be on the increase.[28] Although this is not so different from the situation in the EU, the transition economies are in a unique position of having a fresh playing field. Thus exemptions from competition policy for specific sectors should be resisted strongly. In fact, approximation to EU competition policy acts as a very weak constraint in this area, agriculture and cars being just two quite different examples of where EU practice may not be an ideal target.

Competition offices and policy face an uphill struggle in coming years, largely for political economy reasons. At present the coverage of competition policy is good and growing, but any reversal in this trend could tend to avalanche, leading to damaging rent-seeking behaviour in the design of the coverage of competition policy, either by restricting powers of competition offices or exempting specific sectors. The experience to date suggests that the pressure will be strongest where the interests of pressure groups are most closely aligned with fiscal constraints, so that protectionist trade policies may have the greatest impact on competition policy, especially as the full impact of trade liberalization has not been felt. If so, the need for strong domestic policy, including greater resources for competition offices, is all the greater.

Notes

1. We do not mention exemptions that are standard and identical to those in established market economies, such as those for activities such as the printing of banknotes, lotteries and gaming, etc.

2. See Altrogge (1995) for a detailed discussion of competition policy approaches for agricultural product markets in CEECs.
3. Even despite what the law may say. Under Article 18 of the Czech Act on the Protection of Economic Competition the organs of state administration and the organs of municipalities may not, by their own measures, support or in other ways restrict or exclude economic competition. The Ministry of Economic Competition may require a correction on the part of these organs, but it is not clear that this requirement is enforceable.
4. For example, in the Czech Republic under Article 18 of the Act on the Protection of Economic Competition the organs of state administration and the organs of municipalities may not, by their own measures, support, or in other ways restrict or exclude economic competition. The Ministry of Economic Competition may require a correction on the part of these organs but there is no method of enforcing this requirement.
5. In Poland, decisions of the Anti-monopoly Court suggest that conduct permitted by special legislation (e.g. that governing Chambers) cannot be considered monopolistic. In Slovakia, the Supreme court could decide on the priority of the laws, but there has been no case yet.
6. In the Czech Republic, Article 4 of Act 63/1991 says that patents and trademarks are not valid if the restraint exceeds what is necessary to protect property rights. A similar approach obtains in Hungary, where the international intellectual property rights convention (TRIPS) has been developed. In Poland, there is an exclusion under Article 3.1, provided Article 3.2 can be applied (and detailed guidelines are published in the *Bulletin*, p. 36, 1994). Slovakia is still preparing guidelines.
7. See also comments on pages 34, 119, 122 and 168 regarding different competition issues in the car market. A competition case involving Skoda is discussed on page 129.
8. This is an interpretation by the Competition Council of the existing law and the current amendment proposes a change in the law.
9. Poland and the Czech Republic have had more success in cases in this area. The Polish Office decided against the association of funeral directors and pharmacists and the Czech Ministry found against the society of pharmacists (where excessive registration fees for non-pharmacists were intended as a barrier to entry).
10. Experience suggests the competition offices may have strongest *ex post* powers against overt price-setting and barriers to entry imposed by industry participants. The Czech Republic found the society of pharmacists guilty of restricting entry and found producers of beet and oilseed guilty of price-fixing.
11. Article 61 gives the President of the Office the right of consultation on discussions relating to the scope of the duty of the Competition Office. Article 63 gives the Competition Office the right to bring an action (under the Administrative Code) to the courts and request a review of a decision if an action of some state authority infringes on the freedom of competition. This procedure was used once in the case of refuse collection. The Office also has the opportunity to bring an action to the Constitutional Court to clarify a case in the sense of Articles 9 and 70/A of the Constitution if the office's opinion was not sought or attention was not paid to some legislation relating to competition.
12. In Hungary, the Competition Office even isolated markets where it believed that the increase in duty would create or increase dominance, but the proposal was still rejected.
13. In Hungary in 1992, a certain type of motor vehicle with specific technical characteristics was exempted from increased customs duty. The technical conditions characterized only the Ford Transit and the competitors complained to the Competition Office. As the draft rule had not been sent to the Competition Office for its standpoint by the competent offices (the Ministry of Industry and Trade and the Ministry of Finance), the Competition Office published its own opinion in the newspapers and threatened to bring an action against these ministries at the Constitutional Court. The ministries withdrew the exemption before the matter got to court.
14. There are few statutory monopolies that are not natural monopolies, but the printing of money and postage stamps, legal certification processes, hospital drugs and dangerous chemicals are often undertaken by statutory monopolies without an economies of scale justification.
15. Although fiscal and other pressures have meant that some governments have sold many shares in such companies, in general they retain majority ownership and control.

16. In the sense of Article 90 of the Treaty of Rome.
17. Exceptionally, public radio and television are regulated separately and the Anti-monopoly Office has no role.
18. Janínski (1995, p. 234) notes that 'the results are disappointing partly because of the lack of qualified staff and partly because other acts of Parliament excessively restrict the areas open for investigation and intervention'.
19. Other policy conflicts may exist. In Slovakia, Prime Minister Meciar's cancellation of a coupon-privatization programme in June 1995 may have restricted competition in corporate control. See King (1995).
20. The case where the merger was prohibited was the Gasztrolánc student catering case (VJ-172/1994).
21. This case involved the largest (publicly owned) champagne company being acquired by the second (privately owned company) which was the sole bidder, resulting in a market share of over 60%. The failing firm defence was accepted (perhaps *ex post*) by the privatization board, against the OEC advice.
22. Another case raised geographical issues of jurisdiction and market definition. It involved the purchase of the major cable manufacturing company by the Austrian Siemens, owner of the same facility in Austria and Slovakia. Although there was no effect on domestic concentration, there were concerns for regional competition, especially as Seimens offered twice the price of the nearest bidder.
23. Lavigne (1993) points out that there are no schemes for organizing the decline of whole sectors, for promoting small- and medium-sized enterprises, or for encouraging R&D or modernization that normally characterize industrial policy. Instead, trade policy has been used to substitute for industrial policy, as, for example, with devaluation to encourage exports and increasing tariffs to protect infant industries.
24. Hare's (1994) account of industrial policy in Hungary highlights some general policy dilemmas facing transition economies. Balázs (1994) argues that the lack of systematic policy towards research and development in Hungary has arisen because the government focuses excessively on short-term crisis management. All four countries' policy towards R&D is guided strongly by the EU via its TACIS and PHARE programmes. As of 1995, they became full and equal participants in the EU's R&D agreement.
25. The thresholds are 100000 CZK (2900 ECU) for movable items and 500000 for fixed items (e.g. buildings).
26. Although some state activities of a commercial nature come under the Competition Act, state purchases do not.
27. This includes the Article 113 committee which is particularly vigilant in the calculation of value-added by country of origin and the imposition of duties accordingly.
28. At present, pressure exists in Slovakia for reduced tariffs on car imports from countries other than the Czech Republic (where they are zero), and there have in fact been reductions for some classes of cars. Beer producers in Slovakia have also been lobbying for tariff protection against the Czech Republic. In Hungary, the unstated policy admits to the existence of a trade-off between short- and long-run competition and may be prepared to accept some protectionist tariffs in industries where exposure to international competition would be damaging.

8
The Performance of the Institutions

This chapter evaluates the performance of the institutions that enforce competition policy, dealing specifically with the political independence and accountability of the competition offices which, in turn, leads to a discussion of the overall credibility and consistency of competition policy.

8.1   Political Independence of the Competition Offices

The political independence of competition offices depends upon many factors and varies considerably across the four countries. The first important aspect of political independence concerns the terms upon which people in the competition offices with executive responsibility are appointed and the ease with which such a person can be replaced (see Table 5.7). By this criterion it is clear that Hungary's Competition Office has the greatest independence of the four, Slovakia's the least, with those of Poland and the Czech Republic somewhere in between. The President of the Hungarian Office is a civil servant appointed for a fixed six-year term and may only be removed by a vote of Parliament: there has therefore been only one president since the Office was established in 1990. The Chairman of Slovakia's Anti-monopoly Office is appointed by government and may be removed at any time: the AMO has had five presidents since its foundation. Its fourth Chairman resigned following a dispute[1] with the government in March 1995, a development that has clearly done damage both to the credibility of the agency and to its ability, if not willingness, to take on powerful interest groups. In May 1996, the Slovak AMO's sixth head was appointed.

The frequency with which the head of a competition office changes is, at best, an imperfect measure of political independence, since low turnover may indicate either substantial independence or an unwillingness on the part of the office to offend powerful interest groups. The Czech Ministry has had only one Minister since its foundation, but this Minister, though appointed for a four-year term and theoretically answerable to Parliament, is a full cabinet minister and is likely to be more sensitive than most to general political currents in the country. The Polish AMO is an interesting intermediate case, since its first president served for five years and took a number of controversial and difficult decisions, but resigned after a period of attempting to work with a new government. It is too early to tell what impact this may have had on the activities and the decisions of the office itself. It is nevertheless clear from the Polish case that formal political independence is far from being a necessary condition for a competition office to feel strong enough to take decisions that may offend the government. For example, the AMO took action against a newspaper distribution company (*Ruch*) that had been refusing its services to a publisher Mr Jerzy Urban, who was a vociferous critic of the government, even though it was clear that the AMO would have won many more powerful friends had it decided in Ruch's favour.[2]

A second measure by which we can assess the political independence of a competition office is the manner in which its budget is determined. Here there appears to be little difference between the countries: all four have budgets that are voted by parliament rather than decided by ministers. The budgets appear secure from year to year, although in several instances they have decreased in real terms over time while the output of and general demands placed on the competition offices have been increasing.

A third possible measure of political independence is the range of matters over which a competition office has direct decision-making power as opposed to the right of recommendation. Where an office has power of recommendation, it may choose to exercise that power more or less sparingly. Here there appear to be some interesting differences between offices. In the field of privatization, for example, the Polish Office has the right to take decisions on breaking up large firms before they are privatized. Other offices have only the right to express an opinion, and this right has been exercised very differently in different countries. Both the Czech and Slovak offices have expressed reservations about the privatization of a large number of enterprises, with mixed success. The Hungarian Office, by contrast, has made a negative recommendation in only one case. To some extent this represents an appropriate response to different objective conditions. As we saw in Chapter 2, Hungarian firms are, on average, much smaller and consequently much less likely to be in a dominant position after privatization.

But this difference in action also represents a different choice of political strategy by the offices concerned. The Hungarian Office has chosen to stay out of an area which it knows to be controversial and where its opinion is in danger of being ignored.[3] This suggests there may be something of a trade-off between political independence and the scope of an office's activities. The greater political independence of the Hungarian Office may partly reflect a different political consensus (due to the fact that Hungary's market reforms were further advanced by the time its office was established); but it also represents a different strategy of negotiation between the office and the other political interests with which it must co-exist.

The Hungarian Office is relatively independent in five regards. The head of the office is not a member of the government; is appointed for a fixed term; is not involved in or in a position to influence the outcomes of investigations; investigations are decided by members of the Competition Council who are nominated for life; and policy has been designed to restrict competition policy to non-sensitive areas (hence the different approaches to foreign-registered firms and privatization). At the other extreme, the Czech Ministry is fully integrated into the government and political system: the head of office sits as a full minister at government; he has influence over investigations and decisions; and the office plays a stronger role in approving privatizations At the time of writing there are proposals to transform the Czech Ministry into an independent agency, though it is too early to know if these will prevail. In Poland and Slovakia, an intermediate position prevails, with less independent roles for the heads of offices than in Hungary.

Paradoxically, it seems that the position of the head of the office is most secure at these political extremes, suggesting that an intermediate position may expose the heads of the office to political dispute or controversy without supplying them with the political power to fight their corner. This may be forcing the point somewhat, as the political power of the Czech Minister may derive from his status as member of a minority party supporting the government rather than as a full member of the government.

In its actual implementation, competition policy has involved substantially more controversy than in its initial legislative creation, precisely because competition policy often involves resisting the special pleading of interest groups who may find a more sympathetic ear in other branches of government. Here a degree of independence of a competition office from the interests and concerns of the rest of government is undoubtedly an advantage. However, our evidence has also indicated that formal political independence (in the sense of accountability to parliament rather than to the government) is far from being a necessary condition for independence in the more substantial sense. The Polish Office has been able to demonstrate considerable substantial independence in spite of having no formal independence. The Hungarian Office has complete formal independence, but the substantial independence it has displayed in the domain of its operation may have had something to do with the fact that this very domain has been more delimited than in the other countries (particularly through non-involvement in the privatization process, and through limited concern for matters involving vertical relations between firms).

None of this is to deny that increasing the degree of political independence of competition offices (subject to overall parliamentary accountability) would be of value in many circumstances. But the variation in the degree of effective independence that we observe across countries may well be a symptom rather than a cause of the varying degrees of commitment to the reform process. It is notable that the original draft of the Hungarian competition law of 1990 would have made the office responsible to the government rather than to parliament, and its president would have been appointed by the prime minister. It was precisely in order to achieve all-party consensus in the passage of the legislation that the terms of establishment of the office were changed. In other words, it was because the parties agreed sufficiently on the need for competition policy to be in a day-to-day sense 'above politics' that the office was given substantial independence; it was not a prior decision to grant independence that enabled competition policy to achieve this consensus. Thus substantial and operational independence may be enhanced by formal political independence, but it is naive to expect it to be created out of nothing by constitutional fiat.

8.2   Accountability of the Competition Offices

The competition offices of all four Visegrád countries publish their decisions in the national language and make them available free of charge to experts, law firms, enterprises and the general public, although the Czech Ministry has only very recently begun to publish all decisions; previously it merely issued press releases for more important cases.[4] Summaries are also prepared for press releases, especially regarding cartel and other cases that attract public interest. Important decisions are translated into English in each country, with the Hungarian and Polish offices translating up to 50% in whole or in part, with the selection of cases by the head of the executive division or the international department. In all Visegrád countries, an annual report is prepared and is translated into English.[5] Other publications include commentaries on the law (by the Ministry in the Czech Republic and privately in Poland) and theoretical statements which illustrate interpretations of the law. A regular competition bulletin is published (monthly) in Hungary and in Poland.[6] Reports are prepared for plenary sessions of parliament and for meetings of the OECD Competition Committee.[7] A criticism in some countries has been that the publications of the offices are not sufficiently widely available.

All decisions contain supporting reasoning of, on average, six to twelve

Table 8.1   Appeals against decisions of competition offices, 1992–4

	Czech Republic	Hungary	Poland	Slovakia	All
Numbers of appeals	27	67	167	3	265
1995	na	20	60	0	90
1994	10	19	49	1	79
1993	2	12	34	1	49
1992	5	16	24	2	47
Cases appealed					
Single firm	18	60	150	1	229
Merger	1	0	11	0	12
Cartel	7	4	5	1	17
Other	1	3	1	1	6
Outcomes					
Pending	9	49	3	0	61
AMO decision upheld	8	18	86	3	115
AMO decision rejected or modified	8	0	78	0	86

Sources: Competition offices.
Note:
For the Czech Republic and Slovakia, these data are for appeals to the Supreme Court, for Hungary to the Capital Court of Budapest, and for Poland to the Anti-monopoly Court (hence the high number).
For the Czech Republic and Slovakia, these data do not include 1995.

pages, with the length generally depending on the complexity of the decision. The actual content of the reasoning varies. Decisions of the Hungarian Competition Council give a full explanation of the decision from the complainants' and defendants' points of view whereas in the Czech and Slovak Republics each decision contains a statement of law, brief reasoning and instruction about the appeal process, as is required under the administrative code. A criticism that has been made of the content of decisions and reports is that where a competition office has taken decisions over time that may appear inconsistent, there has been insufficient attempts to issue clear guidelines and interpretations of the law.

The decisions of the courts reviewing competition office decisions have tended to clarify the law, with relatively few decision being altered or reversed.[8] Table 8.1 summarizes the appeals on which we have information, although again the reliability if these data is in doubt and they are not comparable across countries because of the different procedures. Generally the rate of appeal is rising.

There have been no reversals of competition office decisions in Slovakia, despite four appeals. An appeal takes four to five months. The figures reported in Table 8.1 do not include appeals against the initial decision of the AMO, of which there have been 22 in the four-year period, of which 20 concerned single-firm cases. Reversals of the decisions of the Ministry for

Economic Competition in the Czech Republic have been on procedural rather than substantive grounds.

In Hungary, appeals have reduced fines by 33% and cases can take up to two to three years. The court overturned decisions in some consumer protection cases but not in any competition cases. The cases where decisions were overturned were ones where there was a conflict between the competition law and other laws. In at least one instance, the Competition Office decision has been reversed at the first appeal level only to be restored at the higher appeal.[9] Fines are regularly reduced on appeal and the courts' decisions have not made clear a general rationale for this.[10] The delayed payment of fines and the prospective of a reduction in their nominal levels act as an incentive to appeal. The current amendment proposes to change the law in this regard.

In Poland there were 166 judgments by the Anti-monopoly Court to the end of 1995. Approximately 47% involved rejection or modification of the AMO decision, a rather high number. Approximately a third of this group concerns cases that were partly dismissed or overruled on procedural grounds. There have been three extraordinary appeals to the Supreme Courts of which two were dismissed and one was overruled and returned to the AMC (where its outcome is to be determined).[11]

In the Czech Republic there have been eight appeals of which two were accepted on procedural or legal grounds, one was refused, three were not decided, one was withdrawn and in a final case the procedure was stopped.

The final aspect of accountability we consider is the interaction between the offices and the other parts of administration. A significant amount of time in each office is taken up with the writing of position papers, known as standpoints, to draft legislation from government departments. Where there is a potential effect on competition, a detailed standpoint is prepared. Much time is also required to be spent on draft legislation that could have no possible effect on competition. External relations, both national and international, are also undertaken. Each office plays a very strong role in domestic competition advocacy, including publicity, lectures and seminars and media interviews following the issuing of important decisions. At the international level, reports are presented to the EU and the OECD, and papers are given at international conferences. Cases involving 'difficult problems' are summarized for discussion at six-monthly OECD workshops.

8.3   Consistency and Credibility of Policy

We have already outlined, in a necessarily sketchy way, some of the different factors that affect the ability of the offices to take and enforce decisions in favour of competition in the face of lobbying by powerful interest groups.

There can be little doubt that the Slovak office has been hampered by the lack of political backing for a consistently pro-competitive policy, as the 1995 Slovnaft oil merger case illustrates (see page 138). The Hungarian office, with greater political independence, has faced obstacles of a more judicial and technical character. An increasing proportion of cases in which fines were imposed on Hungarian firms have been appealed, which not only tends to lead to the reduction of nominal fines on appeal but also allows payment of the fines to be delayed until inflation has significantly reduced their real value.[12]

The value of political independence has also been somewhat ambiguous in matters concerning the actions of the state itself, especially in the field of licensing. Advice from the Hungarian offices regarding the deregulation of the taxi market was ignored by the government, but the Czech Ministry negotiated deregulatory measures with several municipal authorities.

There is nevertheless evidence, particularly in Poland and Hungary, that the competition offices have been able sometimes to play an important role as a voice for competition even in areas where their counterparts in market economies have little influence. This has been particularly important in foreign trade, as illustrated by two cases involving cars.

In Poland in 1991 the AMO sought and failed to prevent a price increase by a domestic car manufacturer that was believed to be in a monopolistic position (discussed above). Having failed to do so, the AMO 'initiated a formal procedure concerning a relaxation of import barriers for cars. This was in fact done by the government, and imports increased rapidly, bringing a stronger demand barrier on the domestic market' (Fornalczyk, 1993, p. 42).[13] In Hungary, in 1992, a certain type of vehicle with defined technical specifications was exempted from a rule increasing customs duties on cars. As these technical specifications in fact characterized only the Ford Transit, competitor firms complained to the competition office, which had not been consulted on the relevant import tariffs by the competent authorities (the Ministry of Industry and Trade and the Ministry of Finance). The competition office conducted a vigorous campaign against the rule, including publication of its own opinion in the newspapers and threatening to bring an action against these ministries in the Constitutional Court, as a result of which the duty exemption was withdrawn.

For competition offices to conduct such a vigorous campaign against official government policy is hard to imagine in established market economies, and suggests that it is important to view the 'success' of competition not just in the narrow terms of the actions that the competition offices themselves undertake but also in their influence in promoting competition much more broadly throughout the economy, and their role as a voice for competition among the cacophony of special interests. By these standards there have been some impressive achievements. There is also much to be done. As the former President of the Polish AMO commented wryly in 1993:

> Over two years, the Polish government has commenced numerous restructuring programmes in various fields of the economy. The authors of these programmes have tried to avoid discussion of competition problems. Nobody likes competition in his own backyard (Fornalczyk, 1993, p.39).

In all four countries, communication between the competition offices and the other institutions of the state is good. In general, there are several channels of communication open and most competition offices use all of these where possible. The heads of each office play an active part in overall economic policy. The requirement to prepare detailed written standpoints on draft legislation is especially important in this context. Formal and informal communication between officials occurs in Hungary,[14] Slovakia and Poland,[15] but is undertaken solely by the minister in the Czech Republic. Such representational communication is largely uni-directional, so that officials of the trade departments and privatization agencies have no analogous role in competition policy. However, other departments are required to give standpoints to changes in competition law, and it is possible for heads of other agencies or government departments to express their views to the head of the competition office. In Poland and Hungary, the independence of the Anti-monopoly Court and Competition Council, respectively, would prevent any influence being brought to bear on the decisions of these bodies. The same cannot be said unambiguously for the Czech Republic and Slovakia.

Where a policy that affects competition requires new legislation, the competition office is in a much stronger position to comment, both via the head of the office at the economic or government committee and via standpoints on the draft. As discussed above (Chapter 7), both these mechanisms have been used by competition offices in debates about increases in tariffs in several countries. Although the competition offices have generally been less than successful in stopping tariff increases, they have precipitated and contributed to public debates on the issue, increasing the transparency of the decision-making process.

The perception of competition policy within a country has a number of dimensions. First, it is necessary to distinguish between knowledge of the law and knowledge of the institutions. Second, although knowledge of law and knowledge of policy are prerequisite to understanding and appreciating them, appreciation (i.e. understanding that they can bring benefits) is more difficult to measure. Finally, it is necessary to distinguish between consumers, enterprises, public servants and experts in academia and professional practice.

Generally, it would appear that less than 50% of the population are aware of competition offices or legislation, except perhaps in the Czech Republic, where the status of a ministry may give it more 'air-play'. All four offices report consistent and substantial media coverage and that the coverage has been very favourable to the competition office side in most public debates.[16] They also believe that knowledge is growing among consumers, especially as consumer-protection and final consumer-goods cases (notably those concerning agricultural products) receive a great deal of media attention. As evidence of this they point out that that petitions are becoming better and more precise as time goes on and that, although poorly inspired complaints (often about price control) do arrive, especially in the Czech Republic, consumers also manage to make valid complaints on a regular basis, occasionally surprising the competition offices with their detailed knowledge and understanding of the law. Against this trend, the departure of the fourth Chairman of the Slovak office received considerable publicity, but it is not clear whether this exemplified Oscar Wilde's maxim that all publicity is good publicity.

Knowledge among enterprises, law firms and public servants is generally better than among the general public, but still mixed. In general, the presence of (any) foreign capital in a firm is highly positively correlated with awareness of the competition law. *Ceteris paribus*, the larger a firm, the more likely it is to be aware of the law, so that natural monopolies and dominant firms tend to be the best informed (with the possibility that forewarned is forearmed). Native lawyers are relatively unaware of and inexperienced in applying competition law. Courses have now been introduced in many universities' legal programmes so this is expected to change relatively quickly.

The appreciation of competition policy, that is, the acknowledgement that such policy can bring about benefits, is very mixed and may not always be moving in the same direction as knowledge about it.[17] In the public service, competition policy is sometimes held in low esteem, either because of a general poor view of pro-market reforms or because of the low status that competition offices have relative to ministries (the Czech Ministry argues that its esteem is very high because it is a ministry). Public and institutional support for competition policy is very weak in some countries, and this may strengthen the political constraints in the implementation of policy.

Lobby groups are not yet fully developed and in particular have not formulated clear policies on competition issues. Offices were asked to identify the most and least supportive groups and the answers are illuminating. The least supportive or cooperative groups were chambers of professional associations (in the Czech Republic), trade unions (in Hungary and Slovakia), multinationals (in Hungary), state-owned enterprises, enterprises in heavy industries, network industries and agricultural firms, especially agricultural cooperatives (in Poland). On the positive side, the Polish office considered that private firms and small firms were most supportive. Industry lobbies have so far kept simpler targets such as trade protection in their sights and have not yet argued for exemptions from competition rules. In some countries, political support is stronger from right-wing parties than from those on the left (even though distinguishing rhetoric from actual policy is difficult).

8.4   Assessment

The performance of the institutions is mixed.[18] On the positive side, we note the remarkable progress made thus far in attempting to put in place efficient and credible institutions to enforce competition policy. It is clear that the offices are relatively accountable, that they produce high quality output in several different dimensions and that they advocate competition policy in their own countries often with vigorous determination and in spite of powerful opposition. The competition offices appear to be staffed with enthusiastic and well-motivated officials, deeply committed to fostering competition. Good procedures have been put in place for institutional communication, so that the process by which policy trade-offs are made is reasonably transparent, except perhaps in the Czech Republic. This also gives the competition offices a stronger advocacy role in overall economic policy.

On the other hand, there are several reasons for concern. One is that the competition offices may not always do enough to establish clear and understandable guidelines and interpretations of the law. This may be due to the absence of internal evaluation procedures, that would compare how different investigators take decisions. The offices might consider instituting something along the lines of the Board of Experts of the Hungarian Office which tackles and issues statements on different methodological issues. The lack of separation of prosecution and investigation from decision-making creates concern about the quality of decision-making. This can result in the perception, perhaps mistaken, that the decisions reached depend more on the qualifications and preferences of the investigator than on a systematic basis and according to observable criteria. This problem is most serious in the Czech Republic and Slovakia where the immediate appeals procedure is internal. Unlike the first point, this is not something that the competition offices themselves have power to change. However, greater evaluation and refinement of the criteria used in making decisions and the publication and explanation of these criteria would go a long way to mitigate concern regarding the lack of separation of prosecution and decision-making. On a positive note, ministers of the government do not have a power of veto over competition office decisions.

We have also seen a number of ways in which the constraints imposed upon the competition offices by the pressures under which they were established have limited the effectiveness of their subsequent operations. The political weakness and lack of continuity in leadership of the Slovak office has limited its capacity to challenge powerful vested interests. The fact that the Polish office must spend so much of its time on the regulation of natural monopolies has diverted its resources and led to a confusion between the roles of price control and the policing of competition, the protection of competition and the protection of competitors. The Hungarian office has protected its independence by staying out of privatization, an area where the Polish experience suggests decisive intervention may be of considerable benefit. In these and other ways political constraints have been significant. As political circumstances change it may be valuable for the offices concerned to seek cautiously to transcend some of these constraints, and in doing so they may be able to learn useful lessons from each others' experience.

Our most serious concern about the institutions, however, is for the future. There is a great danger that the enormous progress that has been made this far may not be consolidated. To some extent this has been the case in Slovakia. Political interference in the workings of the competition offices can damage morale and, if it results in the departure of the head of the office or other senior executives, can have serious long-term repercussions on the entire organization. The loss of a significant proportion of its skilled personnel from any of the four offices would have serious repercussions on resource constraints and for the quality of competition policy. Given the external pressures in terms of approximation of the law, it is likely that any diminution of competition policy will result from weakening the institutions. This could be accomplished by requiring competition offices to investigate many relatively trivial cases, to keep them clear of potentially sensitive issues.

Notes

1. The dispute concerned an investigation into a proposed merger between the two leading distributors of fuel oil and petrol, a merger to which the Office was opposed but which was subsequently approved by the government. The *Slovak Economic Sheet*, May 1996, reports a 20% increase in annual net profit in the year in question.
2. The validity of this point is independent of our criticism of the decision (page 120).
3. This has been confirmed to us in personal communication.
4. No explanation has been forthcoming for this practice.
5. The Slovak Annual Report for 1994, with its use of clever cartoons, is illustrative of the commitment to competition that is found among the staff of all the offices.
6. The Hungarian Bulletin, *Versenyfelügyeleti Értesítő (Bulletin of Competition Supervision)* contains the decisions of the Competition Council. The table of contents is in four languages (Hungarian, English, French and German) and summaries of significant cases are written in English.

7. In Slovakia, the presentation by the Chairman of an annual report to the Committee for Economics, Business and Privatization of the Parliament was an annual event until 1994.
8. In the Czech Republic there have been eight appeals of which two were accepted on procedural or legal grounds, one was refused, three were not decided, one was withdrawn and in a final case the procedure was stopped. In Hungary, appeals have reduced fines by 33% and cases can take up to two to three years. The court overturned decisions in two consumer protection cases but not in any competition cases. In Poland there have been 129 judgments by the Anti-monopoly Court. In 1990–4, approximately 55% were dismissed, 30% overruled, 15% changed or partly dismissed or overruled on procedural grounds. There have been three extraordinary appeals to the Supreme Courts of which two were dismissed and one was overruled and returned to the AMC (where its fate is awaited). Finally, in Slovakia there have been four appeals but no decision was reversed. The delay is four to five months.
9. For example, in a Hungarian milk cartel case, the Capital Court reversed the Competition Office decision, but the Supreme Court restored the latter.
10. The cases where fines are reduced are more usually those where it has not been possible to calculate the damage caused, so the courts may be concerned with the fact that the legislation does not specify a limit to the level of fines in such cases. It is not inconceivable that the justification for high, especially exemplary, fines is not well-understood.
11. The data for the Anti-monopoly Court in Poland are perhaps more comparable with those for the Competition Council in Hungary (which rejects a minority of the conclusions recommended to it by investigators) and the internal appeals committees in the Czech Republic and Slovakia.
12. The success of this feature of the proposed amendment to the competition legislation may, more than any other element, indicate the extent to which producers' lobbies can effectively muster support against competition policy.
13. Dr Fornalczyk has also argued (personal communication) that this case established an important precedent for giving the AMO a voice in matters concerning tariffs and trade policy in general. 'We lost the battle but we didn't lose the war.'
14. In Hungary, there are representatives on the privatization agency and the committee on tariffs and planned for anti-dumping and state-aid committee. Legislation requires that the competition office be consulted on changes in import surcharges and on anti-dumping duties, although the office does not have a veto in these areas. The Office has no representation on the agricultural products committees.
15. The Polish Annual Report for 1995 gives an impressively long list of committees on which the office had representatives, including the privatization agency.
16. The cases that have inspired the most publicity have been car insurance, soccer cover in the media, the petrochemical privatization, and water and sewage charges in the Czech Republic; misleading advertising, cartels, mergers and abuse of dominance (in that order) in Hungary; and cartel dominance cases, import liberalization, restructurings, and the preparation of regulation in the energy sector in Slovakia.
17. This is admittedly an imprecise concept given that policy may differ from country to country.
18. We are aware of the possibility of capture: much of our information comes from the institutions that we are evaluating. We have used comparative data and obtained supplementary information from other confidential sources, to whom we are grateful for their help.

9

Conclusion

This book has discussed in some detail the role of competition policy in transition and described the competition laws and the institutions that enforce them in the four Visegrád countries – the Czech Republic, Hungary, Poland and Slovakia – the first to develop competition policies. It then examined and assessed the output and case law produced by the competition offices and the courts in those states, and evaluated the overall effectiveness of competition policy as it has emerged thus far.

Our insights and conclusions lie in three general areas: the role of competition policy in transition, the experience of these countries in developing competition policy, and recommendations. Our conclusions may also be of interest to those countries that are at an earlier stage in the transition process and which are currently forging their own policies on competition.

9.1   The Role for Competition Policy in Transition

We argued in Chapter 1 that competition policy, defined in a narrow sense to mean rules on the behaviour of firms (anti-trust rules), is desirable (even) in established market economies, given that anti-competitive behaviour occurs despite the existence of developed legal systems and the presence of relatively free trade and efficient capital markets. In transition economies, there are several additional arguments in favour of such competition policy.

First, those factors that typically encourage product-market competition in established market economies (such as free trade, efficient capital markets, effective systems of corporate control) still continue to be relatively ineffective in transition economies. The privatization process appears to have provided limited impetus for improved corporate control, at least where unaccompanied by an investment of foreign capital. The effect of foreign competition, in factor or product-markets, is constrained by both its low scale and its nature. A few firms (up to 20% in Hungary, but less elsewhere) have some foreign capital but foreign direct investment levels are low and are concentrated in a very small number of firms. Potential competition from imports is an inadequate substitute for domestic competition because of a variety of hidden barriers, some erected by government and some due to underdeveloped distribution systems.

Second, the market structures and behavioural habits may justify concerns that anti-competitive behaviour is more likely in many markets in transition economies. We saw in Chapter 2 that there is weak competition from new entrants, despite the fact that they are reasonably numerous. Capital market imperfections appear to be more significant in restricting the growth of small firms than in preventing their formation in the first place. In addition, foreign investment has primarily involved stakes in firms that are already market leaders, so that it does not assist entry.

Third, competition policy may improve the rate or quality of the transition process itself, bringing dynamic efficiency gains (via a feedback effect). Because the process of restructuring has not been as radical as was expected (e.g. there has been relatively little reallocation of resources across industries and little strategic restructuring by firms), the transition process is being driven to a large extent by product-market competition. In addition, the adoption of competition policy has not been controversial and therefore it has been relatively easy to fashion an early political consensus on competition policy when compared with other reforms.[1] As a result, competition policy may be desirable not only in itself but also as a means of building support for more contentious aspects of reform.

Thus the evidence is that the substitutes for competition policy that exist in an established market economy are absent in these transition economies and that competition policy has a role to play in improving the transition process itself. These are compelling reasons for competition policy to exist in addition to those that are typically advanced in an established market economy.

This evidence also points to a number of priorities for a competition policy in transition. It may need to emphasise cartel detection and market access, to ensure that the market can assist the process of demonopolization. Because of pressures to subvert competition policy to protect weak parties from competition, competition policy in transition should clearly distinguish between the treatment of monopolistic and cartel restraints (the priority of competition policy) and questions of fairness in contracts and industrial policy concerns. This can be achieved by creating a transparent system than enables the determination of the precise trade-off, perhaps with separate responsible bodies, and permits debate and evaluation about the particular trade-off chosen.

9.2   The System of Competition Policy in the CEECs

Each of the Visegrád countries in our study had adopted its legislation and established institutions to enforce it by 1991. Evidence is thus available on the operation of competition policy over a five-year period. This includes a substantial body of case law (over 1000 decisions), details of the operation of the competition offices and information on the development of competition policy. There are many differences between the countries, though in what follows we shall inevitably place particular emphasis on common features.

The laws adopted by each of the countries have reasonably close affinity with one another and with EC competition law. The amendments to the statutes have generally increased the affinity with EC law. In terms of the institutions that enforce these statutes, each country has chosen an administrative body subject to the reviewing courts. The formal political status of these institutions (and their executives) varies considerably.

The case law suggests that the interpretation of the statutes is fairly close in spirit to EU practice. An exception concerns the emphasis given to fairness issues. The statutes prohibit the imposition of onerous or disproportionate contract terms by dominant firms. The competition offices are often involved in allegedly one-sided bargains between parties, and they sometimes find the law to be violated where an adverse impact on competition is not adequately demonstrated, at least not in the reasoning of published decisions. The consequences of such a policy are considerable, given that a majority of all decisions issued by the competition offices over the last five years concerns alleged abuse of dominance. Moreover, such cases absorb a large share of the competition offices' resources, possibly at the expense of pursuing more serious types of anti-competitive behaviour. For instance, the sparseness of hardcore cartel cases is surprising, in view of the long history of cooperative behaviour in command economies among the very people who are now nominally competitors.

Almost all mergers have been permitted, and usually without restrictions. Those restrictions that have been imposed by way of remedy often reflect industrial policy considerations. Indeed, attention to industrial policy objectives often outweighs attention to competition issues, and it is usually not possible to observe what standards of competition are being applied by the competition offices.

Trade policy decisions such as the imposition of tariffs or surcharges (which frequently have an industrial policy motivation) have also affected competition, although in this case the procedure is more transparent. Although trade-policy considerations are often been a priority, the imposition of trade barriers has typically followed a debate in which the effects on competition have been represented, usually by the competition offices.

The competition offices of the Visegrád countries are broadly similar in their functions and in the constraints that they face. Each is responsible for investigating and deciding what competition proceedings to bring. The Hungarian office has additional responsibility for consumer protection and the Polish office for the regulation of natural monopoly. The most serious resource constraint facing the offices appears to be with regard to staff. The offices do not appear to be understaffed in terms of numbers, but they all face similar problems in retaining or recruiting sufficiently experienced professional staff, especially in the face of strong private sector demand. This is potentially a very serious problem for the future, given that the offices may not be able to retain those existing staff who are most experienced and could almost certainly not replace them on equivalent terms.

There is a substantial difference between the offices in regard to the procedures used in deciding cases. In Hungary, decisions are taken by a body that is independent of the investigator. In the other three countries, the investigator makes the first-level decision. Only in Poland is there an independent appeal body.

The dimensions of the political independence of a competition office are extremely complex, and the formal constitutional position of a competition office is only one of a number of factors determining its ability in practice to operate independently of day-to-day political pressures. The considerable *de facto* independence of the Hungarian office is due only partly to the independence of the members of its Competition Council (perhaps a more important feature than the fixed-term appointment of its president). It may also be due to the decision of the Office to stay out of certain politically contentious areas such as privatization. The Czech and Polish offices have been able to act over long periods with substantial *de facto* independence, though both offices have been subject at times to significant pressure in politically sensitive areas. The Slovak office is undoubtedly hampered by the lack of continuity in its leadership, and difficulties of carrying out decisions in the face of political pressures. The evidence suggests that formal independence of a competition office (that is, its answerability to a parliament rather than to a government) is desirable, but may also be difficult to achieve in the absence of political consensus on the role of competition policy in the economy. There is evidence that the pressures on competition agencies are increasing in all countries as interest groups become aware of the implications of their decisions for the distribution of economic benefits. Events in the next few years, or even sooner, may reveal more clearly the degree of the political independence of the offices.[2]

The coverage of the competition statutes in the Visegrád countries is similar to that in many established market economies. Standard exemptions apply for various markets, and the problems that the offices have in applying competition rules, for example, in the face of regulatory barriers to entry or in markets regulated by professional bodies, are very similar to those of competition offices in many other countries. It is particularly clear from the caseload of the offices that state-owned firms have been subject to investigation in the same way as privately owned ones.

The regulation of natural monopoly, and the implementation of public procurement rules and of rules for state aids are at different stages of development in all four countries. The Czech Ministry implements the public procurement rules and the Polish office is in effect the regulator of natural monopoly, but otherwise it is anticipated that these aspects of competition policy, broadly defined, will be the responsibility of other institutions. The competition offices are routinely consulted on development in these areas.

9.3   Recommendations

We make recommendations both to the four Visegrád countries and to EU policy-makers. Before making these suggestions, we would like to emphasize the extraordinary progress that has been made so far, and to acknowledge the leading role that the competition offices and their staff have made, despite enormous obstacles. Moreover, to the extent that our recommendations appear critical, similar recommendations could be made in respect of competition policy in many established market economies.

For the Visegrád countries, there is much that the competition offices could do within the existing structure of the institutions, particularly with regard to case analyses. There is room for improvement in the rigour of the analysis and in establishing a clear distinction between conduct and transactions that obstruct markets from working and perceived unfairness between parties. The process of evaluating the application of competition and setting standards for doing so should be improved, ensuring that the determination of cases is relatively independent of the particular investigator and that standards are known to firms and consumers, perhaps by the issue of guidelines. Areas wherein the analytical framework might be clearer and more rigorous include market definition, the definition of dominance and the identification of anti-competitive effects. It is clear that the offices are aware of these problems and are making considerable efforts in this direction.

Simpler statutes focused on making markets work might have served better the needs of the transition economies. However, even within the existing statutes, the offices could, and we believe should, devote greater emphasis to hardcore cartels and abuses of dominance that restrict entry to or expansion in markets. The offices could avoid involvement in price control and spending much of their time on agreements that have little impact on competition.

The existing institutional structures would also benefit from change, especially to improve transparency. We recommend that each of trade, industrial and competition policies should be managed by independent institutions and that the institutional divisions should correspond to *de facto* distinctions in functions. Also, natural monopoly regulation is better undertaken by a separate authority from the competition office. This is not necessarily what we would recommend for an established market economy, but we see a danger in the possible confusion of competition policy with price control that is specific to transition. At the same time, there needs to be an effective voice for competition in privatization programmes and in trade and industrial policies. Decisions in each of these areas should be accompanied by clear written reasoning (perhaps more substantial than is the case at present) so that the economic trade-off may be clearly observed, debated and evaluated. For similar reasons, the investigation of cases should be separated from deciding them. Even in Hungary, where this separation is made, it is not clear that the Competition Council should be part of the competition office.

In terms of political independence, the possibility of external political interference in competition policy would appear to be a greater danger than any involvement of the competition offices in general political and economic policy-making. We recommend that the people deciding cases and the heads of the competition offices be appointed in a manner that tends to immunize them from external influence or pressure. This is necessary to ensure that neither the selection of cases for investigation nor the decision-making process are distorted by political or other pressures. Some consideration might also be given to ensuring financial independence, so that budgetary pressure cannot be used as a lever against the offices. None of this is to imply that wrong choices were made at the outset of transition, merely that the political constraints on reform are constantly evolving, and compromises accepted at an early stage in the design of competition policy may prove costly later on.

We have deliberated much on the meaning of the term 'approximation' as it is used in the White Paper on the preparation of the CEECs for integration into the internal market of the EU. Approximation means 'to bring or come near, but not exactly' (*Oxford English Dictionary*). Whether the approximation that has occurred is adequate depends on the aims it is designed to serve. In this case it is designed to facilitate the free flow of goods and services, the free movement of factors of production and readiness for EU membership.

Our examination of the case law and other material suggests that the remaining differences between the law and its application in the Visegrád countries and in the EU are not ones that matter for the integration of factor and product-markets or for the readiness of the countries for EU membership. Given the nature of the problems faced by transition economies, further forced approximation of the detail of the law might not be beneficial, in terms of either moving the law and its application closer to that of the EU or in terms of the aims of approximation. It might even reduce the overall readiness for membership.

We have a particular concern in regard to vertical restraints and the issue of EC-style block exemptions. The underdeveloped nature of the distribution system in transition economies is such that an imaginative menu of vertical contractual possibilities may offer the best potential for the development of competition. Existing abuse of dominance provisions in the Visegrád statutes are adequate to deal with vertical restraints. Imposing a rigid formula for vertical restraints would possibly hinder or delay the development of markets and competition in the longer term without bringing countervailing benefits. Nor is it clear that a system of block exemptions would benefit the openness of factor and product markets.

Overall, we consider that the proposals for approximation in detail in the White Paper may not be in the best interests of either the EU or the CEECs and that approximation of competition laws on restrictive agreements, abuse of dominance and mergers should be considered already to have occurred in the Czech Republic, Hungary, Slovakia and Poland. Such a conclusion is reinforced by the consideration, which our analysis of the case law has made very clear to us, that whether competition policy in these countries approximates adequately that in the EU depends much less on the formal letter of the law than upon the priorities chosen by the offices, the political constraints under which they work, and their freedom to pursue their task in a relatively independent manner. There is some reason for concern that, as interest groups within the countries concerned have become aware of the importance of competition policy decisions, the temptation to bring pressure to bear on the decision-makers has grown. The evidence suggests that competition policy has already outgrown its early, comparatively uncontroversial and technocratic image. This is both inevitable and in many respects welcome, but it means that effectiveness and objectivity of competition policy will have to be carefully secured.

Notes

1. Ironically, competition policy may have been less controversial because people thought it meant whatever they wanted it to mean. To many it may have meant restraining the excesses of the market in a general way.
2. At the time of writing, we hope to maintain (links to) more recent information on the subject at the World Wide Web site www.economics.tcd.ie/jfinglet/CEC/update.

Appendix 1

Economic Data

Table A1.1   Allocation of labour across industries, 1989 (%)

	Czechoslovakia	Hungary	Poland	Germany	UK
Coal mining	5.38	4.76	12.14	2.20	1.63
Petroleum and gas	0.11	1.06	0.20	0.08	0.58
Metal ore mining	0.77	0.91	0.72	0.01	—
Other mining	0.63	0.60	1.19	0.49	0.17
Food products	6.19	13.08	9.34	4.79	9.53
Beverages	1.20	1.89	0.72	1.15	1.38
Tobacco	0.14	0.38	0.27	0.22	0.26
Textiles	7.39	6.58	7.98	3.14	4.64
Wearing apparel	3.48	4.69	4.61	2.00	4.09
Leather and products	0.91	0.83	0.97	0.28	0.37
Footwear	2.43	2.34	2.33	0.45	0.93
Paper and products	1.72	1.06	1.14	2.11	2.92
Printing, publishing	0.98	1.44	1.09	2.34	5.85
Industrial chemicals	3.27	2.87	2.68	7.91	2.77
Rubber products	0.95	0.76	0.89	1.32	1.20
Plastic products n.e.c.	0.25	1.28	1.09	3.54	3.21
Pottery, china etc.	0.32	0.91	0.59	0.49	0.86
Glass and products	2.67	1.13	1.19	0.92	0.84
Non-metal products n.e.c.	2.81	2.27	2.68	1.87	2.41
Iron and steel	5.80	4.01	3.57	3.53	2.92
Non-ferrous metals	0.84	1.51	0.77	1.39	1.14
Metal products	6.05	3.85	5.53	8.46	6.26
Machinery n.e.c.	19.03	9.83	11.45	15.13	10.64
Electrical machinery	6.16	10.13	6.34	13.67	9.98
Transport equipment	9.07	5.59	7.46	12.53	9.89
Other industries	1.65	3.17	2.23	0.69	1.57
All industry	100	100	100	100	100
Standard deviation	4.28	3.47	3.24	4.56	3.36

Source: *UN Statistical Yearbook*.

Table A1.2   Average number of employees per firm, 1989

	Czechoslovakia	Hungary	Poland	Germany	UK
Coal mining	3643	6300	4757	1381	1192
Petroleum and gas	3000	2333	2000	125	141
Metal ore mining	4400	1200	1813	200	na
Other mining	1500	500	485	29	19
Mining, quarrying	3267	2310	2590	146	164
Food products	1586	736	449	99	55
Beverages	1097	658	403	95	136
Tobacco	2000	833	1375	320	483
Textiles	3333	630	791	126	37
Spinning, weaving etc.	3239	851	1227	na	53
Wearing apparel	6600	246	335	80	25
Leather and products	2889	196	368	63	13
Footwear	9857	392	797	128	62
Wood products	3050	113	282	na	12
Furniture, fixtures	6100	237	313	na	15
Paper and products	2450	519	708	149	47
Pulp, paper etc.	na	na	1458	301	81
Printing, publishing	1217	144	321	84	15
Industrial chemicals	3000	603	1500	367	87
Basic excl. fertilizers	na	na	889	na	123
Synthetic resins etc.	na	na	2400	na	47
Others chemical products	1182	595	460	na	90
Drugs and medicines	938	1211	565	na	192
Petroleum refineries	3250	1500	2000	na	409
Petroleum, coal products	1250	na	2600	na	69
Rubber products	2077	1667	800	366	107
Plastic products n.e.c.	2333	103	338	115	37
Pottery, china etc.	4500	800	774	216	56
Glass and products	2621	1071	578	199	56
Non-metal products n.e.c.	1633	435	391	59	44
Iron and steel	8684	1152	3064	532	58
Non-ferrous metals	1333	800	1348	229	55
Metal products	2688	185	252	108	22
Machinery n.e.c.	2924	202	655	184	24
Office, computing etc.	na	na	923	467	43
Electrical machinery	2612	439	713	274	50
Radio, television etc.	na	509	833	na	64
Transport equipment	3794	329	947	858	118
Shipbuilding, repair	na	1000	1114	333	42
Motor vehicles	na	4375	1310	na	126
Professional goods	2111	176	385	102	32
Other industries	2136	194	321	85	9
Manufacturing	2772	327	521	162	33
Electricity, gas, steam	2206	2037	1517	435	na
Electricity	2267	2000	na	505	890
Electricity, gas etc.	2206	2037	1517	368	na
All industries	2782	362	603	165	na
Coefficient of variation	0.63	1.41	1.04	1.09	1.97

Source: *UN Industrial Statistics*, 1991.

Table A1.3   Change in production, 1989–93

	Poland	Hungary	Czechoslovakia	UK
Food products (311)	−14.43	−20.54	−32.46	1.80
Beverages (313)	−4.00	−20.54	11.01	0.98
Tobacco (314)	11.22	−20.54	50.00	7.06
Textiles (321)	−48.04	−61.17	−43.70	−14.71
Wearing apparel, except footwear (322)	−23.39	−15.38	−48.82	−9.09
Leather products (323)	−53.44	−50.65	−55.56	−25.56
Footwear, except rubber or plastic (324)	−53.23	−41.58	−40.19	−22.22
Wood products, except furniture (331)	65.14	34.40	−42.98	−12.60
Furniture, except metal (332)	−4.38	−28.45	−31.71	−12.60
Paper and products (341)	−15.13	−34.56	−19.12	5.66
Printing and publishing (342)	−12.44	−2.00	−30.71	3.79
Industrial chemicals (351)	−38.26	na	−29.69	2.40
Other chemicals (352)	−23.85	−48.15	−32.90	14.29
Petroleum refineries (353)	−14.81	−18.28	−27.03	7.27
Misc. petroleum and coal products (354)	−51.92	na	na	−16.85
Rubber products (355)	−26.37	0.00	−35.16	−7.29
Plastic products (356)	30.50	0.00	na	10.11
Pottery, china, earthenware (361)	−25.95	−20.00	−26.89	−15.38
Glass and products (362)	−23.39	−18.18	−25.37	−4.13
Other non-metallic mineral products (369)	−22.11	−26.67	−41.82	−18.26
Iron and steel (371)	−39.74	−60.38	−33.33	−19.53
Non-ferrous metals (372)	−46.67	−61.29	−53.64	−10.38
Fabricated metal products (381)	−26.85	−28.85	−40.98	−8.11
Machinery, except electrical (382)	−43.75	−30.77	−54.01	0.83
Machinery electric (383)	−29.03	−43.66	−58.16	−6.98
Transport epuipment (384)	−31.13	−57.01	−48.69	0.00
Professional & scientific epuipm. (385)	−30.95	−55.37	−56.00	−4.65
Other manufactured products (390)	−64.17	−46.25	−39.50	−6.38
Standard deviation	26.89	22.99	22.47	10.36
Average	−23.59	−29.84	−34.13	−5.73
Coefficient of variation	−1.14	−0.77	−0.66	−1.81

Table A1.4   Average number of employees per firm, 1992

	Czechoslovakia		Hungary		Poland		Germany	UK
	1992	% change from 1989	1992	% change from 1989	1992	% change from 1989	1992	1992
Food products (311)	339	−79	163	−78	479	7	111	58
Beverages (313)	349	−68	114	−83	732	82	105	133
Tobacco (314)	2000	0	333	−60	11 000	700	338	400
Textiles (321)	750	−78	166	−74	1252	58	125	34
Wearing apparel, except footwear (322)	386	−94	62	−75	248	−26	81	23
Leather products (323)	412	−86	67	−62	357	−3	67	14
Footwear,except rubber or plastic (324)	906	−91	124	−68	545	−32	128	60
Wood products,except furniture (331)	291	−90	27	−76	467	66	39	10
Furniture,except metal (332)	290	−95	83	−65	344	10	111	14
Paper and products (341)	568	−77	89	−83	868	23	152	45
Printing and publishing (342)	240	−80	32	−78	424	32	83	15
Industrial chemicals (351)	1360	−55	151	−75	5267	251	896	85
Other chemicals (352)	378	−68	162	−73	648	41	222	97
Petroleum refineries (353)	3500	8	500	−67	2000	0	279	296
Misc. petroleum and coal products (354)	na	na	na	na	1750	−33	na	55
Rubber products (355)	857	−59	99	−94	460	−43	330	90
Plastic products (356)	300	−87	28	−73	252	−26	118	35
Pottery, china, earthenware (361)	526	−88	194	−76	425	−45	233	51
Glass and products (362)	939	−64	275	−74	425	−27	193	44
Other non-metallic mineral products (369)	336	−79	92	−79	219	−44	59	37
Iron and steel (371)	3054	−65	263	−77	2458	−20	502	53
Non-ferrous metals (372)	471	−65	172	−79	1045	−22	216	46
Fabricated metal products (381)	446	−83	35	−81	317	26	107	21
Machinery, except electrical (382)	633	−78	38	−81	415	−37	174	22
Machinery electric (383)	648	−75	80	−82	425	−40	253	43
Transport equipment (384)	1050	−72	68	−79	709	−25	813	108
Professional & scientific equipment (385)	509	−76	39	−78	267	−31	108	29
Other manufactured products (390)	280	−87	38	−80	296	−8	86	8
Total manufacturing (300)	570	−79	68	−79	467	−10	160	31

Appendix 2

The Statutes of the Visegrád Countries

1.1   THE CZECH STATUTE

**Act on the Protection of Economic Competition
No. 63/1991 Coll.
of 30 January 1991 as amended under Acts No. 495/1992 Coll.
and 286/1993 Coll. of 11 November, 1993.**

The Federal Assembly of the Czech and Slovak Federal Republic has adopted the following Act:

SECTION ONE
INTRODUCTORY PROVISIONS

Article 1

1. The purpose of this Act is the protection of economic competition on the market for goods and services (hereinafter referred to as 'products') from and against restriction, distortion or elimination thereof (hereinafter referred to as 'distortion').

2. The protection of economic competition from and against unfair competitive practices is governed by separate legal regulations.[1]

Article 2

1. This Act shall apply to:
   (a) natural or legal persons taking part in economic competition even though they are not business persons (hereinafter referred to as 'competitors').

---

1. Act No. 513/1991 Coll. (Commercial Code), Article 44 and thereinforth, as amended under Acts No. 264/1992 Coll., 591/1992 Coll. and 600/1992 Coll.

(b) state administration and local authorities in terms of their jurisdiction and activities which are directly or indirectly related to economic competition.

2. The provision of this Act shall apply *mutatis mutandis* to business persons' unions, chambers, tradesmen's guilds or other forms of business association (hereinafter referred to as 'business associations') if their activity affects economic competition.

3. This Act shall also apply to activities or conduct abroad as long as the effects thereof influence the domestic market.

4. Unless international agreements binding upon the Czech Republic provide otherwise, this Act shall not apply to conduct whose effects influence foreign markets.

5. Repealed

SECTION TWO
ILLICIT DISTORTION OF COMPETITION
AGREEMENTS DISTORTING COMPETITION

Article 3

1. All agreements between or among competitors, decisions by business associations or concerted practices of competitors (hereinafter referred to as 'agreements') which result or may result in distortion of economic competition on the market for products, are hereby prohibited, null and void unless provided otherwise herein or by a separate legal regulation or unless the Ministry of Economic Competition (hereinafter referred to as 'the Ministry') has granted an exemption.

2. Under the provisions of paragraph (1), the prohibition shall apply particularly to agreements, or their parts, containing:

(a) direct or indirect price fixing or setting of business terms,

(b) an obligation to limit or control production, sales, technical development or investments,

(c) market sharing or division of purchasing sources,

(d) an obligation on the part of at least one party to the agreement to conclude contracts with buyers subject to supplementary obligations which, by their nature or according to commercial usage, have no connection with the subject of such contracts,

(e) an obligation by the parties to the agreement to apply dissimilar business terms in equivalent transactions with individual buyers, thereby placing some buyers at a disadvantage in business relations (discrimination),

(f) an obligation to limit access to the market to competitors who are not party to an agreement.

3. If only part of the agreement is void hereunder, only this particular part shall be void unless it is inferred from the contents of the agreement that such a part may not be separated therefrom.

4. Agreements under paragraph 1 shall not be prohibited if their subject involves:

(a) uniform application of business, delivery or payment terms, with the exception of price fixing agreements or agreements about the components of the price,

(b) rationalization of economic activities, particularly through their specialization, unless it results in a substantial restriction of competition on the market,

(c) a supplying share in the market for the individual product amounting to less than 5% of the national market or to less than 30% of the local market regularly supplied by the parties to the agreement.

5. Agreements under paragraph (4) shall be approved by the Ministry in order to come into force. In their application, the competitors are hereby obliged to provide reasons for approval of the agreement and attach a draft thereof. The Ministry may withhold its approval if there are justifications for withholding such an exemption under Article 5, paragraph (3). The approval shall be deemed granted if the Ministry does not notify its disapproval in writing within two months of the date the agreement was delivered.

Article 4

1. Agreements on the transfer of rights to, or licensing agreements for, inventions, industrial designs, trade marks, trade names, semiconductor product drawings, utility models and protected plant varieties or animal breeds, or parts of such agreements, shall be void under Article 3, paragraph (1) if, in business relations, restrictions exceeding the object and scope of legal protection of industrial property rights are imposed on the licensees or parties acquiring rights . The same shall apply to agreements on the transfer of rights to works or performances protected under the Copyright Act.[2]

2. Nullity under paragraph (1) shall not apply in particular to:

(a) restrictions to the licensee or party acquiring a right if the restrictions are justified by the licenser's or transferor's interest in assuring proper use of the protected subject matter.

(b) the obligation of the licensee, or party acquiring the right, to exchange experience or grant licences to patents related to the use or improvement of the subject matter under protection if this is compatible with the reciprocal obligations of the party providing the right, or of the licenser.

(c) the obligations of the licensee or party acquiring a right related to competition on markets beyond the scope of this Act.

3. Provisions of paragraphs 1 and 2 shall apply *mutatis mutandis* to the transfer of rights or to the granting of licences to subject matter not protected under intellectual or industrial property laws and to production or commercial secrets.

---

2. Act No. 35/1965 Coll. on Works of Literature, Science and Art (Copyright Act) in the wording of the later amendments.
Act No. 529/1991 Coll. on the Protection of Semiconductor Product Drawings.
Act No. 478/1992 Coll. on Utility Models.
Act No. 174/1988 Coll. on Trade Marks.
Act No. 132/1989 Coll. on the Protection of Rights to New Plant Varieties and Animal Breeds.
Act No. 527/1990 Coll. on Inventions, Industrial Designs and Innovation.
Commercial Code Article 8 and subsequent articles.

Article 5

1. Business persons may apply to the Ministry for an exemption from nullity under Articles 3 and 4. In their application, they are obliged to state their reasons and to attach a draft of the agreement.

2. Based on the application, the Ministry may grant, for a specified period of time, an exemption under which it is possible to conclude an otherwise prohibited agreement, if the restriction of competition under such an exemption is necessary in terms of the public interest, particularly with regard to production of goods or promotion of technical and economic development. The exemption from the prohibition may not exceed the limits necessary to satisfy the public interest, while special regard must be paid to consumers' interests.

3. Under the conditions outlined in paragraph 2, the Ministry shall grant an exemption from the prohibition if:
   (a) the agreement does not include an obligation
      i. to sell only such products as are the subject matter of the agreement,
      ii. to sell products identical with or interchangeable with products which are part of the subject matter of the agreement only under certain restrictions in terms of price or quantity,
      iii. to exclude certain competitors from the sale of products or from rendering services which are part of the subject matter of the agreement, even though they are willing to fulfil the prescribed conditions and if their qualifications comply with existing regulations,
   (b) the agreement does not otherwise violate a legal prohibition in any other way, nor is it inconsistent with fair competition ethics,
   (c) restrictions under Article 4, paragraph 1, do not excessively disturb the operation and activities of the licensee or party acquiring a right, and the extent of these restrictions does not substantially impede economic competition on the market.

4. An agreement which has been exempted shall come into force on the date stated in the Ministry's decision. This date may not precede the date on which the application for such an exemption was submitted.

Article 6

The Ministry shall withdraw or limit the exemption at its own initiative or in response to an application, or it shall set new conditions for the duration of the exemption if:
   (a) conditions that were decisive at the time the exemption was granted have changed significantly,
   (b) parties to the agreement are in violation of the rules set forth and directives issued as part of the exemption, or if the parties have abused the exemption.

Article 6a

The Ministry may, in a decree, grant a general exemption from the prohibition under Article 3, paragraph 1, and Article 4, paragraph 1 for certain types of agreement, with the exception of agreements including direct or indirect price fixing. The general exemption may be granted only on condition that the distortion of competition which may result therefrom is outweighed by benefits to other parties on the market, in particular to the consumers.

Article 7

Repealed
Concentrations between Competitors' undertakings[3]

Article 8

1. A concentration shall be deemed to arise through
    (a) a merger or absorption of companies, cooperatives and other legal persons
    (b) a transition or transfer of an undertaking or a substantial part thereof.
2. An operation whereby one or more persons already controlling one undertaking acquire(s) direct or indirect control over the whole or a substantial part of another undertaking shall constitute a concentration within the meaning of this Act. This includes, but is not limited to:
    (a) acquisition of stocks, shares or co-operative members' shares (hereinafter referred to as 'shares'),
    (b) a contract or any other act which allows influence to be exercised on the competitive conduct of the undertakings.
3. A concentration under paragraph 2 shall not be deemed to arise where banks or other competitors, whose business activities include dealing in securities, hold on a temporary basis shares which they have acquired in another undertaking with a view to reselling them.

Article 8a

1. Concentrations which distort or may distort economic competition shall be subject to approval by the Ministry. Competition shall be deemed distorted if the merging undertakings' shares exceed 30% of the total turnover in the nation-wide or local market for the given product.
2. The Ministry shall approve of a concentration if the applying competitors prove that any detriment which may result from the distortion of competition will be outweighed by the economic benefits brought about by this concentration. In other cases, the Ministry shall not approve of a concentration. In its concentration approval decision, the Ministry may stipulate restrictions or obligations necessary for the protection of economic competition.
3. Competitors are obliged to apply to the Ministry for approval of a concentration between undertakings under paragraph (1):
    (a) In the event of mergers or absorptions (Article 8, paragraph 1 [a]), prior to the date of submitting the proposal to record a change in the Companies' register

---

3. Commercial Code, Article 5.

(b) in other cases (Article 8, paragraph 1 [b] and paragraph 2), within a period of one week of signing an agreement, or else such an agreement shall be ineffective.

4. The provisions of Articles 1 through 3 shall not apply to either the National Property Fund of the Czech Republic (Fond národního majetku Èeské republiky) or the Land Fund of the Czech Republic (Pozemkovy fond Èeské republiky) within a period of 12 months from the acquisition of control over another competitor's undertaking under Article 8.

Article 9

Monopoly and Dominant Market Positions

1. If a competitor, either alone or in agreement with other competitors, attains such a position on the relevant market that the competitor is not exposed to any competition (a monopoly position) or to substantial competition (a dominant position), the competitor is obliged to notify the Ministry of this fact without delay.

2. A dominant position on the market is that of a competitor who, over a period of a calendar year, provides the relevant market with at least 30% of its supplies of identical, comparable or interchangeable products.

3. Monopoly or dominant positions may not be abused by the competitor to the detriment of other competitors or consumers, nor to the public interest. Abuse is considered in particular:

(a) direct or indirect imposition of unfair terms and conditions in contracts with other parties on the market, especially enforcing an obligation that is in striking disparity to the counter-obligation provided in return at the time of conclusion of the contract,

(b) making a conclusion of contract subject to acceptance by other parties of supplementary obligations which, by their nature or according to commercial usage, have no connection with the subject of such contracts,

(c) applying dissimilar conditions to equivalent or comparable transactions with individual trading parties on the market, thereby placing them at a competitive disadvantage,

(d) ceasing or limiting production, markets or technical development of products for the purpose of attaining unjustified economic benefits to the prejudice of buyers.

SECTION THREE
JURISDICTION OF THE MINISTRY OF ECONOMIC COMPETITION

Article 10

Repealed

Article 11

1. The jurisdiction of the Ministry entitles the Ministry:

(a) to approve agreements and concentrations between undertakings and to examine monopoly or dominant positions of competitors under Articles 3, 4, 8 and 9,

(b) to decide under Article 5, paragraph 2 on exemptions from prohibitions; to set conditions for the approval of exemptions and to monitor the compliance with these conditions,

(c) to conduct proceedings under Article 6 concerning the withdrawal of exemptions granted and to withdraw exemptions if the set conditions have not been met despite notice, or if the grounds on which the exemption was granted no longer exist,

(d) to prohibit the performance of agreements or parts thereof; to prohibit concentrations between undertakings; to prohibit abuse of a dominant or monopoly position on the market if such a position conflicts with prohibitions under Articles 3, 4, 8 and 9 and provided that no exemption in respect of the agreements has been granted, or if such an exemption has been withdrawn,

(e) to impose, on finding a fault, an obligation to remedy it and to set an appropriate time limit for compliance with the obligation,

(f) to issue decisions on whether particular conduct constitutes an abuse of the monopoly or dominant position held by a competitor under Article 9, paragraph 3,

(g) to institute preliminary measures under Article 12, paragraph 6, regarding a proceeding initiated before the Ministry,

(h) to impose fines on competitors for failure to comply with obligations specified under this Act,

(i) to require that competitors provide materials and information necessary for the activities of the Ministry and, for this purpose, to examine a competitor's legal and commercial documents and to establish whether a conflict with obligations specified under this Act has occurred,

(j) to give public notice of applications for approval of conclusion of an agreement or of concentrations between undertakings, to give public notice of the Ministry's decisions that have come into effect regarding disapproval of agreements and concentrations of undertakings, regarding the abuse of a monopoly or dominant position and regarding fines imposed and other remedial measures.

2. In urgent cases of severe distortion of economic competition by competitors who are in a dominant or monopoly position on the market for a given product, the Ministry may, under paragraph (1[e]), impose an obligation for the transference of a part of the competitor's undertaking, or for its division if the competitor is a legal person; Article 69 of the Commercial Code shall be applied *mutatis mutandis*.

SECTION FOUR
MINISTRY PROCEEDINGS

Article 12

1. A competitor whose rights or obligations set by this Act are subject to decision in the proceedings shall be a party to such proceedings.

2. The party may be represented in the proceedings by a representative of his choice on the basis of a power of attorney. The party may have only one representative at a time representing it in one particular matter.

3. In cases where a separate stipulation provides for a mandatory administrative fee for the performance of an administrative procedure, a formal receipt confirming payment of the fee shall be essential to complete the submission.

4. If the party to the proceedings fails to rectify shortcomings in the submission within the time limit issued by the Ministry, the Ministry shall not conduct the process or it shall discontinue a proceeding already initiated.

5. Competitors are hereby obliged to punctually provide the Ministry with any and all requested materials and information in a full, correct and truthful form and to allow for their verification. They are further obliged to allow Ministry officials access to the facilities, rooms and other premises which are the subject or the place of examination or verification.

6. If it appears necessary from the nature of the matter, the Ministry shall make a decision on the basis of a hearing ordered by the Ministry. The parties to the proceedings must at all times, however, be given the opportunity to communicate their positions on the subject matter of the proceedings conducted by the Ministry. The Ministry is hereby obliged to take measures to ensure that commercial secrets[4] are not disclosed in the process of examination of the documents.

7. Should it be necessary to serve justified interests or should the enforcement of the final decision be curbed or jeopardised in any other way, the Ministry may take a preliminary measure in a proceeding under the above paragraphs to temporarily modify legal relationships until a final decision is issued.

8. Unless stipulated otherwise, proceedings at the Ministry shall be conducted in accordance with the provisions of the Administrative Proceedings Code.[5]

Article 13

Repealed

Article 14

Fines

1. The Ministry may impose a fine of up to 300 000 Czech crowns on competitors who fail to provide the required materials or truthful information within the stipulated time limit, or who fail to allow for the verification procedures specified under Article 12, paragraph 5.

2. The Ministry may impose a fine of up to 100 000 Czech crowns on those who, without a serious reason, fail to attend a hearing ordered under Article 12, paragraph 6, or who otherwise impede the proceedings.

3. The Ministry may impose a fine of up to 1 000 000 Czech crowns for failure to comply with an enforceable Ministry decision.

4. The Ministry is authorized to impose a fine on a competitor who fails to

---

4. Commercial Code, Article 17.
5. Act No. 71/1967 Coll., the Administrative Proceedings Code.

perform other obligations specified by this Act, of up to 10 000 000 Czech crowns or of up to 10% of the net turnover recorded over the last complete calendar year. If a competitor fails to meet the obligations of this Act, and derives proven material benefit from this failure, the competitor shall be fined an amount totalling no less than the benefit derived.

5. The Ministry may impose fines under the above paragraphs no later than one year after establishing that an obligation has not been performed or three years following the year in which the obligation was not performed. The imposition of a fine under this Act does not exclude criminal liability under a separate Act.[6]

6. Imposition of fines under this Act may be repeated within one year of the date that an enforceable decision should have been complied with.

7. The Ministry is hereby authorized to collect fines. The revenues from fines are an income account item of the Czech Republic national budget.

SECTION FIVE

CARTEL REGISTER AND CONFIDENTIALITY

Article 15

Repealed

Article 16

The staff of the Ministry, as well as those entrusted with tasks falling within the jurisdiction of the Ministry, are hereby obliged not to disclose information on facts constituting production or commercial secrets of competitors if such information was acquired in the course of their duties. This obligation shall continue for two years following the termination of employment with the Ministry.

SECTION SIX

LITIGATION ARISING FROM ILLICIT COMPETITION

Article 17

1. Those whose rights have been infringed by illicit restriction(s) of competition may demand that the offender refrain from such conduct, rectify the faulty status, provide appropriate and satisfactory remedy, pay damages and return any unjustified material benefit. For the purposes of enforcing the above claims, provisions of the Civil Code shall be applied unless provided otherwise herein.

2. Once legal proceedings have been initiated in regard to refraining from conduct, or to rectification of faulty status, or after conclusion of such proceedings in a final decision, no further lawsuits for the same claims are permissible by other persons legitimately involved. This is without prejudice to further persons' rights to enter litigation as additional parties under general provisions. Final rulings upon the claims of one legitimate party shall also be binding for others legitimately involved.

---

6. Act No. 140/1961 Coll., the Criminal Code and amendments thereto, Article 127.

3. The Court of Justice may award the party who has won the case the right to publish the final ruling at the expense of the party who has lost the case. Depending upon circumstances, the extent, form and method of publication may also be determined. Applicable provisions of the Civil Procedure Code shall be employed in regard to the court expenses.

SECTION SEVEN
INTERVENTION BY STATE AND LOCAL ADMINISTRATIVE AUTHORITIES
Article 18

1. State and local administrative authorities may not restrict or eliminate economic competition by employing their own provisions, apparent support or other methods.

2. Compliance with the obligations defined under paragraph (1) shall be supervised by the Ministry. Based on evidence and analysis of results, the Ministry may demand that authorities of state and local administration rectify the faults.

SECTION EIGHT
TEMPORARY PROVISIONS
Article 19

State Administration Procedure to Counter the Creation of a Monopoly Position by Competitors in the course of the Transfer of State-owned Property

1. While transferring state property, including the transfer to a state joint-stock company, the state administrative authorities are obliged to set specific conditions under which the monopoly position of an existing competitor shall be discontinued or the creation of a new monopoly by a new competitor shall be prevented. For new competitors whose market share may be expected to exceed the limit defined under Article 9, paragraph 2, the state administration authorities are obliged to prepare an analysis including in particular the following:

   (a) an appraisal, within two years, of whether the competitor is able to abuse a position within the subsequent two years, according to the share occupied in the relevant market, with particular reference to state of technical development, size of competing undertakings, and other parameters characteristic of competitive potential in a particular field,

   (b) an evaluation of the new competitor's competitive potential in relation to the competitors existing involvement in the global market, and anticipated foreign competition on the domestic market,

   (c) an assessment of the new competitor in the light of the regulations which apply to the evaluation of whether or not a competitor is in a dominant market position, after prior consultation with the Ministry or after obtaining relevant materials from the Ministry.

2. State administrative authorities are obliged to submit the analyses to the Ministry for approval. In the event that the state administrative authorities disagree

with the opinion of the Ministry, the case shall be resolved by the cabinet, on proposal from a state administrative authority.

3. Provisions of paragraphs 1 and 2 shall not apply to:
   (a) state-owned public utilities or organizations, or state monopolies stipulated by law,
   (b) competitors rendering local services in regional or local markets, including in particular services to trade, catering, accommodation, repairs and personal services. The provisions of Article 20 apply to these competitors.

Article 20

Local Administration Procedure to Counter the Creation of a Monopoly Position by Competitors in the course of the Transfer of State-owned Property

1. In the process of dividing competitors, local authorities are hereby obliged to ensure that a competitive environment is created on the regional or local markets, and particularly that none of the competitors exceeds the market share stipulated under Article 9, paragraph 2. The same shall apply to cases in which assets of competitors that have not been sold through auctions become the property of a municipality.

2. If the local authorities fail to comply with the provisions of paragraph 1 in specific cases, they shall propose measures for the rectification of this situation to the Ministry, to be executed within two years at the latest.

3. Provisions under paragraph 2 may not be applied to services where the choice of a supplier is beyond the influence of the public in consideration of the transportation distances, disproportionate loss of time involved, and the actual transportation costs. In these cases, the procedures under Article 19, paragraph 1 shall apply to individual competitors.

Article 21

1. Competitors are obliged to report to the Ministry agreements under Articles 3, 4 and 8 concluded before this Act came into force, within three months of this Act coming into force. The Ministry shall decide on the validity of these agreements and the granting of exemption.

2. A competitor who has achieved a monopoly or dominant position before this Act came into force is hereby required to report this fact to the Ministry within three months of this Act coming into force.

3. Failure to perform obligations under paragraphs 1 and 2 shall be construed as a failure to comply under Article 14 with consequences outlined thereunder.

SECTION NINE
CLOSING PROVISIONS

Article 22

The government may decree more detailed conditions to monopoly or dominant position investigations under Article 9, prerequisites of the request for an agreement approval under paragraph 4 of Article 3, prerequisites of the request for granting an exemption under Article 5 and the request for a concentration approval under Article 8a.

Article 23

Articles 119b and 119c of the Economic Code, Act No. 109/1964 Coll. and later amendments thereto are hereby cancelled.

Article 24

This Act shall come into force on 1 March, 1991.

Note: Act No. 495/1992 Coll. came into force on the date of publication, i.e. 29 October, 1992. Act No. 286/1993 Coll. came into force on the date of publication, i.e. 29 November, 1993.

Article II of Act No. 495/1992 reads as follows:

Article II
A proceeding in matters falling under this Act upon the effect hereof, but commenced at the Federal Bureau of Economic Competition before this Act came into effect shall fall under the jurisdiction of the Republic Bureaux and shall be completed thereby. Which of the Republic Bureaux shall be governing depends on the registered office of the undertaking participating in the proceeding. If registered offices exist in both Republics, the proceedings shall be completed by the Slovakian Bureau of Economic Competition unless the respective Bureaux agree otherwise.

The Republic Bureaux shall promptly notify participants in the proceeding of a transfer of jurisdiction to the other country's Bureau if one occurs.

Article II of Act No. 286/1993 Coll. reads as follows:

Article II
Any and all decisions made by business associations prior to the date of effect of this Act shall be null and void within 30 days of this Act coming into effect unless the Ministry grants an exemption upon the association's request or unless a separate Act provides otherwise.

Article III of Act No. 286/1993 Coll. reads as follows:

Article III
Act No. 513/1991 Coll., Commercial Code and later amendments thereto, 264/1992 Coll. and 591/1992 Coll. is hereby amended as follows:
   A new paragraph (6[f]) is hereby inserted into Article 68:
   (f) an undertaking does not perform an obligation imposed by a ruling of the Ministry of Economic Competition under paragraph 2 of Article 11, Act No. 63/1991 Coll. on the Protection of Economic Competition.

Article IV of Act No. 286/1993 reads as follows:

Article IV
The Chairman of the House of Representatives of the Parliament is hereby entitled to publicise the full text of the Act on the Protection of Economic Competition in the Czech Republic Act Collection, as outlined in later stipulations.

Article V of Act No. 286/1993 reads as follows:

Article V
This Act shall come into effect on the date of publication.
Signed:
Milan Uhde, Chairman, House of Representatives
Václav Havel, President
Václav Klaus, Prime Minister

1.2 THE HUNGARIAN STATUTE

Act LXXXVI of 1990
on the Prohibition of Unfair Market Practices[1]

Freedom and fairness of competition are basic preconditions to market competition that makes for economic efficiency. In order to protect this freedom and fairness, forms of conduct that are contrary to fair market practices must be prohibited, and supervision over the merger of enterprises must be introduced through the creation of appropriate organisational forms. Accordingly, the public interest in competition, the interests of the participants of economic cooperation and, in connection with fair market conduct, the interests of consumers, shall be protected by law. In order to realise these goals, Parliament has enacted the following Act.

General Provisions
Article 1

This Act shall apply to economic activities of entrepreneurs on the territory of the Republic of Hungary, unless otherwise provided by any other act.

Article 2

For the purposes of this Act:
  (a) The term 'entrepreneurs' means legal persons, companies with no legal personality, other business organisations and natural persons, each of them engaged in economic activity;
  (b) The term 'economic activity' means any business activity (whether production or service related) perfomed for consideration, the purpose of earning a profit or acquiring property;

---

1. This Act was adopted by Parliament at its session of 20 November 1990.

(c) The term 'competitor' means entrepreneur interested in economic competition; and

(d) The term 'consumer' means customer, purchaser and user.

Article 3

1. Entrepreneurs are required to respect the freedom and fairness of economic competition.

2. It shall be unlawful to engage in unfair economic activity, including, in particular, any conduct that offends or jeopardises the legitimate interests of the competitors and the consumers or is contrary to the requirements of fair business practices.

PART ONE
PROHIBITION OF UNFAIR MARKET CONDUCT

CHAPTER ONE
PROHIBITION OF UNFAIR COMPETITION

Article 4

It shall be unlawful to injure or jeopardise the reputation or credibility of a competitor by making or spreading false allegations, or by falsifying any fact or engaging in any other similar conduct.

Article 5

1. It shall be unlawful to acquire or use a business secret in an unfair manner or unlawfully to disclose it to third parties or the public.

2. A 'business secret' has also been acquired in an unfair manner if it was obtained without the consent of the holder of a business secret and with the assistance of any person who is in a confidential relationship or business relationship with it.

3. For the purposes of this Act:
   (a) The term 'business secret' means any fact, information, solution or data related to any economic activity and in the continuing secrecy of which its holder has a reasonable interest;
   (b) The term 'confidential relationship' includes particularly any employment, other legal relationship with carrying out any work and membership in business organisations; and
   (c) Giving information, negotiating and making offers before a transaction means 'business relationship' even if it will not be followed by concluding a contract.

Article 6

It shall be unlawful to direct an unfair appeal to others which is expressly intended to disrupt an existing economic relationship with a third party or to interfere with the establishment of such a relationship.

Article 7

It shall be unlawful to manufacture or distribute goods and services (hereinafter goods) without the consent of a competitor if such goods use a cover, wrapping or designation (including a designation of origin), or name, by or for which that competitor or its characteristic goods are recognised.

Article 8

It shall be unlawful to withdraw or withhold goods from trade prior to a planned price increase or for the purpose of causing a price increase.

Article 9

It shall be unlawful to condition the delivery or acceptance of goods on the delivery or acceptance of other goods.

Article 10

It shall be unlawful to impair in any way the fairness of tenders, auctions or stock exchange deals.

CHAPTER TWO
PROHIBITION AGAINST CONSUMER FRAUD

Article 11

1. It shall be unlawful to deceive consumers for the purpose of improving the marketability of goods.
2. An act shall be deemed deceiving if, among other things:
   (a) a false statement is asserted or a fact is asserted in a misleading manner with respect to an essential feature of the goods, including, in particular, the composition, use, effects on health or on the environment, as well as the handling, origin and place of origin, source or mode of acquisition of such goods, or, if other misleading or inadequate information is disseminated pertaining to the essential features of such goods;
   (b) a comparison of goods that it likely to mislead is disseminated to the public through advertising or otherwise;
   (c) it is concealed that the goods fail to meet legal specifications, state standards or the normal requirements for such goods, or that the use of the goods requires the creation of preconditions which are significantly different from the usual ones;
   (d) the labels for goods are suitable to mislead consumers with respect to the use or other essential features, origin, place of origin, or source or mode of acquisition of such goods;
   (e) goods that are not available to consumers, or are in short supply or available in inadequate varieties, are advertised, unless in the event goods are advertised to introduce new goods or to liquidate inventories of hard-to-sell goods, such circumstances are disclosed to consumers.

Article 12

1. A comparison of goods shall not be deemed fraudulent if the conditions for impartial and competent inspection have been secured, such inspection is based upon published comparative data and the essential features and prices of the goods compared and the terms of application of the price have been disclosed to the public.

2. A comparison of goods made in accordance with the provisions of paragraph (1) shall be deemed fraudulent if it quotes the results of the inspection out of context, tendentiously and in a one-sided manner.

Article 13

The customarily accepted meaning in daily life and in the given trade of the expressions used shall be taken as a guide when establishing the fraudulence of any information.

CHAPTER THREE
PROHIBITION OF AGREEMENTS RESTRICTING COMPETITION

Article 14

1. Except as provided in the Articles 15 to 17, concerted practices and agreements between competitors (both hereinafter referred to as 'agreements'), that may result in the restriction or exclusion of competition, shall be prohibited, whether or not such an agreement was concluded on the territory of the Republic of Hungary.

2. This prohibition applies particularly to agreements that: fix the price of goods, allocate the market or exclude a given sphere of consumers from purchasing or marketing goods; limit the choice between sources of acquisition or marketing opportunities; restrict the output of goods; impede technical development; hinder market entry; and disadvantage some market participants.

3. Except as provided in Articles 15 to 17, it shall be unlawful for an agreement to purport to fix resale prices if competition could thereby be limited or excluded.

Article 15

An agreement shall not be unlawful if:
    (a) it is aimed at stopping abuse of dominant position or
    (b) it is of minor importance.

Article 16

1. An agreement shall be deemed to be of minor importance if the contracting parties' joint share of the goods subject thereto does not exceed ten percent on the relevant market. This condition must be satisfied for as long as such agreement is in force, or if it is in force for longer than one year, in each calendar year.

2. The term relevant market means the market on which the restriction or exclusion of competition prevails. The relevant market shall be defined by taking into account the goods that form the subject of an agreement and the appropriate geo-

graphical area.

3. Any goods that can reasonably substitute for the goods that form the subject of the agreement must also be taken into account when defining the relevant market. Other factors of substitutability including the price, purpose of use, quality and conditions of fulfilment shall be taken into consideration.

4. The term 'geographical area' means the territory outside which:

(a) a consumer is unable to procure goods or is only able to procure goods under considerably less favourable conditions; or

(b) the seller of goods cannot sell goods or can only sell them under considerably less favourable conditions.

Article 17

1. The agreement is exempted from the prohibition contained in Article 14 if:

(a) the concomitant restriction or exclusion of competition does not exceed the extent necessary to attain economically justified common goals; and

(b) the concomitant advantages outweigh the concomitant disadvantages.

2. For the purposes of exempting an agreement from the prohibition the following are qualified as advantages:

(a) prices turn favourably;

(b) an improvement is achieved in the quality of goods or the high quality attained is maintained;

(c) the terms of fulfilment improve (e.g. shorter times of delivery are secured);

(d) the way of distribution is shortened, purchase and sale are made more rational and the choice of goods improves; or

(e) technological development is promoted and the environmental situation or competitiveness in the external markets improves.

3. For the purposes of exempting an agreement it is qualified to be a disadvantage in particular if the joint share of the parties concluding the agreement in the relevant market of the goods, which form the subject of the agreement, exceeds thirty percent during the validity of the agreement.

Article 18

1. The parties planning to conclude an agreement may request the competition authority (pursuant to Article 52) to issue a decision to the effect that the contemplated agreement is not prohibited under Article 15, or is exempted from such prohibition on the basis of Article 17.

2. Following the issue of a decision pursuant to paragraph (1), the competition authority shall not challenge the agreement and the activities of the parties that are in line with the agreement.

Article 19

The burden of proving that the agreement is not subject to the prohibition under Article 15 or is exempted from such prohibition under Article 17 rests with the person seeking such relief.

CHAPTER FOUR
PROHIBITION OF ABUSE OF DOMINANT POSITION

Article 20

It shall be unlawful to abuse any dominant position so particularly:
  (a) to stipulate unjustified and one-sided advantages or force the other party
      to accept disadvantageous conditions in contractual relations, including
      by the application of standard contractual terms; or
  (b) to refuse without justification to conclude a contract;
  (c) to influence the economic decisions of the other party in order to gain
      unjustified advantages, in particular, with the objective that it should fail
      to enforce any legitimate claims it may have resulting from the contract; or
  (d) to impede market entry or hinder technical progress; or
  (e) to create, without justification, disadvantageous market conditions for a
      competitor, or to influence its economic decisions in order to obtain unjus-
      tified advantages.

Article 21

1. A dominant position shall be presumed to be occupied in particular by any
person
  (a) whose merchandise cannot be purchased from elsewhere, or can only be
      purchased under considerably less favourable conditions than usual, con-
      sidering the trade and goods in question; or
  (b) who orders goods that cannot be marketed elsewhere or can only be mar-
      keted under considerably less favourable conditions than usual, consider-
      ing the trade and goods in question; or
  (c) whose share in the relevant market (Article 16(2)) for the respective goods
      in the period under consideration exceeds 30%.
2. Entrepreneurs between whom there is no competition in the relevant market
during the period under consideration shall be deemed to hold dominant positions.
3. A maximum of three entrepreneurs whose joint share in the relevant market
during the period under consideration exceeds 50% shall be deemed to hold dominant position.
4. In determining whether a dominant position exists, parties taken out from the
prohibition of restriction pursuant to Article 15 or exempted pursuant to Article 17
shall be jointly considered.

Article 22

An unjustified and one-sided advantage exists where particularly there is a considerable difference between contractually stipulated service and consideration. To
establish the existence of such a difference, the conditions under which the contract
was concluded, the contract taken in its entirety, prevailing market conditions, prevailing value relations, features of the transaction, and the method by which service
and consideration were determined, shall be considered.

PART TWO
CONTROL OF CONCENTRATION

CHAPTER FIVE
CONTROL OF CONCENTRATION OF ENTREPRENEURS

Article 23

1. In order for a merger or consolidation of entrepreneurs to occur, preliminary permission of the competition authority must be requested if:
   (a) the joint share in the relevant market of the participants with respect to any goods sold by them in the previous calendar year exceeds 30%; or
   (b) the aggregate turnover of the participants in the previous calendar year exceeded 10 billion forints.

2. The participants are jointly required to apply for permission for a planned merger.

3. If the merger of entrepreneurs has been authorized in a state administrative ruling, the body that issued such ruling shall consult the competition authority in advance.

Article 24

1. The competition authority taking into account the factors contained in paragraph 2 below, shall not authorize a merger that would have the effect of impeding the formation, development or continuation of competition.

2. Paragraph (1) notwithstanding, the competition authority may authorize a merger if:
   (a) the totality of advantageous effects on competition outweighs the disadvantages;
   (b) the transaction does not preclude competition with respect to a substantial part of the goods in question;
   (c) it promotes activities in foreign markets that are advantageous to the national economy.

3. With respect to the advantages and disadvantages paragraphs 2 and 3 of Article 17 should be observed.

Article 25

A permission issued for a merger covers all restrictions of competition necessary to consummate the transaction.

Article 26

1. The rules applicable to mergers shall also be applied if, with respect to any goods marketed by them, the joint market share of the entrepreneur of whom decisive influence has been acquired and the entrepreneur acquiring decisive influence exceeds 30% in the relevant market during the previous calendar year.

2. An entrepreneur shall be deemed to have acquired decisive influence of another if it:

(a) has acquired in excess of 50% of the shares, part of the assets or the voting rights ensuring the right of disposal over property of the entrepreneur being acquired; or

(b) has obtained the right to control the decisions or to manage the business of the entrepreneur being acquired on the basis of a separate agreement.

3. The control is also qualified as decisive influence if this is proven by the actual behaviour of the entrepreneurs.

Article 27

1. Indirect participants acting in the relevant market shall also be taken into account when examining mergers of entrepreneurs and the acquisition of decisive influence.

2. An indirect participant is an entity that:

(a) is under the control of the direct participant pursuant to paragraphs 2 and 3 of Article 26;

(b) controls the direct participant under subparagraph (a);

(c) other than the direct participant under subparagraph (a) of this paragraph is under the control pursuant to subparagraph (a) of the indirect participant under subparagraph (b);

(d) controls the indirect participant under subparagraph (b) pursuant to subparagraph (a).

PART THREE
PROCEDURAL AND ORGANIZATIONAL PROVISIONS

CHAPTER SIX
ENFORCEMENT OF CLAIMS

Article 28

An interested party may:

(a) initiate a private action in the court against the violation of the provisions contained in Chapter One;

(b) initiate a private action in the court or turn to the competition authority with an application against the violation of the provisions contained in Article 3 and Chapter Two; and

(c) apply to the competition authority against the violation of the provisions contained in Chapters Three, Four or Five.

Article 29

1. An interested party may request particularly the following forms of civil relief before the court

(a) an order establishing a violation of law;

(b) an injunction to stop the infringement and forbid any further infringements of the violator;

(c) satisfaction from the violator by public statements or other appropriate means, including, if necessary, appropriate publicity at the violator's expense;

(d) cessation of the injurious situation, restoration of the status quo ante, or rectification of the characteristic giving rise to the injury, or if rectification is not possible, destruction of such goods and of the special instruments used in their manufacture;

(e) damages, as provided for by civil law liability rules.

2. If the competition authority establishes an unjustified refusal to conclude a contract on the basis of subparagraph (b) of Article 20, an interested party may petition the court to find a contract. In so finding, the court may put into force the contract establishing its content under terms that are customary in the trade.

Article 30

1. Except as provided in Article 31, no proceedings shall be initiated later than six months from the date on which the illegal conduct was discovered, but for such cause of action to be actionable, not more than three years may have elapsed from the date on which such conduct was committed. No relief shall be available if this deadline is not met.

2. If the conduct infringing the Act is being performed by putting no end to a situation or to a state, the periods set out in paragraph 1 will be delayed as long as this situation or state exists.

Article 31

1. The competition authority or the organisation representing the interests of consumers may initiate civil proceedings against any person who, by its illegal act, causes to the consumers injury affecting a broad range of them or significant disadvantage, whether or not the identity of consumers injured thereby can be established.

2. Any claim pursuant to paragraph (1) must be brought within one year from the arising of such disadvantage.

3. In a suit brought under this Article, the court may require the violator to reduce the price to repair or exchange the goods or to refund the price. The court may authorize the claimant to publish its decision in a daily newspaper of national circulation at cost of the offending party.

4. A violator is obliged to satisfy the claims of the consumer injured. This does not limit the rights of the consumer to enforce other claims under the provisions of civil law.

CHAPTER SEVEN
PROCEEDINGS
GENERAL RULES OF PROCEDURE

Article 32

The competition authority shall examine the enforcement of the provisions of this Act.

Article 33

1. Proceedings by the competition authority may be initiated at the request of an interested party or ex officio. An application may be submitted by any person who has, or may, sustain injury due to the unlawful activity and whose rights or legitimate interests are affected by the case.

2. If proceedings are initiated at the request of an interested party, such party's application must include all information necessary to adjudicate his claim. If the application does not contain the necessary information, the competition authority may return it once for completing together with notice of a new filing deadline. If the application is so refiled, any procedural deadlines shall be determined with reference to the repeated receipt of the application.

Article 34

1. Unless otherwise stipulated by this Act the provisions contained in Act IV of 1957 on general rules of state administrative procedure shall be applied to the proceedings of the competition authority.

2. Unless another deadline is established by the Act the competition authority is required to issue a decision within sixty days from the date of receipt of an application in the event proceedings are initiated at the request of an interested party, or from the date an investigation is initiated in the event such proceedings are initiated *ex officio* or from the date of delivery in the event such proceedings start due to judicial referral. The competition authority may once extend the deadline by up to sixty days. It shall notify this measure to the parties before the original deadline expires.

3. The competition authority, as well as any person commissioned by it during the proceedings, is obliged to keep confidential any business secrets of which it thereby becomes aware.

Article 35

1. The procedure used by the competition authority is composed of the following stages:
  (a) investigation, and
  (b) trial and decision-making in Council (Article 55, para. 1).

2. When cause exists, the competition authority may hear the body that represents the professional interests of the sides party to the case, and, if requested by an interested party, shall hear such professional body.

Article 36

1. The competition authority or any person commissioned by it to conduct an investigation, is authorized, in the conduct of its lawful duties:
  (a) to compel the entrepreneur to release information, without undue delay with regard to the nature of the case and to gather information on the spot;
  (b) to conduct an investigation at the entrepreneur, with the power, inter alia, to obtain access to documents related to the economic activity notwithstanding any state secrets, service secrets or business secrets that might be contained therein;
  (c) to make duplicates or extracts of such documents.

2. The person conducting such an investigation may impound the original documents of an entrepreneur only if a serious violation of law is suspected, and there is a belief that such documents would otherwise be tampered with or destroyed.

3. The person conducting such an investigation shall be entitled to full access to the examined entrepreneur's premises and may compel oral or written information from any of such entrepreneur's employees.

4. Other entrepreneurs, as well as state or social organs, shall be required to release to the investigator any information, and documents needed by it, if necessary for the investigation.

Article 37

1. Upon concluding its investigation, the competition authority shall hold a trial in council.

2. The date for the trial shall be set so as to afford the applicant and other persons affected by the case (hereinafter referred to as the 'parties') opportunity to inspect the documents on which the investigation is based and to prepare for trial.

Article 38

1. The parties may attend the trial in person or by means of their representatives, and may reflect to statements of the competition authority, of the trial proceedings and of any documents submitted. The parties may adduce their own evidence until the conclusion of the trial.

2. The trial council is authorized to take temporary measures prior to reaching a decision if such measures cannot be deferred in order to protect the legal or economic interests of the parties or in view of the formation, maintenance or development of competition being jeopardized.

3. The proceedings except for proceedings concerning abuses of market power and consumer fraud, shall be closed to the public.

Article 39

1. The trial council shall make its decision at the conclusion of the trial. A decision may, however, be taken by neglecting the trial, if the parties agree herewith. The decision shall be delivered to the parties concerned.

2. The trial council may publish its decision made in the merits of the case in the official gazette of the Office of Economic Competition.

Article 40

1. Except as provided in Paragraph (2), the following fees must be paid in connection with proceedings concerning the supervision of competition:
   (a) 1000 forints in proceedings initiated by natural persons other than entrepreneurs;
   (b) 100 000 forints in proceedings relating to concentrations;
   (c) 10 000 forints in all other cases.

2. No fee shall be payable for proceedings concerning supervision of competition if such proceedings were initiated at the competition authority:

    (a) as a result of obligatory preliminary notification of a foreseen price increase, or

    (b) in cases in which the court has transferred the case in order to imposing fine [Paragraph (2) of Article 47].

3. Fees set in Subparagraph (a) of Paragraph (1) must be paid in stamps and fees set in Subparagraph (b) and (c) of Paragraph (1) must be paid in cash to an account established by the Ministry of Finance.[2] The fee payable in connection with proceedings concerning the supervision of competition must be paid at the time an application is filed. The failure to include the proper fee shall be grounds for the return of such application in which case procedural deadlines shall be calculated with reference to the date of repeated receipt of the application.

4. Fees payable in connection with such proceedings shall be paid by the person whose illegal conduct has been established. If the proceedings were initiated in cases relating to concentrations on the basis of an application requesting permission to consummate such a transaction , or ex officio, the fee for the proceedings must be jointly refunded by the parties involved in the concentration.

5. Other rules of law pertaining to the fees payable in connection with proceedings concerning supervision of competition shall apply in the event such supervision is conducted by the State Securities Supervision, the State Banking Supervision, or the State Supervisory Authority of Insurance.

6. The competition authority may exempt the party from the requirement to pay the fee in connection with such supervision in the event that the payment of such a fee would constitute a burden incommensurate with the party's income or assets.

7. Other costs incurred during the proceedings by the competition authority shall be advanced by the State and be borne by the person whose illegal conduct is confirmed. If no violation of law is found to have occurred, such other costs arising during the proceedings shall be borne by the person who requested the proceedings.

Article 41

1. Decisions of the competition authority shall not be subject to appeal. The interested party may request the court to review the decision made in the merits of the case within thirty days from the issuance of the decision. Statements of claim shall be submitted at the competition authority.

2. The filing of a complaint, except with respect to a decision imposing a fine shall not delay the execution of such a decision.

3. The complaint requesting a review of a decision of the competition authority together with the documents shall be transferred by the competition authority to the court within eight days of receipt thereof.

4. The competition authority may publish its decision made in the merits of the case even if the review of the decision by the court has been requested.

Decisions of the competition authority

Article 42

1. The competition authority:

---

2. Note: NgE. Competition supervision proceeding fee intake account 232–90103–7577.

(a) may refer a matter to the court in the event a violation of the provisions of the Articles 4 to 10 of this Act seriously affects or jeopardises the fairness of competition;

(b) shall issue decisions in merits of the cases in other matters.

2. If an interested party has filed a complaint with the competition authority against a violation of the provisions contained in Article 3 or Articles 11 to 27, and it has established the occurrence of an unfair act of competition (Articles 4 to 10), it shall inform the interested party of its right to proceed to a law court with its claim.

Article 43

1. By its decision, the competition authority
   (a) may establish the fact of infringement;
   (b) may prohibit the continuation of practices violating the provisions of the Act;
   (c) in the event any illegal practices threaten imminent harm, may enjoin the person posing a threat from performing such practice, or may order him to take measures necessary to prevent damages, and, if necessary, to establish safeguards;
   (d) may establish that the agreement (planned agreement) restricting competition shall not be prohibited, or may rule on the applicability of an exemption pursuant to the provisions of Paragraphs (2) and (3) of Article 17;
   (e) may permit concentrations of entrepreneurs, on conditions as it may impose, or prohibit such transactions;
   (f) may impose a fine on persons violating the provisions of this Act;
   (g) may prohibit planned price increases of certain goods falling into the scope of compulsory notification.

2. If the competition authority files a complaint with the court against a violation of the provisions of the Act, it may enforce civil law claims regulated in Article 29, Paragraph (1), subparagraph (a), (b) and (d).

Article 44

1. The competition authority is required to conclude any proceedings initiated in connection with the prohibition of agreements restricting competition within forty-five days counted from starting the proceedings or from putting the case over by court. It may once extend the deadline by up to forty-five days; it shall notify this measure to the parties before the original deadline expires.

2. If the competition authority fails to meet the deadlines under Paragraph (1) in proceedings initiated pursuant to Paragraph (1) of Article 18, the application shall be deemed fulfilled.

Article 45

1. The competition authority is required to notify the applicant of its decision on the application related to a concentration within ninety days from the date on which the application was delivered. It may once extend the deadline by up to six months; it shall notify this measure to the parties before the original deadline expires.

2. If the competition authority fails to meet the original or extended deadline, the permission shall be deemed granted.

3. In the course of assessing an application for a permission, the opinion of the minister concerned must be solicited.

Article 46

If no permission was requested to consummate a concentration, and the concentration could not have been permitted even on application, the competition authority shall by decision, invalidate the concentration within ninety days from the date it learned of it and shall notify the parties concerned, as well as the court of registration. The competition authority may once extend this deadline by up to six months.

Article 47

1. The competition authority shall, by decision, impose a fine on any person found to have violated the provisions of this Act.

2. The court that, by its valid decision, finds a violation of the provisions of this Act shall send its decision to the competition authority for the purposes of imposing a fine.

Article 48

1. The amount of the fine shall exceed by at least 30%, but no more than 100% of either the value of the material advantage gained through unlawful conduct or the sum of the damage suffered by consumers and competitors. In special cases, the amount of the fine may be less than 30%.

2. In the absence of unlawful material advantage or damage, the amount of the fine shall be set with regard to the totality of the circumstances, including, in particular, the extent to which competitive interests were jeopardized.

JUDICIAL PROCEEDINGS

Article 49

1. The provisions of Chapter XX of the Civil Procedure shall be applied in an appropriate manner to court proceedings initiated on the basis of a complaint (Article 41) against the decision of the competition authority with such exceptions as specified in the Act. The court may overturn the decision of the competition authority.

2. If proceedings by the competition authority have been initiated on an application, the court proceedings reviewing the decision shall be initiated against the applicant as well.

3. In the event competition supervision proceedings were initiated by request, and significant injury of procedural rules occurred in the course of such proceedings, the court may, by its decision, if it is otherwise unable to remedy such injuries by means of its judicial procedure, instruct the competition authority to initiate new proceedings.

Article 50

Except as provided pursuant to Paragraph (2) of Article 63, all suits initiated under this Act fall within the competence of the county court. The Metropolitan Court is competent to hear a suit brought under the provisions of Paragraph (1) of Article 49.

Article 51

If an interested party filed a complaint with the court against the violation of provisions contained in Articles 3 to 13; and in the course of such proceedings the court established:
- (a) that also an abuse of dominant position (Articles 20 to 22) was committed, the court shall also rule thereon;
- (b) a restriction or exclusion of competition (Articles 14 to 19), resp. an unlawful concentration of entrepreneurs (Articles 23 to 27), was also committed the court shall transfer the case to the competition authority.

CHAPTER EIGHT
OFFICE OF ECONOMIC COMPETITION

Article 52

1. Except as provided in Paragraph (2), the Office of Economic Competition shall perform the duties of supervising competition in accordance with the provisions of this Act and the Act on Price Setting.

2. The State Securities Supervision, the State Banking Supervision and the State Supervisory Authority of Insurance shall perform the duties of supervising competition in matters concerning money and securities markets and insurance activities and shall apply separate procedural rules and rules relating to legal consequences.

Article 53

1. The Office of Economic Competition is a budgetary institution with a nationwide competence.

2. The Office of Economic Competition is headed by a president.

3. The president and the two vice presidents of the Office of Economic Competition are appointed for a term of six years on the proposal of the prime minister and may be dismissed by the president of the Republic.

Article 54

1. The authorization of the president and the vice presidents of the Office of Economic Competition shall terminate upon:
- (a) the expiration of the appointed term;
- (b) such official's dismissal;
- (c) such official's resignation;
- (d) such official's death.

2. The authorization of the president and the vice presidents of the Office of Economic Competition shall be terminated on dismissal if
 (a) such official commits a crime, the verdict for which becomes valid;
 (b) such official becomes permanently unfit for his office;
 (c) such official has an incompatibility with his/her position that has not been resolved.

Article 55

1. The decisions of the Office of Economic Competition are made by the Competition Council, which proceeds by means of its councils composed of at least three members.

2. The president of the Competition Council shall be a vice president of the Office of Economic Competition.

3. The members of the Competition Council are appointed for an unspecified term and may be dismissed by the president of the Office of Economic Competition.

4. The president and the members of the Competition Council are accountable only to law.

Article 56

1. The president, vice presidents and the administrators of the Office of Economic Competition and the members of the Competition Council must not pursue any other activities for profit other than activities dedicated to scientific, educational, artistic, authorial and inventive (i.e. falling under patent law protection) pursuits, as well activities arising out of legal relationships aimed at instructorial and editorial revision, and must not serve as senior officials of companies or members of a supervisory board or board of directors.

2. Persons specified in Paragraph 1 may not be relatives of each other (Civil Code, Article 685, Paragraph (b)) and may not participate in an investigation of an entrepreneur with whom they have business relationship or with whom a close relative of them is in an employment or other legal relationship of labour law.

Article 57

1. Arising of incompatibilities must be notified without delay as follows:
 (a) if arising for the president or a vice president of the Office of Economic Competition, to the prime minister;
 (b) if arising for administrators of the Office of Economic Competition or members of the Competition Council, to the president of the Office of Economic Competition.

2. Notifiers are required to eliminate the incompatibility within eight days from the date of notification.

Article 58

1. The president of the Office of Economic Competition shall report to Parliament annually or, if specially requested by the competent Parliamentary committee, at least annually, on the activities of the Office of Economic Competition and, on the basis of his experience in applying the Act, on the manner in which the freedom and fairness of economic competition is observed.

2. The president of the Office of Economic Competition shall, upon special request, issue a written expertise to Parliament on any matter before Parliament affecting economic competition.

Article 59

The president of the Office of Economic Competition:
  (a) shall guide the activities of the Office of Economic Competition, and secure that the Office of Economic Competition operates in accordance with law;
  (b) shall participate in sessions of Parliament;
  (c) shall represent the Office of Economic Competition;
  (d) shall issue the bylaws of the Office of Economic Competition;
  (e) shall employ persons to work in the Office of Economic Competition.

Article 60

Ministers are obliged to solicit the opinion of the Office of Economic Competition on every draft bill that would have a restrictive effect on competition, including, in particular, market activities or access, or that would provide exclusive rights or regulate prices or marketing.

Article 61

1. The president of the Office of Economic Competition shall participate in sessions of the Government that address questions affecting the scope of the Office of Economic Competition and shall have the right to be consulted thereupon.
2. The Office of Economic Competition shall release information with respect to its activities requested by the Government and by ministers except for information on proceedings still pending.

Article 62

The ministries, the State Property Agency, municipalities and other state administrative agencies shall release information to the Office of Economic Competition at its request in connection with their activities related to the supervision of competition.

CLOSING PROVISIONS

Article 63

1. Should the ruling of some state administrative agency violate the freedom of competition, the competition authority shall have the right to apply for redress.
2. The competition authority may appeal to the court for a review of any ruling referred to in Paragraph (1) above within thirty days from the date such injury of law is discovered. No legal remedy shall be available to redress a ruling later than six months after it has become valid. No relief shall be available if this deadline is not met.

Article 64

Legal consequences applied and civil claims enforced because of the infringement of the provisions of this Act shall not prejudice, pursuant to other legal regulations, to the application of other legal consequences of the civil law respectively to the possibility of starting regulatory or criminal procedures.

Article 65

The competition authority may also examine agreements resulting in restriction or exclusion of competition concluded before the date on which this Act entered into force and may issue decisions pursuant to Paragraph (1) (b) of Article 43, if the parties continue any illegal conduct under such an agreement after this Act became effective.

Article 66

All proceedings outstanding for the purpose of imposing fines as of the date this Act becomes effective shall be wound up.

Article 67

1. This Act shall take effect on 1 January 1991.
2. Immediately upon the effectiveness of this Act:
   (a) Paragraph (6) of Article 3 of Act IV of 1957 on the general rules of state administrative proceedings shall be replaced by the following provision:
   '(6) This Act shall be applied to matters affecting national defence, foreign exchange authority, foreign trade administration and social insurance, as well as to matters regulated by the Acts prohibiting unfair market practices and declaring certain provisions of price setting, unless otherwise provided by law,'
   (b) Article 321 of the Act VI of 1988 on companies shall be supplemented with the following provision:
   'In such an event, the provisions of the Act prohibiting unfair market practices shall also apply,'
   (c) Article 10 of the Act VI of 1977 on public undertakings shall be supplemented with the following provision:
   'In the event of a merger (amalgamation, combination), the provisions of the Act prohibiting unfair market practices relating to the control of concentration shall also apply,'
   (d) Paragraph (1) of Article 60 of the Act XIII of 1989 on the transformation of economic organisations and companies shall be supplemented with the following provision:
   'In the event of a merger (amalgamation, combination), the provisions of the Act prohibiting unfair market practices relating to the control of concentration shall also apply,'
   (e) Article 45 of the Act III of 1971 on the co-operatives shall be supplemented with the following Paragraph (3):
   '3. In the event of a merger (amalgamation, combination), the provi-

sions of the Act prohibiting unfair market practices relating to the control of concentration shall also apply,'
(f) Act III of 1967 on the agricultural co-operatives shall be supplemented with the following Article 128/A:
'Article 128/A. In the event of a merger (amalgamation, combination), the provisions of the Act prohibiting unfair market practices relating to the control of concentration shall also apply.'

3. Upon the effectiveness of this Act, the following regulations shall cease to have effect:
- Act IV of 1984 on prohibiting unfair economic activities;
- Council of Ministers Decree 32/1984 (31st Oct) on economic fines and Council of Ministers Decree 69/1987 (7 December) amending it;
- Council of Ministers Decree 37/1984 (5th Nov) on market supervision and Article 3 of Council of Ministers Decree 25/1988 (8th Apr) amending it

1.3   THE POLISH STATUTE

Uniform text announced in Journal of Law No 80, item 405 of 12 July 1995

The Law
of 24 February 1990
on Counteracting Monopolistic Practices

In order to ensure the development of competition, protection of business entities exposed to monopolistic practices and protection of consumer interests, the following shall be enacted:

CHAPTER 1
GENERAL PROVISIONS

Article 1[1]

This Law governs the principles and procedures of counteracting monopolistic practices of business entities and the associations thereof, which cause or may cause effects within the territory of the Republic of Poland, and specifies the organs competent in the above matters.

Article 2

Whenever the Law refers to:
1.[2] business entities – shall mean natural and legal persons, as well as organiza-

---

1. Wording as determined by Art. 1 item 1 of the Law of 3 February, 1995 on amending the Law on counteracting monopolistic Practices (*Journal of Law*, No. 41 , item 208), which came into force on 19 May, 1995.
2. Wording as determined by Art. 1 item 2 letter (a) of the Law specified in annotation 1.

tional units having no legal personality, running business activities or entities organ-ising or rendering public utility services, which are not considered business activ-ities (*Journal of Law* No. 41, item 324; of 1990 No. 26, item 149 and No. 86, item 504, of 1991 No. 31, item 128, No. 41, item 179, No. 73, item 321, No. 105, item 452, No. 106, item 457 and No. 107, item 460, of 1993 No. 28, item 127, No. 47, item 212 and No. 134, item 646 and of 1994 No. 27, item 96 and No. 127, item 627).

2. associations – shall mean chambers, confederations and other organisations associating business entities,

3. agreements – shall mean those contradictory to this Law:
   (a)[3] contracts concluded between business entities, between associations of business entities and between business entities and associations, or certain clauses thereof,
   (b) settlements between two or more business entities or associations thereof undertaken in any form,
   (c) resolutions or other acts adopted by associations of business entities,

4. prices – shall also mean any pricewise charges, trade margins, commissions and retail margins,

5. goods – shall mean things, all forms of energy, services, construction projects and facilities, securities and other proprietary rights,

6. monopolistic position – shall mean such a position of the business entity posi-tion, where the entity does not encounter any competition on the domestic or local markets,

7. dominant position – shall mean the position of a business entity based on the fact that the entity does not encounter any competition on the domestic or local markets; the business entity is presumed to hold a dominant position when its share in the market exceeds 40%.

8.[4] competitors – shall mean the business entities which introduce or may intro-duce, or purchase or may purchase, at the same time and on the same market, the goods either the same or different, providing the users of such goods consider them substitutes,

9.[5] average salary – shall mean the average monthly salary within the industry sector in the last month of the quarter preceding the day of issue of the decision by the Anti-monopoly Office, announced by the President of the Chief Office of Statistics by way of separate regulations.

10.[6] revenue – shall mean 1/12 of the revenue attained in taxation year preceding the day of issue of the decision by the Anti-monopoly Office as provided under the regulations on income tax from legal persons or from natural persons.

Article 3[7]

This Law does not violate any exclusive rights ensuing from the legal regulations concerning proprietary rights or copyright, and in particular from the legal regula-

---

3. Wording as determined by Art. 1 item 2 letter (b) of the Law specified in annotation 1.
4. Appended by Art. 1 item 2 letter (c) of the Law specified in annotation 1.
5. Appended by Art. 1 item 2 letter (c) of the Law specified in annotation 1.
6. Appended by Art. 1 item 2 letter (c) of the Law specified in annotation 1.
7. Wording as determined by Art. 1 item 3 of the Law specified in annotation 1.

tions on inventions, trademarks, decorative patterns, protection of topography of integrated circuits, copyrights and associated rights and agreements concluded by employees and trade unions with employers and aimed at protection of employee rights.

2. This Law shall apply to:
   (a) License contracts and other acts of exercising exclusive rights specified under item 1,
   (b) contracts concerning technical or technological information not disclosed to the public, with regard to which necessary action has been taken to ensure their confidentiality,

if the above contracts and agreements result in an unjustified reduction of freedom of business activities of the parties and significant reduction of market competition.

CHAPTER 2
MONOPOLISTIC PRACTICES

Article 4[8]

Monopolistic practices shall be defined as agreements aimed in particular at:
1. direct or indirect fixing of prices and determining the principles of pricing between competitors in their relations with third parties,
2. dividing the market according to territorial, assortment or subjective criteria,
3. fixing or reducing the volume of output, sales or purchases of goods,
4. limiting access to the market or eliminating from the market those business entities which do not participate in such an agreement,
5. the establishing, by the competitors or their associations, of conditions of contracts entered with third parties.

Article 5.1[9]

1. Also considered monopolistic practices are the events of abuse of the dominant position in the market, and in particular:
   (a) counteracting the formation of conditions essential to the creation or development of competition,
   (b) division of the market according to territorial, assortment or subjective criteria,
   (c) sale of goods in a manner resulting in granting privileges to some business or other entities,
   (d) refusal to sell or purchase goods, thus discriminating against some business entities due to lack of alternative purchase or sale sources,
   (e) unfair influence upon the formation of prices, including the prices of resale, and sale below cost aimed at eliminating competitors,

---

8. Taking into consideration the numbering changes introduced by Art. 1 section 4 of the Law specified in annotation 1 and in the wording determined by the aforementioned regulation.
9. Numbering as determined by Art. 2 of the Law of 7 July, 1994 on the amendments to the Co-operative Law and on the amendments to various other Laws (*Journal of Law*, No. 90, item 419), which came into force on 26 September, 1994.

(f)[10] imposition of onerous contract conditions yielding unjustified benefits to the business entities imposing such terms,

(g)[11] making the conclusion of a contract conditional upon the acceptance or fulfilment by the other party of other services not associated with the subject matter of the contract, which otherwise the other party would not have accepted or fulfilled given freedom of choice.

2.[12] The granting by a cooperative to its members in their mutual dealing of certain bonuses, relieves and other economic benefits shall not be considered a monopolistic practice.

Article 6[13]

The practices specified under Art. 4 and Art. 5 above shall be forbidden, unless they are necessary for technical, organisational or economic reasons to running business activities and they do not cause any significant reduction of competition; the obligation to document such circumstances is vested in the entity adducing such circumstances.

Article 7.1

1. The business entities activities holding a monopolistic position shall also be forbidden to:

(a) reduce, despite their existing capacity, the volume of output, sales or purchase of goods, particularly where it leads to a rise in prices,

(b) suppress the sales of goods to lead to a rise in prices,

(c) charge excessive prices.

2. The interdictions specified under item 1 shall also apply to business entities holding a dominant position, unless their market share and the practices apply thereby lead to results similar to the results of behavior of business entities which hold a monopolistic position.

Article 8.1[14]

1. Where the monopolistic practices specified under Art. 4, Art. 5 and Art. 7 have been found, the Antimonopoly Office shall issue a decision ordering such practices to be abandoned and specifying the terms of such an abandonment.

2. The whole or the appropriate parts of the contracts concluded in violation of Art. 4, Art. 5 and Art. 7 shall be null and void.

3.[15] where, as a result of the monopolistic practices, specified under item 1, the prices have been increased, the Anti-monopoly Office may issue a decision ordering a reduction of prices and determining the period of validity of the price and the conditions of its change by the business entity at that time. For the period the

---

10. Appended by Art. 1 section 5 of the Law specified in annotation 1.
11. Appended by Art. 1 section 5 of the Law specified in annotation 1.
12. Appended by Art. 2 of the Law specified in annotation 1.
13. Wording as determined by Art. 1 section 6 of the Law specified in annotation 7.
14. Wording as determined by Art. 1 section 7 letter (a) of the Law specified in annotation 1.
15. Wording as determined by Art. 1 section 7 letter (b) of the Law specified in annotation 1.

increased price has been charged, the Anti-monopoly Office may also specify, in such a decision, the undue amount or the undue amount and the additional amount; the provisions under Art. 20 of the Law of 26 February, 1982 on Prices (*Journal of Law*, 1988, No. 27, item 195; 1990 No. 34, item 198; 1991, No. 100, item 442; 1993, No. 11, item 50; and 1994, No. 11, item 536) shall apply, respectively.

Article 9.1

1. The Anti-monopoly Office may issue a decision forbidding the execution of an agreement, which:
    (a) introduces an assortment-wise specialization of production or sales; or
    (b) provides for joint sales or joint purchases of goods,
if such an agreement is detrimental to the interests of other business entities or consumers.

2. The Anti-monopoly Office shall issue a decision forbidding the execution of agreements specified under item 1 if it leads to a significant reduction of competition or of the conditions necessary for its emergence within given market, thus failing to bring economic benefits, consisting, in particular, of:
    (a) a considerable reduction of production or sales costs; or
    (b) improvement in the quality of goods.

Article 10.1[16]

1. The decisions taken by the Anti-monopoly Office shall be subject to appeal filed to the Voivodship Court in Warsaw – the Anti-monopoly Court – within two weeks of the date the decision has been delivered.

2. The proceedings in the case of appeals against the decisions of the Antimonopoly Office shall be carried out pursuant to the provisions of the Code of Civil Procedures relating to the proceedings in business matters.

3. The Anti-monopoly Office may order immediate execution of its decisions.

4.[17] The decisions of the Anti-monopoly Office which can be appealed against, shall be subject to the provisions under items 1 and 2, respectively, providing the appeal is filed within 7 days.

CHAPTER 3
INFLUENCE UPON FORMATION OF ORGANIZATIONAL STRUCTURES OF BUSINESS ENTITIES

Article 11.1[18]

1. The Anti-monopoly Office shall be notified of any intention to merge or to transform an business entity in cases specified under items 2 and 3 within 14 days from the execution of action which the Law associates with such obligation.

---

16. Wording as determined by Art. 1 section 8 letter (a) of the Law specified in annotation 1.
17. Appended by Art. 1 section 8, letter (b) of the Law specified in annotation 1.
18. Wording as determined by Art. 1 section 10 of the Law specified in annotation 1.

2. The obligation to deliver the notice of intention to merge, provided under item 1 concerns:

(a) the merger of business entities, whose total annual sales volume – in the calendar year preceding the year of notification on the intention to merge – exceeds 5 million ECU,

(b) the acquisition or take-over by a business entity, once or repeatedly within 12 subsequent months, of an organised part of the property of another business entity, if the total value of such property exceeds 2 million ECU,

(c) the take-over or acquisition of stocks or shares of another business entity, resulting in the reaching or exceeding the limit of 10%, 25%, 33% or 50% of votes at a general assembly or assembly of shareholders, if the total annual sales volume of both business entities – in the calendar year preceding the year of notification on the intention – exceeds 5 million ECU;

(d) the take-over or acquisition by financial institutions, whose business activities consist of trading securities, of stocks or shares of another business entities, resulting in the reaching or exceeding the limit of 10%, 25%, 33% or 50% of votes at the general assembly of partners or assembly of shareholders, if the total annual volume of sales of the acquired entity's goods – in the calendar year preceding the year of notification on the intention – exceeds 5 million ECU, unless the taking into possession or acquisition of stocks or shares was performed with the intention to resell them before the lapse of 1 year, relinquishing the execution until that time of rights ensuing from the possession of such stocks and shares, apart from the right to receive dividends and the right to dispose of such stocks and shares,

(e) assuming by the same person the positions of a director, assistant director, board member, member of supervisory board, member of auditing commission or chief accountant in competing business entities, if the total annual volume of sales of goods – in the calendar year preceding the year of notification on the intention – exceeds 5 million ECU,

(f) take-over in other manner, directly or indirectly, of control over another business entity, if the total annual sales volume of goods – in the calendar year preceding the year of notification on the intention – exceeds 5 million ECU.

3. The obligation to deliver a notice of intention to merge banks, within the scope specified under item 2 applies to banks if the total volume of the bank equity exceeds 50 million ECU as of the end of calendar year preceding the year of delivering the notice of intention to merge.

4. The total annual volume of sales of goods specified under item 2, encompasses the sales performed as both the dominating entity and a dependent entity pursuant to the provisions under Art. 2 section 9 of the Law of 22 March, 1991 – The Law on Public Dealing in Securities and Trust Funds (*Journal of Law* of 1994, No. 58, item 239; No. 71, item 313 and No. 121, item 591).

5. The value of ECU specified under items 2 and 3 shall be converted to Polish Zlotys according to foreign exchange rates announced by the National Bank of Poland NBP:

(a) on the last day of the calendar year preceding the year of notification of intention, specified under item 2 sections (a) and (c)–(f) and item 3,

(b) on the day preceding the notification of intention to purchase the property, specified under item 2 section (b),

6. The provisions under items 1 and 2 do not apply to stocks admitted to public trading.

7. The intention to merge business entities shall be notified by business entity organs pursuant to provisions under Art. 11e.

8. The notice of intention to merge shall contain information concerning the influence of merger upon the change of position of business entities and its consequences to the competition, and in particular to:

(a) the type, cause and scope of merger of business entities,

(b) the particulars characterising the business entities partaking in the merger, their associations with other business entities and the scope and field of their activities,

(c) the market shares of such entities in various markets.

Article 11a[19]

1. The Antimonopoly Office may:

(a) return within 14 days the notice of intention to merge, shall it fail to meet the conditions specified under Art. 11, item 8 and the conditions which should be met by the notice of intention to merge or transform business entities,

(b) order the party delivering the notice of intention to merge, to remedy the indicated errors in the notice and to supplement the essential information, instructing it that exceeding the relevant deadline may result in the administration of a fine pursuant to provisions under Art. 16 item 2 section 1,

2. The Anti-monopoly Office may also present the business entities – prior to issuing a decision forbidding the merger – the conditions, upon which such merger may be executed, stating the deadline for taking a position regarding the proposal filed; the failure to reply in time or taking a negative position with regard to the conditions presented, results in issuing a notice or decision specified under items 3 and 4.

3. If there are no reservations regarding the intention to merge, the Anti-monopoly Office, within a time limit not longer than 2 months, shall inform the party notifying on the intention.

4 The Antimonopoly Office, within a time limit not longer than 2 months, may issue a decision:

(a) forbidding the merger of business entities, shall such action cause the business entities to attain or reinforce their dominating market position,

(b) forbidding the assumption by the same person of functions specified under Art. 11 item 2 section e, if such an action results in a significant deterioration of competition; it is hereby presumed that significant deterioration of competition occurs when the joint market share of such entities exceeds 10%.

5. In case of an intention to merge banks, the Anti-monopoly Office, within a

---

19. Appended by Art. 1 section 11 of the Law specified in annotation 1.

time limit not longer than 2 weeks, shall notify the party in question of the lack of reservation or it may, within the above specified time limit, issue a decision forbidding the bank merger.

6. The time limits specified under items 3–5 do not include the waiting time for removing gaps, supplementing information or taking a position regarding the conditions filed by the Antimonopoly Office, specified under item 1 section 2 and item 2.

Article 11b[20]

The Court of Registration, acting upon the grounds of separate provisions, shall make an entry into register, if:

(a) the Antimonopoly Office notifies the applicant of the lack of reservations regarding the intention to merge, specified under Art. 11a items 3 and 5,

(b) the business entity demonstrates that the intention to merge business entities is not notifiable.

Article 11c[21]

1. The intention to transform a commercial law company, a state-owned company into a single-shareholder State Treasury Company and a utility company into a municipal company is notifiable to the Antimonopoly Office within 14 days from the execution of actions associated by the law with the obligation to notify.

2. The obligation to deliver a notice of intention to transform, pursuant to provisions under item 1, applies to entities whose annual sales volume of goods attained in the calendar year preceding the year of notice of intention exceeds 5 million ECU.

3. The Anti-monopoly Office may, within a time limit no longer than 2 months, issue a decision forbidding the transformation, if the company resulting from such transformation maintains a dominating market position.

4. The provisions under Art. 11 item 4, items 5 and 7, Art. 11a items 1–3, items 5–6 and Art. 11b shall be applied respectively.

Article 11d[22]

The business entities with regard to which the intention to merge or transform is notifiable, until the receipt of a notice from the Anti-monopoly Office on the lack of reservations concerning the intention to merge or transform, or until the deadline for the issuing of a decision prohibiting the merger or transformation, shall be obligated to refrain from undertaking actions which result or may result in attaining or reinforcing a dominating market position by the merging or transformed entities or one of such entities, even if such actions do not constitute monopolistic practices according to the provision of the Law.

Article 11e[23]

The Council of Ministers shall determine, by way of ordinance, the detailed conditions which should be met by the notice of intention to merge and trans-

20. Appended by Art. 1 section 11 of the Law specified in annotation 1.
21. Appended by Art. 1 section 11 of the Law specified in annotation 1.
22. Appended by Art. 1 section 11 of the Law specified in annotation 1.
23. Appended by Art. 1 section 11 of the Law specified in annotation 1.

form business entities, and the organs of the entities obligated to notify of such intention.

Article 12.1

1. State-owned enterprises and cooperatives, as well as commercial law companies holding a dominating market position, may be subject to division or dissolution if they permanently restrict the competition or the conditions for its formation.

2.[24] Where it has been established that business entities fulfil the conditions specified under item 1, the Anti-monopoly Office may issue a decision ordering the division of an enterprise or a cooperative or the dissolution of a company, specifying the terms and the time of such a division or dissolution. Prior to issuing a decision ordering the division of a state-owned company or a dissolution of a single-shareholder State Treasury Company, the Antimonopoly Office shall acquire an opinion from the founding organ or an organ representing the State Treasury.

3.[25] It shall be the duty of state-owned enterprise bodies, cooperative bodies or company bodies to execute the decision, and such execution shall take place under the provisions regulating the manner of division or dissolution of a given entity, respectively; executing the division does not require the consent or opinion envisaged under these regulations. State-owned enterprises, created as a result to such divisions, shall be created by a founding organ.

4. Where it has been found that a business entity has assumed a dominant position in the market, the Anti-monopoly Office may issue a decision ordering the limiting of its business activities, specifying the conditions and dates of such reductions.

5. The provisions under item 1 do not exclude the possibility of division or dissolution of business entities pursuant to other regulations.

Article 13[26]

The provisions of Art. 10 shall be applied, respectively, to decisions and resolutions taken regarding the merger, transformation, division and dissolution of business entities and the limiting of their business activities.

CHAPTER 4
LIABILITY FOR VIOLATING THE PROVISIONS OF THE LAW[27]
Article 14.1[28]

1. In the decisions issued on the grounds of Art. 8 items 1 and 3 and Art. 9, the Anti-monopoly Office may impose a fine payable to the State budget. Such a fine shall not be applied where the Anti-monopoly Office has made a decision establishing the value of the undue amount and the additional amount, specified under Art. 8, item 3.

---

24. Wording as determined by Art. 1 section 12 letter (a) of the Law specified in annotation 1.
25. Wording as determined by Art. 1 section 12 letter (a) of the Law specified in annotation 1.
26. Wording as determined by Art. 1 section 13 of the Law specified in annotation 1.
27. Wording as determined by Art. 1 section 14 of the Law specified in annotation 1.
28. Wording as determined by Art. 1 section 15 letter (a) of the Law specified in annotation 1.

2.[29] The fine specified under item 1 shall amount up to 15% of the revenues of the business entity thus penalized.

3. The fine specified under item 1 shall be paid out of the taxable income or from other form of surplus of revenues over expenditures less taxes.

4.[30] The provisions under item 1 apply respectively to associations. Where the association does not attain any revenues, the fine may be determined by the Anti-monopoly Office at the level of fifty-fold the average salary.

Article 15[31]

1. When the business entities fails to execute the decisions specified under Art. 8 items 1 and 3, Art. 9, Art. 11a items 4 and 5 and Art. 11c, or court judgments altering such decisions, it shall be obligated, for each commenced month of failure to execute such a decision or a court judgement, to remit a fine to the amount of 1% of revenues. The decision on this issue shall be taken by the Antimonopoly Office, however it cannot be made if 3 years have lapsed from the date of making the decisions specified under the preceding sentence.

2. In case of failure to execute the decision specified under Art. 12 items 2 and 4 or a court judgment altering such decisions, the fine shall amount from 1 to 10%; the provisions under item 1 shall apply respectively.

3. The fiscal penalties specified under items 1 and 2 shall be remitted to the State budget.

4. The provisions under Art. 10 and Art. 14 item 3 shall be applied respectively.

5.[32] The provisions under item 1 shall be applied respectively to associations. Where the association does not attain any revenues, the fine for each commenced month of failure to execute the decision or court judgement is determined by the Anti-monopoly Office at the level of fiftyfold the average salary.

Article 15a[33]

1. The Anti-monopoly Office may by way of a decision impose upon a business entity a fine to the amount of:
   (a) 1% of the revenues for each commenced month of failure to fulfil the obligation to notify pursuant to provisions under Art. 11 and Art. 11c, stipulating sections 3 and 4,
   (b) 15% of the revenues by way of executing the actions specified under Art. 11d,
   (c) 15% of the revenues, if following the take-over or acquisition of stocks or shares, the rights vested in such stocks or shares are executed with violation of Art. 11 item 2 section 4,
   (d) 1% of the revenues for each commenced month of possession of stocks or shares after the lapse of one year, specified under Art. 11 item 2 section 4,

---

29. Wording as determined by Art. 1 section 15 letter (b) of the Law specified in annotation 1.
30. Wording as determined by Art. 1 section 15 letter (c) of the Law specified in annotation 1.
31. Wording as determined by Art. 1 section 16 letter (a) of the Law specified in annotation 1.
32. Appended by Art. 1 section 16 letter (b) of the Law specified in annotation 1.
33. Appended by Art. 1 section 17 of the Law specified in annotation 1.

unless it demonstrates that with maintenance of appropriate care it could not have disposed of them earlier due to circumstances it cannot be held responsible for.

2. The Anti-monopoly Office, by way of a decision, may impose upon a person failing to execute the obligation to deliver notice, specified under Art. 11 item 2 section 5, a fine to the amount of fivefold the monthly salary for each commenced month of failure to fulfil such obligation.

3. The provisions under Art. 10, Art. 14 item 3 and Art. 15, shall be applied respectively.

Article 16.1[34]

1. Where a person managing a business entity or an association fails to execute decisions made under the Law and the court judgements, the Anti-monopoly Office may make a decision imposing upon such a person a fine up to the tenfold value of its average salary.

2. The following shall be subject to the fine specified in item 1 above:
   (a)[35] a person managing a business entity for failing to submit particulars and information as required by the Antimonopoly Office or where the particulars and information are unreliable,
   (b)[36] A person who acts on behalf of legal person or companies and other organisational units having no legal personality and undertaking measures leading to merger, transformation or formation of business entities if it has not notified of its intention as specified in Art. 11 and Art. 11c, or the notice of intention contains unreliable particulars or information.

3. The provision under paragraph 1 above shall not apply where the managerial function in the business entity is performed by a person running a business activity in one's own name.

4. The provisions under Art. 10 and Art. 15 item 3 shall be applied respectively.

CHAPTER 5
ANTIMONOPOLY ORGAN

Article 17.1

1. The Anti-monopoly Office shall be established as a central organ of State administration for the matters relating to counteracting monopolistic practices, subordinated to the Council of Ministers.

2. The Anti-monopoly Office shall be headed by the President, appointed and recalled by the Chairman of the Council of Ministers.

3. The Vice President of the Anti-monopoly Office shall be appointed and

---

34. Wording as determined by Art. 1 section 18 letter (a) of the Law specified in annotation 1.
35. Wording as determined by Art. 1 section 18 letter (b) tier one of the Law specified in annotation 1.
36. Wording as determined by Art. 1 section 18 letter (b) tier one of the Law specified in annotation 1.

recalled by the Chairman of the Council of Ministers upon request of the President of the Anti-monopoly Office.

4. The organization of the Anti-monopoly Office shall be defined by the statute bestowed by the Council of Ministers.

Article 18.1

1. The President of the Anti-monopoly Office may establish regional offices of the Antimonopoly Office and may determine the seat and the territorial and material competence thereof.

2. The branch offices of the Anti-monopoly Office shall be headed by directors appointed and recalled by the President of the Anti-monopoly Office.

3. Deputy directors of the regional offices of the Anti-monopoly Office shall be appointed and recalled, upon request of the directors of those regional offices, by the President of the Anti-monopoly Office.

Article 19.1

1. The scope of initiatives of the Anti-monopoly Office shall include:
   (a) inspection of the observance by business entities of provisions on counter-acting monopolistic practices.
   (b) examination of price formation under conditions of reduced competition,
   (c) issuing in cases envisaged by this Law, decisions relating to counteracting monopolistic practices, shaping the organisational structures of business entities and decisions determining the liability of entities for application of such practices.
   (d) keeping a register of business entities whose market share on the domestic market exceeds 80%.
   (e) conducting research into the level of economic concentration and presentation to the interested entities of conclusions relating to actions aimed at balancing the market.
   (f) elaborating of and providing opinions on the drafts of legal acts pertaining to monopolistic practices, development of competition and conditions for the creation thereof.
   (g) preparation of government policy drafts for competition development,
   (h) fulfilment of other tasks provided for under this Law and separate Laws.

2. The decisions specified under item 1 section (c) shall be undersigned by the President of the Antimonopoly Office or by a person authorised by the President.

Article 19a[37]

1. All business entities and associations of business entities, holding in their possession the documents, particulars and information essential to resolving a case pending before the Anti-monopoly Office shall be bound to make such items available to the Anti-monopoly Office or to submit such items to the Anti-monopoly Office at its demand.

---

37. Appended by Art. 1 section 19 of the Law specified in annotation 1.

2. The obligation resulting from item 1 also applies to issues specified in Art. 19 item 1 sections 6, d and e.

3. The information obtained by virtue of items 1 and 2 shall be governed by Art. 20 item 2, respectively.

Article 20.1[38]

1. The business entities shall be obliged, upon demand of the Antimonopoly Office performing inspection, to ensure proper conditions for the performance thereof.

2. The subject of the inspection, specified in Art. 19 item 1 section (a) is to determine, whether the inspected business entity observes the provisions on counteracting monopolistic practices, and in case of infringements thereof and the making of decisions or court judgements – whether those decisions and court judgement have been executed.

3. The employees of the Anti-monopoly Office, authorized to perform inspections, shall be authorised to:
   (a) enter all premises of the business entity under inspection,
   (b) inspect all documents of the business entity under inspection and demand copies and extracts from such documents,
   (c) demand explanations, also in written form, from the employees of the business entity under inspection,
   (d) collect particulars and information concerning the operations of the business entity under inspection, carried out also within other organizational units without the need for obtaining an additional authorization,
   (e) participate in the sessions of collective bodies of the business entity under inspection,
   (f) secure documents and other evidence,
   (g) make use of experts' opinions.

4. The information collected in the course of inspection by the employees of the Antimonopoly Office and persons authorized thereby shall be classified as restricted.

Article 20a[39]

1. The information collected in the course of duty actions by the employees of the Anti-monopoly Office and persons authorized thereby shall be classified as confidential as provided by the regulations on combating unfair competition if the business entity or association has undertaken the necessary action to maintain their confidential character.

2. The information specified under item 1 cannot be utilized for the needs of other proceedings carried out based on separate regulations,

3. The provisions under item 2 shall not apply to criminal litigation carried out by law execution bodies or courts, civil litigation exclusive.

---

38. Wording as determined by Art. 1 section 20 of the Law specified in annotation 1.
39. Appended by Art. 1 section 21 of the Law specified in annotation 1.

Article 21.1[40]

1. Administrative proceedings in cases envisaged under this Law shall be instituted *ex officio* or upon request of an empowered body. No proceedings shall be instigated if, until the end of year in the course of which the monopolistic practices have been abandoned, a year has lapsed. A refusal to instigate the proceedings is issued by way of a decision.

2. The bodies empowered to apply for the proceedings to be instituted are:
   (a) business entities, whose interests have been or may be infringed upon by a monopolistic practice as well as associations thereof,
   (b) State and social inspection organs,
   (c) social organizations whose statutory tasks include protection of consumer interests,
   (d) municipality organs.

3. The request to institute proceedings shall be submitted in writing and shall be justified.

4. No administrative proceedings shall be instituted if they result from the information contained in the request (application) and possessed by the Anti-monopoly Office that provisions of Art. 4, Art. 7, Art. 9, Art. 11 items 4 and 5, Art. 11c and Art. 12 items 2 and 4 have not been infringed. In such a case the Anti-monopoly Office shall inform the applicant in writing that the administrative proceedings will not be instituted for the reasons quoted. The proceedings shall be, however, instituted, if within 2 weeks the body empowered or obligated supports its request (application).

Article 21a[41]

1. The Anti-monopoly Office, at the request of a party or a body may to the necessary extent reduce the right of the remaining parties to inquire into the evidence material appended by the parties to the case files, if rendering such material accessible results in disclosure of significant secrets of the company.

2. The Anti-monopoly Office may by way of a resolution obligate the applicant or the party which applied for undertaking the actions associated with costs, to remit an advance payment for the costs of proceedings, under the pain of abandoning the application or relinquishing the examination of evidence.

3. The Anti-monopoly Office shall make the decision on costs of proceedings by way of a resolution.

4. The proceedings before the Antimonopoly Office shall be carried out pursuant to provisions under Art. 98–100 and Art. 235–315 of the Code of Civil Procedures.

Article 21b[42]

The decisions taken on the grounds of Art. 21a items 1 and 3 may be appealed against. The provisions under Art. 10 shall be applied respectively.

---

40. Wording as determined by Art. 1 section 22 letter (a) of the Law specified in annotation 1.
41. Wording as determined by Art. 1 section 22 letter (b) of the Law specified in annotation 1.
42. Wording as determined by Art. 1 section 22 letter (b) of the Law specified in annotation 1.

CHAPTER 6

SPECIAL, TRANSITIONAL AND FINAL PROVISIONS

Article 22.1

1. Making the particulars available by the business entity and providing explanations in foreign proceedings based on a charge of performing competition-restricting actions, may be prohibited by the Minister of Foreign Economic Relations.

2. A business entity shall notify the Minister of Foreign Economic Relations on any foreign proceedings specified under item 1 above, instituted abroad, if in the course of the proceedings it is obliged to disclose the particulars or to provide explanations.

3. The Minister of Foreign Economic Relations shall impose the ban, specified under item 1 above, if the foreign proceedings might result in a decision causing negative effects on Poland's economy or Polish business entities in the field of foreign trade or business activities carried out in whole or in part within the territory of the Republic of Poland.

4. The ban, specified under item 1 above may:
   (a) be addressed to particular business entities, groups of business entities or associations of thereof,
   (b) refer to specific foreign proceedings or various proceedings of a given type,
   (c) cover particular data and explanations or specific kind thereof.

The provisions under items 1 to 4 above shall also apply to the particulars made available and explanations provided by business units to the Polish law enforcement organs, within the framework of legal assistance performed upon request of foreign State authorities on the grounds of international agreements.

Article 23

Where in cases envisaged under this Law, a business entity lodges an appeal against a decision of the Anti-monopoly Office, to the antimonopoly court, a party shall not be entitled to set the decision aside by legal means specified under the Code of Administrative Proceedings, relating in particular to instituting the proceedings *de novo*, quashing, amendment or declaration of invalidity of the decision.

Article 24

Whenever separate provisions refer to an antimonopoly organ, it shall mean the Anti-monopoly Office.

1.4   THE SLOVAK STATUTE

The Act No. 188
of the National Council of the Slovak Republic
of 8 July 1994
on Protection of the Economic Competition

The National Council of the Slovak Republic has adopted this Act:

Part I
Introductory Provisions
Article 1

Purpose of the Act

The purpose of this Act is to protect economic competition in the markets for products and services (hereinafter only 'goods') against prevention, restriction or distortion (hereinafter only 'restriction on competition') as well as to create conditions for its further development, in order to promote economic progress for the benefit of consumers.

Article 2

Scope of the Act
1. This Act shall apply to:
   (a) entrepreneurs,[1] other natural persons and legal persons who undertake economic activities and their associations (hereinafter only 'entrepreneurs');
   (b) state administrative authorities and municipalities in their administrative activities which are linked to economic competition.
2. This Act shall apply to all activities and negotiations, with the exception of restrictions on competition to the extent ensuing from special laws.[2]
3. This Act shall also apply to activities and negotiations taking place abroad, if they lead or may lead to a restriction on competition in the domestic market.
4. This Act shall not apply to a restriction on competition with exclusive effects in a foreign market, unless international agreements binding for the Slovak Republic state otherwise.

Part II
Types of the Unlawful Restrictions on Competition and Concentration Agreements Restricting Competition

Article 3

1. Agreements and concerted practices between entrepreneurs as well as decisions of their associations whose object or effect is or may be the restriction on competition (hereinafter only 'agreements restricting competition') are prohibited, if this Act does not state otherwise.
2. There are prohibited agreements restricting competition that involve in particular:

---

1. Article 2, Paragraph (2) of the Commercial Code.
2. E. g. Article 2 of the Act No. 222/1946 Coll. of Laws on Postal Services;
   Articles 5 and 7 of the Act No. 2/1991 Coll. of Laws on Collective Bargaining;
   Article 18 of the Act of the National Council of the Slovak Republic No. 566/1992 Coll. of Laws on the National Bank of Slovakia;
   Article 1 of the Act of the National Council of the Slovak Republic No. 7/1993 Coll. of Laws on Establishing of the National Insurance and on Financing of Health Insurance, Sickness Insurance and Retirement Insurance.

(a) direct or indirect fixing of prices;
(b) commitment to limit or control production, sales, technical development, or investment;
(c) division of the market or of sources of supply;
(d) commitment by the parties to the agreement that different conditions of trade, relating to the same subject matter of the contract will be applied to individual entrepreneurs that will disadvantage some of them in competition;
(e) conditions that conclusion of contracts will require the acceptance of supplementary obligations which are not related to the subject of these contracts either by their nature or according to commercial usage.

3. The agreements restricting competition prohibited in accordance with Paragraph (1) shall be void. If the reason for nullity is related only to a part of the agreement, then only that particular part is void. If the portion of the agreement restricting competition cannot be separated from the remainder of the agreement, then the entire agreement is void.

Article 4

1. Agreements for the transfer of rights or the grant of licences over inventions, industrial designs, trade marks, names of entrepreneurs, protected varieties of plants or breeds of animals, utility models and protected topographies of semi-conductor products[3] or part of these agreements are prohibited and void in accordance with Article 3, if restrictions on competition imposed to an acquirer of these rights are not necessary for the safeguarding of existence of these rights.

The same shall apply to agreements granting rights to works and performances protected under the Authorship Act.[4]

2. The provision of Paragraph 1 shall apply similarly to transfer of rights or the granting of licences over objects of industrial ownership and to manufacturing and commercial knowledge and experience (know-how) that are not protected by special laws.

Article 5

1. The ban in accordance with Articles 3 and 4 shall not apply to agreements restricting competition that at the same time:
(a) contribute to improving the production or distribution of goods or to promoting technical or economic progress;
(b) allow users a fair share of the resulting benefit;

---

3. Act No. 527/1990 Coll. of Laws on Inventions, Industrial Designs and Rationalization Proposals;
   Act No. 174/1988 Coll. of Laws on Trade Marks;
   Article 18 of the Commercial Code (protection of names of entrepreneurs);
   Act No. 132/1989 Coll. of Laws on Protection of Rights to New Varieties of Plants and Breeds of Animals;
   Act No. 478/1992 Coll. of Laws on Utility Models;
4. Act No. 35/1965 Coll. of Laws on Literal, Scientific and Artistic Works (The Authorship Act) as amended.

(c) do not impose on the parties to the agreement restricting competition such restrictions which are not indispensable to the attainment of these objectives; and

(d) do not afford the parties to the agreement restricting competition the possibility of eliminating competition in respect of a substantial part of the goods in question.

2. Anti-monopoly Office of the Slovak Republic[5] (hereinafter only the 'Authority') may require entrepreneurs to prove that their agreements restricting competition fulfil the conditions set out in Paragraph 1.

3. Entrepreneurs can apply to the Authority for a decision, whether the agreements restricting competition within the meaning of Articles 3 and 4 fulfil the conditions described in Paragraph 1, (negative clearance).

4. The Authority shall issue a decree with detailed provisions of the conditions described in Paragraph 1.

Article 6

The Authority shall modify or withdraw the decision in accordance with Article 5, Paragraph 3, if:

(a) circumstances decisive for its issuing have changed substantially;

(b) the decision was based on untrue or incomplete data, or was induced by a deceit.

Article 7

Abuse of a Dominant Position in the Market

1. A dominant position in the market is held by one entrepreneur or by several entrepreneurs, who are not subjected to substantial competition, or as a result of their economic strength they can behave independently from other entrepreneurs and consumers and can restrict competition.

2. If it is not proved otherwise, it shall be presumed that an entrepreneur is not subjected to substantial competition within the meaning of Paragraph 2, if his share of supply or purchase of identical or interchangeable goods in the relevant market is at least 40%.

3. Relevant market is a geographical and temporal equilibrium of supply and demand of such group of goods, which are for the satisfaction of certain needs of users identical or mutually interchangeable. Relevant market is defined in product, geographical and time dimensions.

4. Abuse of a dominant position in the market is prohibited.

5. The abuse of a dominant position in the market is in particular:

(a) direct or indirect enforcement of disproportionate conditions in contracts;

(b) restricting the production, sale or technological development of goods to the detriment of consumers;

(c) applying different conditions for equal or comparable transactions to indi-

---

5. Articles 20 and 23 of the Act No. 347/1990 Coll. of Laws on Organization of Ministries and Other Central State Administrative Bodies of the Slovak Republic as amended.

vidual entrepreneurs in the market, which constituting a competitive disadvantage;

(d) making the conclusion of the contract conditional upon another party accepting additional conditions, unrelated to the object of the contract both in substance and in customary commercial practice.

CONCENTRATION

Article 8

1. A concentration shall be a process of an economic combining through:
    (a) merger or amalgamation of two or more previously independent entrepreneurs or transfer of an enterprise, or a part of an enterprise to another entrepreneur; or
    (b) acquisition of control by one or more entrepreneurs over an enterprise of another entrepreneur or over a part of it.

2. Acquisition of control within the meaning of Paragraph 1, part (b) is the possibility to exercise decisive influence on an enterprise's activities, especially by means of:
    (a) ownership or the right to use the whole enterprise or a part thereof;
    (b) rights, contracts or other means which permit the exercise of decisive influence on composition, voting or decisions of the organs of the enterprise.

3. A creation of an enterprise jointly controlled by several entrepreneurs (joint venture) shall be deemed to be an acquisition of control within the meaning of Paragraph 1, part (b).

4. A concentration shall not be deemed where:
    (a) credit and other financial institutions or insurance companies temporarily acquire securities providing control over an enterprise of another entrepreneur or over a part thereof with the view to reselling it, provided they do not exercise voting or other rights with a view to determining the competitive behaviour of that enterprise;
    (b) temporary acquiring of control over an enterprise of another entrepreneur or over a part thereof is ensuing from special laws.[6]

Article 9

1. Concentration is subject to control by the Authority, if:
    (a) the combined turnover of the participants of the concentration is at least 300 million Slovak crowns and at least two of the participants of the concentration achieved turnover, each one at least 100 million Slovak crowns for the previous accounting time period;[7] or
    (b) the joint share of the participants of concentration exceeds 20 per cent of

---

6. Article 11 of the Act No. 92/1991 Coll. of Laws on Conditions of Transfer of the State Property to Other Persons as amended;
    Articles 4a and 8 of the Act No. 328/1991 Coll. of Laws on Bankruptcy as amended;
    Article 68 of the Commercial Code (on liquidation of an undertaking).
7. Article 3 of the Act No. 563/1991 Coll. of Laws on Book-keeping.

the total turnover in identical or interchangeable goods in the market of the Slovak Republic.

2. The combined turnover or joint share within the meaning of Paragraph (1) shall be the sum of turnovers of:

(a) participants of concentration;

(b) entrepreneurs, in which the participant of concentration owns more than half of the capital, or has the power to exercise more than half of the voting rights, or the power to appoint more than half of the members of organs of the enterprise, or the right to manage the enterprise;

(c) entrepreneur who owns or has the rights described in part (b) in an enterprise of the participant of concentration;

(d) all other entrepreneurs in which the entrepreneur mentioned in part (c) owns or has the rights described in part (b).

3. If a mutual fund or investment company acquires control over an enterprise of another entrepreneur, the combined turnover or joint share within the meaning of Paragraph 1 shall be the sum of turnovers of entrepreneurs in which the mutual fund or investment company – including all mutual funds administered by the investment company – owns more than 10% of the capital, or has the right to exercise more than 10% voting rights, or has the right to manage the enterprise.

4. The concentration which is subject to control within the meaning of Paragraph 1 must be notified to the Authority within 15 days after the submission of the bid in a public tender, or the conclusion of the agreement, or the acquisition of control over an enterprise of another entrepreneur or over a part thereof by other means.

5. The notification of concentration in accordance with Article 8, Paragraph 1 part (a) and Paragraph (3) shall be submitted by the participants jointly, and in other cases shall be submitted by the entrepreneur who acquired control over an enterprise of another entrepreneur or over a part thereof. The notification must contain:

(a) a written agreement or description of the means, by which concentration will occur;

(b) identification data on participants of concentration to the extent in which they are registered in the Commercial Register;

(c) data on property and personnel linkage of each of the participants involved in concentration;

(d) calculations of shares in the relevant markets, balance sheets and financial statements of the participants of concentration for the previous accounting time period including entrepreneurs by property or personnel linked to them;

(e) reasons and effects of concentration and its impact on competition;

(f) the list of main suppliers, buyers and competitors of the participants of concentration in the relevant markets.

6. It is prohibited for the participants of the concentration which is subject to control within the meaning of Paragraph 1, to realize any such measures connected with concentration that could lead to irreversible changes, and this in time period before the notification to one month after the notification. The Authority may at the request of the participants of concentration grant an exemption from the ban, if there is a danger of damage to the participants of concentration or other legal

persons or natural persons. The decision may be made subject to conditions in order to preserve market structure before concentration.

Article 10

1. On the basis of the notification of concentration, the Authority shall issue within one month from its submission a decision on concentration, and in case the Authority shall not issue a decision, it shall issue a preliminary ruling that will prolong suspension of concentration in accordance with Article 9, Paragraph 6. If the Authority has issued a preliminary ruling, the decision on concentration will be issued within three months after the issuing of the preliminary ruling. If the Authority shall not decide within stipulated time period, then it means that it shall acquiesce to the concentration. The stipulated time period does not begin if the notification is incomplete and the Authority shall call participant's attention on insufficiency of the notification in written form.

2. The Authority shall prohibit the concentration if it creates or strengthens a dominant position in the market unless the participants prove that the harm which results from the restriction on competition will be outweighed by overall economic advantages of the concentration.

3. If the concentration is not contrary to this Act, the Authority shall issue a decision that it agrees with concentration. The Authority can impose conditions for completion of concentration connected to competition.

4. The Authority shall change or withdraw a decision in accordance with Paragraphs 1 to 3, if:
   (a) the concentration was completed other than as notified, or the participants of concentration have acted in contravention of the conditions established in decision;
   (b) the decision was based on untrue or incomplete data submitted by the participants of concentration or was induced by deceit.

5. If the concentration which is subject to control within the meaning of Article 9, Paragraph (1) was consummated without notification, the Authority may impose measures for remedy, including division of an enterprise of the participants on concentration. The Authority shall act in this way only if the conditions for prohibition of concentration according to the Paragraph (2) are met.

PART III
THE AUTHORITY

Article 11

1. The Authority is entitled:
   (a) to investigate and to determine the position of entrepreneurs in the relevant market;
   (b) to issue the decision whether the agreement restricting competition is prohibited and void in accordance with Articles 3 and 4;
   (c) to issue the decision on obligation to refrain from fulfilment of agreement restricting competition and to remedy a breach;

(d) to decide whether the agreement restricting competition fulfils conditions described in Article 5;

(e) to issue the decision, whether certain behaviour is by its nature an abuse of dominant position in the market in accordance with Article 7;

(f) to issue the decision on obligation to refrain from the abuse of a dominant position in the market and to remedy a breach, if it is in contrary with Article 7;

(g) to issue the decision whether a concentration is under control of the Authority in accordance with Articles 8 and 9 and to issue the decision granting an exemption from the ban to realise measures within the meaning of Article 9, Paragraph 6;

(h) to issue decisions on concentration in accordance with Article 10;

(i) to issue preliminary rulings in accordance with Articles 10 and 12, Paragraph 6;

(j) to impose fines on entrepreneurs in accordance with Article 14;

(k) to publicize notifications of the concentrations, decisions of the Authority, which have come into force and additional corrective measures;

(l) to control implementation of decisions issued in proceedings by the Authority;

(m) to require state administrative and local bodies to remedy the state of affairs in accordance with Article 18;

(n) to conduct general inquiry into particular economic sectors, if restriction on competition has occurred in them;

(o) to propose other measures for protection and support of competition.

2. In the execution of this Act the employees of the Authority have the right to request from entrepreneurs all materials and information which are necessary for activities of the Authority, in particular:

(a) business records or legal documents and to take copies or extracts from them;

(b) to ask for oral or written explanation on the spot;

3. When fulfilling the goals of this Act the employees of the Authority have the right to enter any premises, land and means of transportation of entrepreneurs.

4. The Authority may request from other state administrative bodies materials and information about the entrepreneur, which are protected by special laws.[8]

5. The Authority shall represent the Slovak Republic in international negotiations about agreements in the area of the economic competition.

PART IV
PROCEEDINGS BEFORE THE AUTHORITY

Article 12

1. Proceedings before the Authority shall begin on its own initiative or if petitioned by an entrepreneur.

---

8. E.g. Article 36 of the Act No. 322/1992 Coll. of Laws on State Statistics;
   Article 28 of the Act No. 248/1992 Coll. of Laws on Investment Companies and Mutual Funds.

2. The participants in the proceedings shall be the petitioner and the entrepreneurs about whose rights, interests protected by the law or duties stipulated by this Act shall be decided.

3. In cases in which a special law stipulates an obligation to pay an administrative fee, the petitioner must submit a receipt indicating payment of the administrative fee.

4. The Authority may stop the proceedings, if

   (a) the petitioner does not eliminate insufficiency of the petition or does not submit requested materials and information within the time period stated by the Authority;

   (b) the petitioner has withdrawn its petition;

   (c) reason for proceedings did not exist or ceased to exist.

5. If the nature of the case requires, the Authority shall make its decision following a hearing, to which the participants shall be invited. The Authority is obliged to ask participants in the proceedings to make submissions on the subject matter of the proceedings and on the outcome of the investigations carried out by the Authority.

6. In proceedings begun in accordance with the preceding Paragraphs, the Authority is entitled to issue a preliminary ruling temporarily governing legal relations until the final decision is reached, if this is necessary to safeguard legitimate interests or if execution of the final decision would otherwise be thwarted or seriously hampered.

7. Unless stated otherwise in this Act, proceedings before the Authority are governed by the provisions of the Administrative Procedure Act.[9]

Article 13

1. If a party to the proceedings disagrees with the final decision of the Authority, it may bring an action before the Supreme Court requesting a review of the decision.[10]

2. The deadline for bringing an action in accordance with Paragraph 1 is 30 days from the date on which the decision was delivered to the party to the proceedings.

Article 14

Fines

1. The Authority is entitled to fine entrepreneurs for breaching duties stipulated by this Act according to its importance up to 10% of their turnover for the previous accounting time period and if it is not possible to calculate the turnover, up to 10 million Slovak crowns. If it is proved that the entrepreneur obtained material profit from breaching a duty, the fine shall be at least equal to this profit. The Authority cannot impose a fine to entrepreneurs that applied for the decision within the meaning of Article 5, Paragraph 3.

2. The Authority may impose a fine up to 1 million Slovak crowns to an entrepreneur who does not submit in the determined time period the requested

---

9. Act No. 71/1967 Coll. of Laws on Administrative Proceedings (The Administrative Procedure Act).
10. Article 244 of the Civil Procedure Code.

material or true information or who do not allow their inspection or entry in accordance with Article 11, Paragraphs 2 and 3.

3. The Authority may impose a fine up to 100 000 Slovak crowns to entrepreneur who does not participate in hearings without having any serious reason for not doing so, or who by their action make the process of the proceedings more difficult.

4. The Authority may impose a fine up to the amount described in Paragraph 1 to the entrepreneur who does not keep with the decision of the Authority which came into force.

5. The fines, described in the previous paragraphs, may be imposed even repeatedly.

6. The fines in accordance with Paragraphs 1, 2 and 4 may be imposed by the Authority within one year of discovery of the breach, however, at least within three years following the day in which the breach of duty occurred.

7. If an entrepreneur fails to pay the imposed fine before the set deadline, he shall be obliged to pay a penalty 0.5% of the amount of the imposed fine per day of delay.

PART V
OBLIGATIONS OF THE ENTREPRENEURS AND CONFIDENTIALITY

Article 15

Entrepreneurs are obliged to deliver to the Authority requested materials and information and to submit its investigations in accordance with Article 11, Paragraph 2, to cooperate with the Authority in its examination and to allow employees of the Authority to enter any premises, land and means of transportation of entrepreneurs.

Article 16

1. Materials and information acquired by the Authority from entrepreneurs may be used only for the purpose for which they were requested.

2. All employees of the Authority as well as those entrusted with occurred tasks that fall within the competence of the Authority, are required to keep as confidential all facts relating to the commercial secrets[11] which they have learned in connection with the implementation of their professional duties.

PART VI
CIVIL LAW LITIGATIONS ARISING FROM UNLAWFUL RESTRICTION ON COMPETITION

Article 17

1. Consumers whose rights have been violated by unlawful restriction on competition may require the violating party to refrain from behaviour or to remedy

---

11. Article 17 of the Commercial Code.

the breach. This right may also be claimed by a legal person authorised to protect the interests of consumers.

2. After the commencement or the final conclusion of litigation to halt such unlawful conduct or rectify such a detrimental situation, lawsuits brought by other entitled persons involved in the same matter shall not be admissible; these other entitled persons may, however, join the proceedings as subsidiary participants according to special provisions.[12] A legitimate ruling on such claims – providing it is made to only one claimant – shall similarly be applied to the other entitled persons.

3. The procedure for raising claims in accordance with Paragraph 1 is governed by civil law regulations, if not stated otherwise by this Act. The court may permit the party who won the case the right to have the judgment publicized at the expense of the losing party and if necessary, may determine the scope, manner and form of the publication. The cost of the proceedings shall be governed by the respective provisions of the Civil Procedure Code.[13]

PART VII
INTERVENTIONS BY THE STATE ADMINISTRATIVE AUTHORITIES AND MUNICIPALITIES

Article 18

1. State administrative authorities and municipalities may not, by their own actions, by support or in any other way, restrict competition.

2. The Authority shall supervise the observance of Paragraph 1. Based on evidence and an assessment of the effect, the Authority may require state administrative authorities or municipalities to remedy the state of affairs.

PART VIII
SUPPORT OF ECONOMIC COMPETITION DURING THE PRIVATIZATION PROCESS

Article 19

1. State organizations and state administrative bodies are required, when transferring state property to other persons within the meaning of the special law[14] to proceed in the way that secures appropriate de-concentration of privatized enterprises. Where the state organization's market share has exceeded the threshold stipulated in Article 7 Paragraph 2, the state administrative body which is the establisher or creator of the state organization (hereinafter only 'establisher') shall ensure the carrying out of an assessment, containing in particular:

    (a) determining of market share of the state organization and expected market share of a new enterprise in the relevant market;

---

12. Article 93 of the Civil Procedure Code.
13. Article 137 of the Civil Procedure Code.
14. Act No. 92/1991 Coll. of Laws on Conditions of Transfer of State Property to Other Persons as amended.

(b) an assessment of the competitiveness of the new enterprise taking into account its existing involvement in the world market and foreseeable foreign competition in the domestic market, particularly taking into account the technological level, the size of the competing enterprises and other considerations characteristic of competitiveness in a certain field of industry;

(c) turnover of the state organization for the previous accounting time period.

2. The Authority shall be required to advance its view to the draft of the privatization project submitted by the establisher in accordance with the special law[15] from the viewpoint appropriate de-concentration described in Paragraph 1 within 8 working days. If the establisher disagrees with the ruling of the Authority, then the case will be decided by the government of the Slovak Republic, following an appeal of the establisher.

3. If the Ministry for Administration and Privatization of National Property of the Slovak Republic (hereinafter only 'Ministry') when approving draft of the privatization project shall proceed in the way that it changes conditions for appropriate de-concentration contained in the draft of the privatization project, the Ministry shall be required to submit a draft of the privatisation project to the Authority for review. The Authority shall be required to advance its view to it from the viewpoint of the appropriate de-concentration described in Paragraph 1 within 8 working days. If the Ministry disagrees with the ruling of the Authority, the case will be decided by the Government of the Slovak Republic, following an appeal of the Ministry.

4. If direct sale of property of the state organization or a part thereof shall be proposed and the combined turnover of the state organization, or as the case may be its privatized part and the entrepreneur who would acquire this property in accordance with draft of the privatization project will reach threshold settled in Article 9, the entrepreneur shall proceed in accordance with suitable provisions of Articles 8 and 9. When determining turnover the Article 9 shall be applied analogous. Notification of intention to acquire the property shall be submitted by entrepreneur at whatever time, at least when submitting draft of the privatisation project to the establisher. The Authority shall proceed in accordance with suitable provisions of Articles 8 to 10 analogous.

Article 20

Actions by Municipalities to Prevent the Creation of Dominant Position of Entrepreneurs During the Transfer of Municipal Property

Municipalities during the transfer of municipal property are required to care of the creation of a competitive environment in respective regional or local markets.

Article 21

1. Decisions of the associations of entrepreneurs accordance with Articles 3 which were adopted before this Act came into force and their effects continue for

---

15. Article 8 Paragraph (1) of the Act No. 92/1991 Coll. of Laws as amended.

the next time, shall be harmonised to this Act by entrepreneurs within three months time period after this Act shall come into force, otherwise they shall be void.

2. Proceedings before the Authority which had begun before the day in which this Act came into force, will be resolved according to the recent provisions of the Act.

PART IX
FINAL PROVISIONS

Article 22

The Government of the Slovak Republic by its order may set the limits described in Article 9 Paragraph 1 for some industries or may modify these limits according to a development of the economic conditions.

Article 23

Provision of the Article 7 on dominant position in the market and relevant market shall apply analogous to other provisions of the Act, in which these terms are applied.

Article 24

The Act No. 63/1991 Coll. of Laws on Protection of Economic Competition as amended by the Act No. 495/1992 Coll. of Laws shall be hereby repealed.

Article 25

This Act shall come into force on August 1 1994.

References

Aghion, P. (1993), 'Some issues in competition and competition policy in transition', in S. Estrin and M. Cave (eds), *Competition and Competition Policy: A comparative analysis of Central and Eastern Europe*, Pinter, London.

Altrogge, P. D. (1995), 'Competition policy in agriculture and food processing: some lessons for transitional economies', *World Competition*, **18** (1), 71–98.

Anderson, R.W. (1996), 'Transition banking: Poland 1989–1994,' in E. Miklaszewska (ed.), *Competitive Banking in Central and Eastern Europe*.

Atkinson, A. and Micklewright, J. (1992), *Economic Transformation in Eastern Europe and the Distribution of Income*, Clarendon Press, Oxford.

Balázs, K. (1994), 'Transition crisis in the Hungarian R&D sector', *Economic Systems*, **18** (3), 281–306.

Baldwin, R. (1994), *Towards an Integrated Europe*, CEPR, London.

Bayer, J. (1991), 'Antikommunizmus Magyarorszagon, 1990' ('Anticommunism in Hungary, 1990'), in S. Kurtan, P. Sandor, and L. Vass (eds.), *Magyarorszag Politikai Evkonyve 1991 (Hungarian Political Yearbook)*, Okonomia Alapitvany and Economix plc, Budapest.

Belka, M., Estrin, S., Schaffer, M. and Singh, I. (1995), 'Enterprise adjustment in Poland: evidence from a survey of 200 private, privatised and state-owned firms', mimeo, World Bank.

Bermann, G., Davey, W,. Goebel, R. and Fox, E. (1993), *European Community Law: Cases and Materials* (also supplement (1995)), West Publishers, New York.

Blejer, M. and Coricelli, F. (1995), *The Making of Economic Reform in Eastern Europe*, Edward Elgar, Aldershot.

Bolton, P. and Roland, G. (1992). 'Privatisation policies in Central and Eastern Europe', *Economic Policy*, **15**, 275–309.

Boner, R. A. and Krueger, R. (1991), *The Basics of Antitrust Policy: A Review of Ten Nations and the European Communities*, World Bank Technical Paper 160, Washington, DC, USA.

Bouin, O. and Grosfeld, I. (1995), 'Crédibilité des réformes et ajustment des entreprises en Pologne et en république tchéque, *Revue Economique*, **46** (3), May, 775–86.

Bresnahan, T. (1989), 'Empirical studies of industries with market power', in R.

Schmalensee and R. Willig (eds), *Handbook of Industrial Organization*, North-Holland, Amsterdam.

Bresnahan, T. and Reiss, P. (1991), 'Entry and competition in concentrated markets', *Journal of Political Economy*, **99**, 5, 191–202.

Calvo, G. and Coricelli, F. (1992), 'Stabilization in Poland', *Economic Policy*, **14**, 175–226.

Carlin, W., Van Reenen, J. and Wolfe, T. (1994), 'Enterprise restructuring in the transition: an analytical survey of the case study evidence from Central and Eastern Europe', EBRD, Working Paper No. 14, July.

Cecchini Report on the European Single Market, European Commission.

CEPR (1990), 'The impact of Eastern Europe', *Monitoring European Integration*, No. 1.

Corrado, C., Benacek, V. and Caban, W. (1995), 'Adjustment and performance of the textile and clothing industry in the Czech Republic, Poland and Portugal', CEPR Discussion Paper No. 1260.

Davies, S. and Lyons, B. (1996), *Industrial Organisation of the European Community*, Oxford University Press, Oxford.

Deacon, D. (1996), 'Vertical Restraints under EU competition law: new directions', in B. Hawk (ed.), 1995 *Fordham Corp. L. Inst.* (forthcoming).

Dewatripont, M. and Roland, G. (1995),'The design of reform packages under uncertainty', *American Economic Review*, **85**, 1207–23.

Dixon, H. and Rankin, N. (1994), 'Imperfect competition and macroeconomics: a survey', *Oxford Economic Papers*, **46**, 171–99.

Earle, J., Estrin, S. and Leshchenko, L. (1995), 'The effects of ownership on behaviour: is privatization working in Russia?' mimeo, World Bank.

Edwards, J. and Fischer, K. (1994), *Banks, Finance and Investment in Germany*, Cambridge University Press, Cambridge.

Elster, J. (1994), *Rebuilding the Boat in the Open Sea: An essay on constitution-making in Eastern Europe*, University of Chicago, Department of Political Science, manuscript.

EBRD (1994), *Transition Report. Economic Transition in Eastern Europe and the Former Soviet Union*, EBRD, October.

EBRD (1995), *Transition Report: Economic Transition in Eastern Europe and the Former Soviet Union*, EBRD, November.

Estrin, S. and Cave, M. (1993), *Competition and Competition Policy: A Comparative Analysis of Central and Eastern Europe*, Pinter, London.

European Economy, (1991), *The Path of Reform in Central and Eastern Europe*, Commission of the European Communities, special edition No. 2, 1991.

European Economy (1994), *The Economic Interpenetration between the European Union and Eastern Europe*, Commission of the European Communities, No. 6, 1994.

Eurostat (1995), *Country Profile: Hungary 1994*, Statistical Office of the European Communities.

Eurostat (INDE).

Faini, R. and Portes, R. (eds.) (1995), *European Union Trade with Eastern Europe: Adjustment and Opportunities*, CEPR, London.

Feinberg, R.M. and Meurs, M. (1994), 'Privatisation and antitrust in Eastern Europe: the importance of entry,' *Antitrust Bulletin* **39** (3).

Fingleton, J. (1993), 'Competition policy and employment: an application to the Irish economy,' *Economic and Social Review*, October.

Fingleton, J. (1995), 'Competition and efficiency in the services sector,' in J. W.

O'Hagan (ed.), *The Economy of Ireland: Policy and Performance of a Small European Country*, Gill and Macmillan, Dublin.

Flek, V. (1995), 'The strategy of marketisation and problems of competitiveness of industry in the former Czechoslovakia,' in M. Jackson and W.B. Biesbvonck (eds), *Marketisation, Restructuring and Competition in Transition Industries in Central and Eastern Europe*, Avebury, Aldershot.

Fornalczyk, A. (1993), 'Competition policy in the Polish economy in transition', in S. Estrin and M. Cave (eds), *Competition and Competition Policy: A Comparative Analysis of Central and Eastern Europe*, Pinter, London.

Fox, E. (1986), 'Monopolisation and dominance in the United States and the European Community – efficiency, opportunity, and fairness', *Notre Dame Law Review*, **61**, 501.

Fox, E. and Sullivan, L. (1987), 'Antitrust – retrospective and prospective: where are we coming from? Where are we going?' *New York University Law Review*, **62**, 936.

Fung, K. C. (1992), 'Economic integration as competitive discipline', *International Economic Review*, **33**, 837–48.

Gambetta, D. (ed.) (1988), *Trust: Making and Breaking Cooperative Relations*, Blackwell, Oxford.

Gambetta, D. (1993), *The Sicilian Mafia: the Business of Private Protection* (translation of *Mafia Siciliana*), Harvard University Press, London.

Geroski, P. (1992), 'Entry, exit and structural adjustment in European industry', in K. Cool, D. Neven and I. Walter (eds), *European Industrial Restructuring in the 1990's*, Macmillan, London

Good, D., Roller, L.-H. and Sickles, R. (1993), 'US airline deregulation: implications for European transport', *Economic Journal*, **103**, 1028–41.

Grosfeld, I. and Roland, G. (1995), 'Defensive and strategic restructuring in Central European enterprises,' CEPR Discussion Paper No. 1135.

Hamilton, C. and Winters, A. (1992), 'Opening up international trade with Eastern Europe', *Economic Policy*, **14**, 77–116

Hare, P. and. Hughes, G (1991), 'Competitiveness and industrial restructuring in Czechoslovakia, Hungary and Poland', *European Economy* (The Path of Reform in Central and Eastern Europe – Special Edition No.2).

Hawk, B. (1995), 'System failure: vertical restraints and EC law', *Common Market Law Review*, **32**, 973.

Hayri, A. and McDermott, G.A. (1995), 'Restructuring in the Czech Republic: beyond ownership and bankruptcy', paper presented at the EEA conference in Prague, March.

Hirschausen, C. von (1995a), 'From privatisation to capitalisation: industrial restructuring in post-socialist Central and Eastern Europe', in R. Withley, G. Schmidt and E. Dietrich (eds), *Industrial Transformation in Europe*, Sage, London.

Hirschausen, C. von (1995b), 'Industrial restructuring in post-socialist Central and Eastern Europe: privatisation, enterprisation and diversity of corporate governance', paper presented at the Fourth Freiberg Symposium on Economics, 'Microeconomics of Transition and Growth', 28–30 August, 1995.

Hoekman, B. and Djankov, S. (1996), 'Intra-industry trade, foreign direct investment and the reorientation of Eastern European exports', mimeo, World Bank.

Hoekman, B. and Mavroidis, P. (1994), 'Linking competition and trade policies in Central and East European countries.'

Hussain, A. and Stern, N. (1993), 'The role of the state, ownership and taxation in transition economies', STICERD Development Economics Research Programme Discussion Paper, July.

ILO Statistical Yearbook, 1993 and 1994.

Jackman, R. (1995), 'Economic policies, employment and labour markets in transition in Central and Eastern Europe', Centre for Economic Performance, London School of Economics, Discussion Paper no. 265.

Janínski, P. (1995), 'Regulation and systemic transformation,' *Communist Economies and Economic Transformation*, **7** (2), 213–237.

Johnson, S. and Kowalska, M. (1994), 'Poland: the political economy of shock therapy', in S. Haggard and S. Webb (eds), *Voting For Reform: Democracy, Political Liberalisation and Economic Adjustment*, Oxford University Press and the World Bank, New York.

Joskow, P. L., Schmalensee, R. and Tsukanova, N. (1994), 'Competition policy in Russia during and after privatisation', *Brookings Papers on Economic Activity: Microeconomics*, 301–81.

Katsoulacos, Y. and Talka, L. (1995), 'Investment funds and stock exchange developments ; an analysis of firms' restructuring decisions in the Czech republic', mimeo, London Business School.

Khemani, S. (1996), 'Competition policy in the CIS', mimeo.

Khemani, S. and Dutz, M. (1996), 'The instruments of competition policy and their relevance for economic development', in C. Frischtak (ed.), *Regulatory Policies and Reform: A Comparative Perspective*, The World Bank, New York.

King, N. (1995), 'Slovak's shift on privatisation plan allows managers to buy firms cheaply', *Wall Street Journal*, 21 July 1995.

Konings, J., Lehman, H. and Schaffer M., (1995), ' Employment growth, job creation and job destruction in Polish manufacturing 1988–1991', LICOS mimeo, 1995.

Layard, R., Nickell, S. and Jackman, R. (1991), *Unemployment: Macroeconomic Performance and the Labour Market*, Oxford University Press, Oxford.

Lavigne, M. (1993), 'A comparative view on economic reform in Poland, Hungary and Czechoslovakia', UN Economic Commission for Europe, Discussion Paper, Vol. 3, No. 2.

Lizal, L., Singer, P. and Svejnar, J. (1995), 'Manager interests, break-ups and performance of state enterprises in transition', mimeo, CERGE.

Mayhew, K. and Seabright, P. (1992), 'Incentives and management of enterprises in economic transition: capital markets are not enough', CEPR Discussion Paper No. 640.

Miklaszewska, E. (1996), *Competitive Banking in Central and Eastern Europe*, Poland.

Neven, D. and Seabright, P. (1995), 'Trade liberalization and the co-ordination of competition policy', in L. Waverman (ed.), *Competition Policy in a Global Economy*, Routledge, London.

Newbery, D. M. (1995), 'The Distributional impact of price changes in Hungary and the United Kingdom', *Economic Journal*, **105** (July), 847–63.

Newbery, D. M. and Kattuman, P. (1992), 'Market concentration and competition in Eastern Europe', CEPR Discussion Paper No. 664.

Nuti, M. (1988), 'Perestroika: transition from central planning to market socialism', *Economic Policy*, **7**, 353–90

OECD (1993), *Etudes Economiques de l'OCDE: Hongrie 1993*, Paris.

OECD (1994a), *Industrial Policy in OECD Countries: Annual Review*, Paris.

OECD (1994c), *Etudes Economiques de l'OCDE: Les Républiques Tchèque et Slovaque 1994*, Paris.

OECD (1994c), *Etudes Economiques de l'OCDE: Pologne 1994*, Paris.

OECD (1995), *Etudes Economiques de l'OCDE: Hongrie 1995*, Paris.

Pinto, B., Belka, M. and Krajewski, S. (1993), 'Transforming state enterprises in Poland: evidence on adjustment by manufacturing firms', *Brookings Papers on Economic Activity*, **1**, 213–70.

Putnam, R. (1993), *Making Democracy Work: civic traditions in modern Italy*, Princeton University Press, Princeton, NJ.

Quarterly Statistical Bulletin (1995, 1) Czech Republic

Romania Statistical Yearbook

Rutkowski, M. and Sinha, S. (1995), 'Employment flows and sectoral shifts during the transition shock in post-socialist countries', World Bank mimeo.

Schaffer, M. (1992), 'The Polish state-owned enterprise sector and the recession in 1990', *Comparative Economic Studies*, **34**, 58–85.

Schmalensee, R. (1989), 'Inter-Industry studies of structure and performance,' in R. Schmalansee and R. Willig (eds), *Handbook of Industrial Organization*, North-Holland, Amsterdam.

Seabright, P. (1995), 'A taxonomy of vertical restraints', mimeo, Cambridge.

Shiller, R., Boycko, M. and Korobov, V. (1991): 'Popular attitudes towards free markets: the Soviet Union and the United States compared', *American Economic Review*, **81**, 385–400.

Skoczny, T. (1995), *Polish Antimonopoly Case Law*.

Smith, E. (1995), 'Lessons from the EEA: trans-national competition policy and integration', paper presented at a conference in Prague, March.

Statistical Yearbook – the Czech Republic.

Statistical Yearbook – Hungary 1990 and 1994.

Statistical Bulletin – Hungary 1995.

Varese, F. (1994), 'Is Sicily the future of Russia? Private protection and the rise of the Russian mafia', *Archives Européennes de Sociologie*, **35**, 224–58.

Voszka, E. (1993), 'Restructuring of large state-owned enterprises in Hungary 1988–1993', mimeo

White Paper on Enlargement (1995), European Commission.

Wijnbergen, S. van and Marcincin, A. (1995), 'Voucher privatization, corporate control and the cost of capital: an analysis of the Czech privatisation programme', CEPR Discussion Paper No. 1215.

Zemplinerova, A. (1994), 'Restructuring of the Czech industry', mimeo.

Zemplinerova, A. and Stibal, J. (1995), 'Evolution and efficiency of concentration in manufacturing,' in J. Svejnar (ed.), *The Czech Republic and Economic Transition in Eastern Europe*, Academic Press, San Diego.

Index